Jeff Kelly has worked as a prison officer for twelve years in a local prison housing some of the country's most dangerous prisoners. He was a hostage negotiator. Jeff's background would never have suggested a career in the prison service and many associates from his past have been on the wrong side of the bars. However, it is the life skills learnt on the south London council estates that gave Jeff the skills to perform the role of a prison officer with authority, firmness, fairness and above all with good humour and compassion.

BANG 'EM UP

Jeff Kelly

BANG 'EM UP

Vanguard Press

VANGUARD PAPERBACK

© Copyright 2009
Jeff Kelly

The right of Jeff Kelly to be identified as author of
this work has been asserted by him in accordance with the
Copyright, Designs and Patents Act 1988.

I have changed some of the names to protect the guilty – and others
have been changed to protect me from a good kicking!

A CIP catalogue record for this title is
available from the British Library.

ISBN 978 1 84386 560 5

Vanguard Press is an imprint of
Pegasus Elliot MacKenzie Publishers Ltd.
www.pegasuspublishers.com

First Published in 2009

Vanguard Press
Sheraton House Castle Park
Cambridge England

Printed & Bound in Great Britain

Disclaimer

This book is based on the true life experiences of Jeff Kelly whilst he served as a prison officer.

To protect the rights of those whose paths have crossed the author, all of the characters and some of the events have been altered and names, dates and places have been changed.

This book is dedicated to the hard work of all staff who work within our prison service; they work with some of the country's most dangerous and violent prisoners. Every day thousands of prison staff perform a difficult task with great professionalism and dedication.

Glossary of Prison terms, Jargon and Slang

Like any institution anywhere in the world the prison service has expressions and jargon used to describe a process that are sometimes unique to the service; there are some regional variations and the glossary below covers the southern region. I have also included prison slang, which is always changing with the times.

Adjudication: Daily process where the governor deals with disciplinary matters.

App: Prisoners have to put in an 'app' (application) to the governor for anything different from normal daily routine eg, for goods to be brought into prison, or simply to apply for anything.

Apple: Apple Core=Score, what's the situation?

Association: Time when prisoners are allowed out of their cells to meet, talk, play pool, watch TV, etc.
This is also the time that prisoners can make phone calls.

Bacon: Bacon Bonce= Nonce. A sex offender.

Bang 'em Up: Lock the prisoners in the cells

Banged up: locked in a cell.

Baron: Prisoner who controls illicit articles through bullying and other exploitative practices of the prisoners.

Basic: There are three levels of prison regime: basic, standard and enhanced, based on behaviour in prison. The higher the regime, the more privileges the prisoner has, such as an increased number or length of visits.

Bertie: Bertie Smalls=Grass, informer.

Bird: prison sentence, i.e. I'm doing bird (Bird Lime=time)

Block, Choky or 'seg': Prison segregation unit where prisoners are sent for bad behaviour or sometimes for their own protection, or simply to protect others.

Burglars: security or 'DST' ('Dedicated Search Team').

Burn: Cigarettes.

Canteen: This is the prison shop, where prisoners will be able to order extra food, toiletries, tobacco, etc once per week.

Catch a ride: To ask a friend with drugs to get you high. "Can I catch a ride?"

Category A, B, C and D: Prisoners are categorized.

Closed visit: Visit supervised by officers where the prisoner and visitor are separated by a screen.

Cucumbers: Cucumbers=Numbers, on rule 43, a Bacon.

Goppers: Prisoners, as they are gopping (not nice).

Grass: prisoner who provides guards information about other prisoners.

IMB (Independent Monitoring Board): These are lay people appointed by the Home Office to act as watchdogs and look after the interests of prisoners.

In possession: Prisoners are allowed a strictly limited number of articles 'in possession' to keep in their cells. Anything above the limit is usually kept in 'private property' or handed out on a visit.

Jam Roll: Parole

Jimmy or Jimmy Boyle: Foil used by drug users to smoke heroin.

Jolt: A long sentence.

Jug up: to scald someone, usually with a mixture of boiling water and sugar.

Kangaroo: "Screw" Prison officer.

Knockback: A setback such as losing an appeal, being refused parole, etc.

Legal letter: Prisoner's letter to or from their solicitor.
This is covered by prison rule 37A and cannot be opened except in the prisoner's presence. Both correspondents need to write Rule 37A on the envelope.

Legal visit: Lawyers are allowed to visit clients in prison without using a visiting order.

Listeners: Prisoners trained by Samaritans to listen in confidence and offer emotional support to other prisoners.

MDT (mandatory drug testing): Random urine testing for drugs.

Mule or Donkey: A person who smuggles drugs into the prison.

On the leg: A prisoner who is always chatting with and befriending prison officers.

On The Rule: This is a prison rule under which some prisoners are segregated for their own protection, either because they have large debts to other prisoners or because they have committed an offence such as a sex offence, which would put them at risk from others.

Paper or wrap: A small quantity of drugs packaged for selling.

Patches: a prison uniform with prominent yellow panels worn by prisoners captured after an escape or following an attempted escape.

Personal officer: Each prisoner should have a personal officer to look after his or her interests.

Peter, Pad or flowery Dell: Cell.

Pie and liquor: The vicar.

Pony parcel: Shit wrapped in newspaper and thrown out of the window

Private spends: Money sent in by relatives, which can be spent in the prison canteen (shop).

PVO (privileged visiting order): Sent out to visitors at the prisoner's request. Prisoners can be allowed these extra visits in return for good behaviour.

Screw: Prison officer.

Shank: Homemade knife.

Shipped out: Moved from one prison to another, often without warning (when it is known as being 'ghosted' as it is done usually in the middle of the night).

Shit and a shave: A short sentence.

Shit up: A prisoner who is staging a demonstration by covering his cell in shit.

Shit watch: A person who is suspected of hiding drugs in his anus will be placed on a shit watch.

Spin: A search of either the person or the cell.

Stretch: a sentence or a year (a '10 stretch' is a 10 year sentence).

Sweatbox: Cellular vehicle for court escorts.

Tariff minimum term: The part of a life sentenced prisoner's sentence, which must be served 'for retribution and deterrence'. At the end of the tariff period the prisoner may be released on licence.

The Box: An isolation cell in the segregation unit, used as a safe containment area.

The enchanted: prisoners on the 'Enhanced Privilege Level'.

Town visit/community visit: Some prisoners are judged to be suitable to go out for the day to a place within a certain radius of the prison (usually 20 miles) in the company of family or friends.

Tram lines: a distinctive scar caused by a prison-made weapon, which uses two razor blades melted into a toothbrush.

VO (visiting order): This is sent out by the prison, at the request of the prisoner, to family and friends who the prisoner wants to get a visit from.

VPU (vulnerable prisoners' unit): Where prisoners at risk are held 'On the rule'.

Chapter One

To be a Screw

"Now, listen up. I am very busy tonight. Therefore I am going to limit you to one question and one question only. So do not waste it."

"Good evening, Mr Kelly. How are you?"

"I am fine. Next!"

This was my tongue-in-cheek style that carried me through all the years I served as a prison officer. You may ask why I ever chose to become a prison officer, considering I am a Battersea boy whose family would say that they had already had enough brushes with the law and experience of life on the wrong side of the bars.

The thought of being a prison officer would not normally have ever crossed my mind. I was a fully qualified Master Plasterer, after all. However, this was 1992, and work was a bit thin on the ground in the building industry. Daily rates for a self-employed plasterer were very low, with no holiday pay, sick pay or pension. So I decided to look for a career that would provide me with some job security as well as holiday and sick pay. I focused my job search on the three main disciplined services that would provide me with all I was looking for and pay a decent wage. Of course, ensuring that the wage was decent also meant that there would be an element of risk to the type of work performed. These jobs were the police, fire and prison services.

I had fancied being a fireman, as everyone likes a fireman, especially the ladies. My second choice was to become a police officer as there would be a certain amount of respect for the position and I could retire at 55 years of age. My third and least likely choice was to be a prison officer; although I had worked in Brixton Prison on a refurbishment contract plastering their administration area, so I thought that experience had given me some insight into the job.

So I set about applying for all three in an attempt to start a new career that had an element of job security about it. I was certain that I would enjoy the strange notion of receiving a pay packet, instead of having to turn up at a customer's or a builder's house demanding the money that I was owed. I always had a sense that this approach to getting the money that was due to me would ultimately lead me to two out of three of the services I was currently contacting, not as an employee, however, but more as a user of their services.

The fire service replied and informed me that the next recruitment drive would not be until the following year. Glossy brochures and application forms for the police and prison services arrived on the same day. I could see from the police brochure and application form that I would not be paid as much to be a policeman as I would a prison officer and would have to have my tattoo removed from my arm. It was not that I had a tattoo that held some fond memories or proclaimed undying love for my wife and kids; it was far more to do with the fact that I was terrified of hospitals and needles and an absolute coward when it came to any clinical assault on my body.

So the prison service it would have to be. My next problem was how I would tell my wife and family that I had decided to become a Kanga (Kangaroo=Screw). I thought about telling my mother and father that this was one sure way of getting to visit my brother who was serving one of his many terms at Her Majesty's Pleasure. Or I could just tell it as it was – that I needed to feed my kids and pay the mortgage and did not want to have to travel to the other side of London to work for £35 per day as a self-employed plasterer when I could have a job that provided a pension, sick pay, holiday pay and a career with a chance of promotion and an opportunity to meet a wide range of people I might not normally ever meet. In the end, my mum and dad came round to my way of seeing things – not, however, before my father had choked on his cup of tea when I told him and immediately demanded a DNA test. My wife, on the other hand, was considerably less pleased and thought I was a traitor to the criminal classes that I often worked and drank with. This was all rather strange as, although she had grown up in the East End of London, all her family were law-abiding citizens, quite unlike mine.

In order to join the prison service, you have to first pass an aptitude test. At the time, it was like some kind of IQ test which assessed your reading, writing and observational abilities. I practised every day by testing myself on all kinds of magazine puzzles and eventually the day of the test arrived. I was to report to HMP Downview where the aptitude test would be carried out. The first test was to find out just where exactly in the country HMP Downview was. I was surprised to find that this prison was in Banstead, just five miles from my home.

I was going to take my aptitude test at a Category C prison. As I was quick to find out, prisons are categorised based on the security level of the prisoners they can accommodate.

All male prisoners – but oddly not female prisoners – are given a security categorisation when they enter prison. These categories are based on the likelihood of whether they will try to escape, and their danger to the public if they did escape. The four categories are:

- category A: prisoners whose escape would be highly dangerous to the public or national security;
- category B: prisoners who don't require maximum security, but for whom escape needs to be made very difficult;
- category C: prisoners who can't be trusted in open conditions but who are unlikely to try to escape; and
- category D: prisoners who are trusted enough to wander freely but must show up for daily roll calls.

To explain this in non prison service jargon, a category A prison has some of the meanest, murdering, raping and most violent scum on the earth. A category B prison holds those who want to become the meanest, murdering, raping and most violent scum on the earth. A category C prison holds those who believe they could become the meanest, murdering, raping and most violent scum on the earth if only they had the bottle or the brain. And a category D prison has those who would never dream of becoming the meanest, murdering, raping and most violent scum on the earth and yet have either raped or conned someone or have come to the end of a very long sentence during which time they have been the meanest, murdering, raping and most violent scum on the earth.

Meanwhile, I arrived at the gate of HMP Downview to be tested. I was feeling confident that I had practised enough on the magazine puzzles. I also had a chance to look at the other candidates and noticed that there was a bit of a mixed bag. There were ex-guardsmen (you could spot them straightaway, as they were the ones with the shiniest shoes and wearing their blue, red, blue regimental ties and a vacant look from too much guard duty outside St James Palace). There were a few builders. Some had made the effort to dress up smart and others had clearly turned up in between jobs just so that they could carry on collecting their dole by providing evidence that they were indeed looking for work. Finally, auxiliary prison officers made up the rest of this motley crew – these were people who were already working in prisons assisting the work of prison officers, whilst not being paid as much as them and not being expected to be in any direct unsupervised contact with prisoners.

We were all briefed by the training Principal Officer (PO) on how to complete the test and were told to start. The test was a type of IQ psychometric test of different shapes and groups of numbers or spelling and grammar. As soon as I turned the test paper over I went straight into panic mode as this did not look like any competition or puzzle I had practised on in *Take a Break*. I looked around the room to see if anyone else was starting to panic but, other than seeing the very blank expressions on the two guardsmen's faces, everyone was hard at it. So I simply resigned myself to believing that I would not pass the test, would therefore not become a prison officer, and started to say goodbye to the job security, pension and holiday and sick pay. Having said goodbye to it all, it was then that I began to relax and decided to at least have a go at it, guessing at those things that I did not know.

The test was over and we were informed that, if our name was called out, we were to proceed to the room to our right. My name was not called out, nor was one of the builders who had turned up in his overalls, the two auxiliary prison officers and the bus driver. The guardsmen were called and it was then that I became very despondent thinking that I had been beaten by two giddy guardsmen. The PO then returned and told us that we had all passed that stage of the selection and we could therefore put this part of the laborious process behind us. Somehow, in my humiliation at having been beaten by a guardsman, or so I thought, the PO's words registered with me as: The rest of you miserable gits have all failed to pass this simple task so piss off and close the door behind you!

The next part of the selection was the interview itself and I was told to report to HMP Highdown Prison. I had every confidence that I could sell ice to Eskimos so to sell myself to a couple of prison governors at an interview would be easy. Once again, I was faced with the task of finding out where this particular prison was, as I had been informed that, should I be selected, I would be working there. Once again my luck was in – HMP Highdown was just next door to HMP Downview. The only difference being that HMP Highdown was a local category B prison housing category A prisoners.

I was right about the interview. It was conducted by two very experienced prison governors who had come up through the ranks and who clearly knew their stuff. They had asked all the set questions and I had made sure that I had given them the answers that they wanted to hear, like, "If you discover that a fellow passenger is smoking with his friends on a bus that does not allow smoking, what would you do?" I responded that, naturally, I would ask them to stop, pointing out that the notice said 'no smoking' and then I would report them to the driver. Under any circumstances other than this interview situation, I would, of course, have kept quiet, either letting them get on with it or asking them for a light myself, rather than grass them up and risk a community beating for my efforts.

Immediately after the interview, I was told that I had passed. One of the governors who had interviewed me then leant forward and asked me if I would really have grassed them up or tried to stop them from smoking, to which I replied, "Like hell would I!" With some visible relief on his face, he responded, "Thank fuck for that! We've enough dangerous twits in the service already," before asking me for a light whilst leaning on the No Smoking sign.

After a few weeks of waiting to have my appointment processed, the day finally arrived that I had to report to the main gate of HMP Highdown to take up my new post as a prison officer. Now the fact that it is called the main gate has always confused me. This was a category B prison, which also housed category A prisoners, some of whom were the meanest murdering, raping and most violent scum on the earth. So why should there be anything other than a prison gate, let alone a main gate? In a prison, there is no back door, side entrance, tradesman's entrance or even a cat flap so the term, 'main gate', has always remained a puzzle to me.

So, on the 30th January 1994, I presented myself at the prison main gate, where I was met by the other successful candidates from the selection process and a few others, ten of us in all. As well as the ones who were selected with me, there was also an ex 2 Para sergeant, an ex army physical trainer who had also trained the police, an ex Royal Green Jackets soldier, a prison works officer and another civilian.

After some very boring introductions, the obligatory swearing of our allegiance to Her Majesty and her Government and the signing of the Official Secrets Act, we were launched into the training programme that would make prison officers of us all. We were divided into three groups, given a programme and set of objectives to follow. We were expected to write up our observations in our notebooks and present them to the training staff to mark. It was like being back at school and some of the comments that were written in my notebook – in red, of course – were merely grammatical corrections rather than the accuracy of my observations. They were in fact quite lucky to have been able to read any of the drivel that I had written, given that the most I had ever written since leaving school was a birthday card.

Most of our first two weeks were concerned with understanding the aims and objectives of the prison service. Although we soon understood how to repeat them in parrot fashion, none of us had a clue as to what they actually meant. We also embarked on a training programme that was carefully put together by expert prison physical exercise instructors (PEIs) to get us ready for the rigorous training programme that was awaiting us at the prison service college.

This was all straightforward enough until our ex-army PEI decided to make a complaint about the type of training that the prison PEIs were dishing out to us. I have served with the army as a combat signalman and understand how the mind of PEIs work. It is quite simple. They have an inferiority complex, seeing themselves as the body beautiful and yet often being uncomfortable with their own sexuality. They therefore want to ensure that they know everything about keeping fit and gays (although we suspected that this was more to do with their homophobia than any desire to actively embrace cultural diversity). They are not renowned for being the brightest penny in the pocket and will react when compromised or challenged. Therefore when told to run around the gym and touch all four corners, they will think it amusing to enquire why it has taken you so long to achieve this simple task. I could never resist responding with, "Sorry, Sir. I thought you said twice round the gym!" This would, in turn, appeal to their limited sense of humour and they would then see you as the class clown who could be relied upon to feed them their lines.

Our ex-army PEI unfortunately decided that a different approach would be best and made a formal complaint about the prison service's unsafe training methods. Perhaps not surprisingly, the PO in charge of the gym decided to address the ex-army PEI's unhappiness with the whole group at the next debriefing session. We would all have been impressed by the ex-army PEI's stance had it not been for the fact that this was only the end of week one and we still had one more week to endure the inept training methods of the prison's PEIs. Again, perhaps not surprisingly, we suddenly found ourselves being thoroughly beasted by testosterone-pumped-up, utterly pissed off gym queens. None of us could quite find it in ourselves to thank Paul Hockey for having raised his concerns about the safety of the prison training after that.

I had already started to align myself to Mick Blake who was an ex-Green Jacket soldier. He shared the same sense of humour as me and an equal dislike for PEIs. There was also a character called Dean who would twitch a lot and make some very impressive claims to being the fittest all-round sportsman of our team. Then there was Sue, an ex-auxiliary prison officer who also twitched a lot. We wondered whether this twitching would befall us all as we progressed with our training but quickly decided instead to open a book on when they would both twitch together at the same time. There was also Robert who was the works prison officer and who wanted to become a real prison officer, for reasons even he thought were unsound and probably drink induced. There was also a guy called Mark who was an auxiliary prison officer and who had also attended the same school as me. The school had been opposite Wandsworth Prison and we wondered if this was to prove to be an omen.

Finally, there was Fred Bloom, an ex-Para who had very strange whisks of hair growing on his cheeks. One day our training team, which consisted of a principal and a senior officer

(SO), decided to take the piss out of Fred. There was something about Fred's eyes that told a different story, so Mick and I decided not to join in with this jovial banter. There was something about Fred that we could not quite put our finger on – over and above the fact that he was an ex-Para, a regiment that has a reputation that no one in their right mind would mess with.

During these two weeks of induction, we were assigned to different houseblocks, residential units where the prisoners are held. Each houseblock has three spurs, which hold about 50 prisoners giving a total of about 150 prisoners per houseblock. Highdown had four houseblocks, each with different regimes. Houseblock one was the induction houseblock for new prisoners; houseblock two had two spurs for workers and one spur for vulnerable prisoners; houseblock three also contained foreign nationals; and houseblock 4 served as home to those on a long sentence.

Now, the official line that we gave prisoners or visitors was that the B spur of houseblock two is home to vulnerable prisoners and not just sex offenders. A prisoner could be on this spur, we would explain, because he is being picked on by other prisoners, for example, or because he has had threats made against him and is frightened of being on the normal spurs. The truth, however, was that the vast majority of prisoners on B spur of houseblock two were sex offenders, commonly known by prisoners and officers alike as 'nonces'. The name was derived from 'a nonsense crime' as other prisoners could not understand what kind of animal could commit such crimes. Locally they were known as 'bacons', which is from the rhyming slang of bacon bonce meaning nonce. Most prisoners would commit serious harm to any prisoner that they believed was either a nonce or who was from B spur on houseblock two.

One of the spurs on houseblock three was set aside for foreign nationals. Due to the prison's close proximity to Gatwick Airport, we seemed to get quite a few foreign nationals, all of whom had clearly given the wrong answer at Gatwick when asked by customs staff: "Did you pack your own bag, sir?" Instead of replying "Yes", which they all did, they should have said: "This is not my bag. I have never seen this bag in my life before. Where is my matching lizard skin bag?"

Houseblock four held workers and long-termers. These were prisoners who were either coming to the end of their sentence or who were at Highdown so that their families could visit them. Ordinarily, they would have been serving their time at a prison too far away for their families to visit. However, the prison service has a scheme whereby a prisoner who has not been able to have visits because of how far away family are, can be moved to a more local prison for a month or so. This enables the prisoner to use his accumulated visiting orders when he is transferred to a more local prison, making it possible for family members to visit during the time he has been transferred.

I was assigned to look at houseblock two. At this stage we were all dressed in suits, which would indicate to a prisoner that we were civilians visiting the prison for some reason. This gives them an ideal opportunity to either try to scare or shock us or to complain about their treatment. I was observing the daily routine of the serving of lunch; commonly know as 'feeding time'. This is a controlled process where the prisoners are let out of the spurs, six at a time, to collect their lunch. The reason that lunch is controlled in this way is to minimise the outbreaks of fights and to ensure that prison officers outnumber those that are collecting their lunch. I was trying not to appear as scared as I was actually feeling, particularly since this was my first contact with real, live prisoners. I was determined to stay as close to the 'real' officers as I could, when all of a sudden, a very scary looking prisoner with lots of misspelt tattoos that had either been done by a chronic dyslexic or by himself whilst looking in a mirror, came over to me and asked, "What do you think you're fucking looking at?" And then, just as suddenly, he said, "Wait a minute. Don't I know you?" Drawing on all my courage, I decided to stare him in the eye and inform him that, yes, I was looking at him but no, I did not know him. To which he responded, "Well, that's all right then," and calmly went back to his cell with his lunch. The officer next to me told me not to worry about him because he was mad and commended me for keeping my cool. Little did the officer know that I was indeed shaking in my boots, not because the incident had scared me particularly but because I did actually know the guy, having employed him as a plasterer's labourer previously. I knew only too well that he was seriously mad: he had bitten off the ear of one of the bricklayers on the site we were working on.

The two main things that hit you when you start working in a prison are the noise and the smell. There are different levels of noise depending on the activities and the regime the prisoners are following. Association is when the prisoners are out of their cells and are associating with the other prisoners on their spur. With about 50 prisoners to a spur and each houseblock having three spurs, you can imagine the noise level of 150 prisoners all talking and shouting at the same time. In fact, the noise levels often exceed the danger levels set for health and safety. One of the skills of a good prison officer is to be able to distinguish between the din and identify when there is a real problem like a fight, an assault or a diversion. "It is not a skill you can be taught; you can only learn it through experience on the houseblocks. But it is a truly important skill and one that can literally save lives."

The next function involving noise is when the prisoners are on movements, a process that is carried out twice per weekday when prisoners are allowed to move to education classes or work. During this time the officers have to ensure that they are heard above the din that the prisoners are already creating. This often ends up in a shouting competition with officers always having to come out as the loudest.

Then there is 'bang up'. This is obviously when prisoners are put away in their cells and the cell doors are locked. The process of 'banging up' is always associated with lots of shouting from officers and prisoners and the closing of the cell doors creates a banging sound, hence the term 'bang up'. Once the prisoners are safely 'behind the wood' (this term comes from the days when the cell doors were made of wood. Now, of course, they are made of steel) you always have a period where the prisoners will shout to each other from their cells. Others may choose to share their taste in music with everyone else in the prison whether they like it or not.

There are only three occasions during the prison regime when there is relative peace and quiet: first, when the majority of prisoners have moved off the wings to education and workshops, leaving the lazy and incapable prisoners to climb back into bed to sleep off a busy night's shouting; second, between the hours of 1am and 6.30am, when the majority of prisoners are asleep; and then, third, there are the times when we are going to storm a cell with a Control and Restraint team in what is called a planned intervention (more commonly known as a C&R take out, which is explained in detail further in the book). During these times the cons (prisoners) are all trying to hear what we are up to and who is going to get it and are very keen not to miss one second of the entertainment. Once the 'take out' has begun, you just get shouting from friends of the prisoner who had, unknown to himself, volunteered for the 'good news', a control and restraint planned intervention, or 'take out', as it is often referred to by prison officers. As soon as we start to move the prisoner off the wing to the segregation unit, we will get the 'window warriors' shouting abuse and threats toward the staff involved. A 'window warrior' is the name given to a prisoner who will only be brave enough to shout abuse out from within the confines of his cell when he believes that we do not know who is doing it.

The only other noisy times worth a mention are when staff are allowed to go home at the end of their day. There are three times of the day when staff will finish a shift: at lunch time, tea time and in the evening when staff are informed that the roll (head count) of the prison is correct and they can go home. This involves leaving the wing and making your way to the gate past the cells. The prisoners will then choose this time to verbally abuse staff, which can often turn into a good exchange of insults particularly as the prison officer is normally in good spirits having finished his shift. I have been subjected to and have participated in many of these banters. On one occasion, I was leaving the prison after a very long shift and a prisoner from houseblock four shouted out, "Oi, Mr Kelly, you fat cunt," to which I replied, "The only reason I am so fat is because every time I fucked your mother, she gave me a biscuit." This type of repartee caused much entertainment for officers and prisoners alike.

On another occasion, I was on the upper walkway with a colleague called Crane, who was also, shall we say, of a comfortable size, when a prisoner shouted to me, "Mr Kelly, you fat bastard."

We both stopped in our tracks and Crane turned to me and said, "Mr Kelly, did you hear what that prisoner has just called you?"

"Yes, I did," I responded.

With that, the prisoner retorted, "You are a fat bastard as well, Crane."

So I turned to my colleague and said, "Mr Crane, did you hear that?"

"Yes," he responded.

"And did you hear the lack of respect?" I asked.

"Yes," he said. "The con clearly has more respect for you as he called you Mr Kelly and simply referred to me as Crane."

The prisoners would usually shout the same boring comments from the cells and most officers simply kept their heads down and hurried along to get out of the prison. However, having been brought up to believe that manners are all important, I always liked to acknowledge the fact that a prisoner had taken the time to single me out and abuse me. It seemed only polite to acknowledge this and repay the insult. Most of the time they would shout such sophisticated and well thought out insults such as, "Mr Kelly, you fat bastard!" or something equally distasteful but no less sophisticated. I would always try to reply in a slightly more original way and, on several occasions would correct the prisoner by pointing out that, although I might be a fat bastard, I was also in fact a "free, lager drinking, wife fucking, fat bastard."

Most of my replies to the prisoners would never give real offence and I like to think that they were at least entertaining enough to make prisoners and officers laugh or bring a smile to their faces. There was, however, one group of staff that most prisoners did take offence to and that was the Governor grades.

The noise and insults can be very daunting to anyone new who has never been in a prison before and I knew that it would take some time before I would get used to it. Just as I would need to get used to the noise, the smell of a prison is also quite unique and takes some getting used to. Although the main smell you experience is not too dissimilar to any other institution or hospital, the smell of the wings depends on the time of the day and the function of the wing.

The most common smell is food, which always smells very unappetising. Although, considering it cost around £1.40 per day to feed each prisoner, the quality of the food at HMP Highdown was very high. The other most common smell is the prisoners' sweating bodies because they are not able to use the showers either because they are banged up, or because they don't know how to keep themselves clean or, more often than not, because they can't be bothered to wash regularly. Then there is the smell from the different wings. The hospital wing (known as the healthcare unit) always smelled very clean, as the last people they tended to keep in the unit were those prisoners who actually needed to be there. At the time of my induction, houseblock two had a unique smell of perfume, as this is where the sex offenders were held. Houseblock one smelled of detox. This was the induction houseblock that housed new prisoners. At the time of my induction into the prison service the amount of prisoners coming into prison with a serious drug problem was about 75 per cent and growing fast. The smell of a de-toxing prisoner is quite unique. It is a mixture of sick, sweat and shit because this is all a de-toxing prisoner does for two weeks until he can afford to buy some more drugs on the inside.

The smell reaches its worse when you have to open the cell door of a 'three up' (a cell holding three prisoners, which was only designed for two) first thing in the morning to wake up a prisoner for court. We were a modern prison and all our cells had a lavatory in them. However, three sweating, de-toxing prisoners all shitting and spewing in one bog would challenge even modern day plumbing and the stench in the cell would encourage you to breathe through your ears. Most prisoners would still be wearing their own clothes as they refused to wear the 'No dad' prison clothes and trainers ("No, dad. Please don't make me wear them!"). The chances are that they had been wearing these clothes for about two weeks. Combine all of this with the stench of rotten food that has been discarded everywhere but in the bin, with cigarette smoke from a mixture of teabags and tobacco rescued from cigarette butts, and you will begin to understand the stench of 'detox'.

I have attempted to explain some of the sights, sounds and smells of a prison so that, as I take you further into the life of a prison officer, you will have some idea of the ambience of what is home to those serving time at Her Majesties Pleasure.

For the next stage of our training, we had to attend the prison service training college at Newbold Revel. This was a very grand, old style, stately home near Rugby. It was the flagship college of the prison service. Its other one was based in Wakefield. The course was to run for nine weeks and it was residential. However, they did not have enough room to accommodate all of the new recruits so some of us had to be put up at a nearby Trust House Forte hotel. Unlike the prison service accommodation, this hotel had a gymnasium, a swimming pool and a sauna – we poor recruits who were an overspill from the main accommodation did our best to get used to such surroundings and facilities!

I woke up early on the first morning and had quite a thirst from the previous night's drinking so went in search of a cold drinks machine. As I turned the corner into the main corridor of the hotel, I found one of the recruits from another prison dressed in his full No.1 uniform, very shiny boots and service cap, marching around the hotel. I kept low and returned to my room and risked quenching my thirst with the tap water from the bathroom rather than engage in conversation with this nutter. It turned out that he was yet another guardsman – an ex-household cavalryman (or donkey walloper as they are known in the trade).

In the morning, after a short coach ride, we arrived at the college for our first day and were met by training staff who instructed us to collect overalls, boots and PE kit from the stores. Whilst queuing up, the storeman recognised Fred Bloom and when we later asked him where he had met Fred before, he divulged that it was when he was a storeman in Hereford. By then, we had also found out from another ex-Para, who had served in the same regiment as Fred, that he remembered Fred being posted to another regiment for a couple of years. Putting two and two together, we came up with five and deduced that Fred must be ex-SAS. We all felt pleased with our deduction but, more importantly, with our foresight of not joining in with the piss take he had received from Highdown staff who we feared would live to regret it.

We were divided into sections and found ourselves split into different groups, with each group having someone from a different prison, each of which was trying to boost their staffing levels following the Manchester Strangeways riot. The worst prison riot in Britain took place at Strangeways between the 1st and 25th of April 1990 and left some of the original buildings and some of the prison records virtually destroyed. There were 147 staff and 47 prisoners injured, one prisoner was killed and a prison officer had died of a heart attack. These riots led to the Woolfe Inquiry. The prison was rebuilt and is now known simply as HMP Manchester, in line with current thinking on prison that advocates getting rid of prison names so, for example, Birmingham's Winson Green prison is now just known as HMP Birmingham.

One of the reasons why the riot caused so much damage was because there was not enough control to take back the prison quickly as there was simply not enough staff. At the time, most prison officers had to work overtime to make up their low wages and ensure that prisons were staffed but there was still a very dangerous combination of overcrowding and understaffing. At the time of the Strangeways riot, the prison population stood at 44,000. It now stands at 75,000 and it is predicted to reach 83,000 by 2008. However, a pay deal called 'fresh start' has been introduced and prison officers can no longer work overtime with one of the Woolfe report's recommendations being to increase staffing levels within prisons and to build new ones around the country.

My section was, perhaps aptly named, 'F' section and we began with the normal creeping death introductions where, in turn, we had to stand up in front of our colleagues and give our name, the prison we were from, our hobbies and something unusual about ourselves. Most of the section were ex-forces and the guy next to me stood up, came smartly to attention, gave his name, former rank and announced he was from North Sea Camp. (North Sea Camp [NSC] is an open category D male prison. It originally opened in 1935 as a Borstal and became an adult male prison in 1988. The prison is set in a rural location four miles from Boston.) He then informed the class that his hobby was reading history and the unusual thing about him was that he researched the many and varied methods of execution. With this, he promptly sat back down again, bracing himself in the 'sitting at attention' position.

There was a slight, somewhat uncomfortable, silence before the instructor looked at me. I stood up and announced that my name was Jeff but that I had not always been called Jeff. My original name was Susan but after many successful operations, I was now trying to be accepted as a man. I informed my section that I was from Happy Highdown and that my main hobby was masturbation. Thankfully, this had the desired effect and the class and, to my relief, the tutor, roared with laughter, thus lightening the mood left from the introduction by Corporal Pierrepoint, as he quickly came to be known. The irony though is that he quite enjoyed his nickname because, unknown to us, Pierrepoint was indeed his hero while I was left being referred to as Susan, which can only be my own fault for trying to be funny, I guess.

The classes were extremely boring with the topics being designed to teach us how to be nice and non-threatening to prisoners. Most of the lessons appeared to teach us how to suck eggs such as non-verbal communication skills and understanding when a prisoner is most likely to thump you – quickly followed by first aid in the event that the prisoner did thump you! Other riveting topics included: how to apply handcuffs; escorting prisoners to court; court procedures; control and restraint; adjudications; prison rules; the Criminal Justice Act; keep fit; how to open and close a door; and marching. It has to be said that the one lesson we could have done with but which we had to learn for ourselves was: how to stay awake through these boring classes while suffering from a monumental hangover.

Most of the course was based on acronyms like KISS, Keep It Short & Simple which was a pity, as they could save a fortune if they followed this advice themselves. Fred Bloom had decided to set up a study group and had suggested that Mick and I be a part of his club. In some respects we felt a certain pride that this ex-SAS guy had chosen us to be in his club but, for the most part, we simply didn't have the bottle to say no and duly turned up at his room to be tested on subjects we were supposed to be learning that day. We would find Fred in a dressing gown, aquavit and pipe in hand, and he would invite us to sit down (or, more accurately, would instruct us to sit down) while he remained on the bed, firing off lots of questions at us. We would do our best to guess the answers and when we got them wrong, he would give us such a stare that would unnerve us for the rest of the session but would certainly make us concentrate and try that little bit harder next time.

After only a few nights at the hotel, we were given our own bar. This was due, I am sure, to the celebratory mood we found ourselves in each evening and the complaints from other guests to the management about how much they were being disturbed by our boyish and good natured antics. The manager wanted to ensure that his other guests could have some peace and quiet from us bunch of 'would-be' screws but he could also see the potential income that he would receive from our drinking habits. The hotel had a function room away from the main part of the hotel with its own bar, so that's where we were to be found most evenings, ensuring that any good that may have been done in the gymnasium or the swimming pool was rapidly undone by the vast amounts of alcohol that was being consumed on a nightly basis.

The manager of the hotel went out of his way to ensure that we were happy with the arrangements and, for a small charge, he even arranged for a supper to be laid on one evening. Having asked him how much it would cost and him having replied £1.50, we devoured a bowl of chilli con carne for at least 30 people and left him the required £1.50. That was the last time we saw a supper like that.

We also discovered that the bar was not as well stocked as it should have been. When we would ask for certain mixers, for example, the barmaid would have to go all the way over to the main building to fetch the mixer. While she was gone, most of the 'would-be' screws would top up their pints. Even though we had, what we would call 'high spirited' ways of obtaining food and drink for little or no money, the manager still made a very good profit from us and has received numerous bookings from the Home Office since our memorable stay there.

Marching was a class all of its own as we were to be given instructions on how to march properly. However, most of us, in one way or another, had already been trained in how to march by the various different branches of the armed forces, with some of us having a very unique way of performing what is known as 'drill'.

We were asked for a volunteer to demonstrate how to move a body of people in a disciplined manner from point A to point B. In good forces' fashion, no one volunteered and so, in similar forces' fashion, a volunteer was chosen who the trainers knew had served in the forces. They chose Mick but what they failed to realise was that Mick was an ex-Green Jacket (Light Infantry) and would have a style of marching at a most horrendous pace, resulting in half the class not being able to keep up and the group being split in two. The instructor then decided to pick on a civilian called Paul, who had a liking for Monty Python sketches.

"Don't stand there gawping like you've never seen the Hand of God beforehand!" screamed the trainer who was clearly reaching the end of his tether by now. "Right! Today we're going to do marching up and down the square. That is unless any of you has got anything better to do? Well! Anyone got anything they'd rather be doing than marching up and down the square?" he yelled.

"Well yes!" said one bright and brave spark. "We'd rather be inside having a cup of tea!"

"All right then. Off you go," conceded the by then beaten trainer.

And so, that was the end of that class.

Some of the classes were more interesting to us than others. Control and Restraint classes were in this category and were performed in the dojo. C&R was a method of set moves and disciplines that were loosely based on a martial art called Aikido. It consists mainly of a series of moves that use pressure points on the human frame to deliver extreme pain to the recipient in order to secure compliance from that person so that they are under control. The intention is that, once they are compliant, the pressure can be eased off.

Before this method of control came in, prison officers used to use what was know as MUFTI, Minimum Use of Force Tactical Intervention. This was more commonly known as Maximum Use of Force Towards Inmates. MUFTI methods were never very successful as they usually involved using a mattress as a shield, then piling into the cell to give the prisoner the 'good news'. However, this always resulted in more prison officers getting hurt than prisoners either through 'red mist syndrome' or pure, simple, unadulterated revenge. So they decided to teach us C&R.

Some of us welcomed this training and gave it our full attention. We were the ones who understood the value of knowing a new method of being able to handle yourself in what could potentially be a very dangerous situation when being on the receiving end of violence from prisoners. Others, however, who, we thought, should have joined the probation service, were very nervous and were not learning the methods. It was clear that they would not use these methods as the vital lesson for a prison officer of 'bottle and loyalty to your mates' was simply not on their agenda. Some of the female trainees were very good at the art of C&R although they believed that we men would

41

have phenomenal and unlimited amounts of flexibility in our wrists, which caused quite a few injuries.

We had to be careful not to sustain an injury that would prevent us from completing the course, otherwise we would end up being 'back squaded' and have to do the whole course again. One of the PEIs who was teaching us C&R methods was a very likeable guy, for a PEI, most of whom are utterly devoid of any character or humour. Nick, however, was someone who was not only an excellent teacher but also possessed a great sense of humour and even looked like Jasper Carrot. During the training he would come out with some very predictable jokes that would always set me off laughing before the punch line: like the time when he instructed us all to lie on our bellies and place our hands behind our backs before asking us to lift our heads six inches off the floor. He then asked us to lift our legs and feet six inches off the floor. He then said, "Right now, you should all be resting on your cocks. Are you all now resting on your cocks?" he asked. One of the female trainees said that she was not resting on her cock and when Nick asked why not, she replied because she did not have one. "Well, would you like one?" retorted Nick.

The C&R lessons became even more fun when we were taught how to use a shield with a four-man intervention team. This is a team of four officers who would be trained to go into the cell of a prisoner needing to be restrained, either because he could hurt himself or others. In prison lingo, the prisoner would be referred to as 'kicking off'. The four-man team prepares by donning protective overalls, toe protector boots, leg guards, helmet and padded gloves. One of the team carries a short shield. The shield is a 4mm thick lexan polycarbonate with a clear centre panel for maximum visibility. This shield would be used as protection against a prisoner who might be attempting to rearrange the position of our heads with a lump of 2x2 table leg that the prison regime now insists all prisoners have in their cells. To ensure that we would have confidence in the protection that this shield would give us, we were split into twos and, whilst one of us held the shield up, the other would set about the shield with a pickaxe handle. I was paired with one of the officers who, we all believed, should have joined the Salvation Army and, on my third blow, I managed to split the shield in two. With this, the officer threw down his shield, burst into tears and ran from the room never to be seen again.

The skill with any cell 'take out', as this process was called, is to work as a team, not to hesitate and, if you are the shield officer (usually the biggest), hit the prisoner as hard as you can while the rest of the team disarms him and uses the standard C&R methods of control. We were all given the opportunity to practise each position in the team and even given the chance to take the role of the prisoner in the cell. I found that acting as the prisoner was great fun and, as well as donning the same protective clothing as the officers, I also got to wear a protective face guard, which enhanced my fierce look even more. The cell door cracked open and I was confronted with the smallest bunch of trainee prison officers I had ever seen. I was screamed at to drop the weapon, to which I replied that I had only just been given it and wanted to see how well it worked. With that, they came charging into the cell. I simply threw the pickaxe handle at their feet, barged into them knocking them over and ran out of the cell. This was not what the instructors wanted and, at the end of my C&R report, I was to find the words: 'Officer Kelly is very competent in the use of C&R and would make an extremely difficult and challenging prisoner.'

During one of our many physical training exercise classes we had a team sport game called Danish long ball. This was a kind of dodge ball game where we were split into two teams. One of the PEIs would bowl the ball to us, we would kick the ball out into the gym and then try and run to the other end before someone else picked the ball up and threw it at us. This must have been this particular PEI's favourite game as he was very good at bowling the ball, catching it as soon as it was kicked, and then throwing it straight at you. It soon became my turn and, when the ball was bowled to me, I kicked it straight into his face causing a spectacular nosebleed. I thought that my best course of action would be to run to the end of the gym, straight out through the door and then lie low in the canteen until the heat had died down or his nose had stopped bleeding, whichever came soonest.

Another part of our training covered the correct use of handcuffs and how to apply them to prisoners and officers who were to be handcuffed to prisoners during escorts to court or hospital. The prisoners had to be searched first before the handcuffs were applied. One of the training staff, who considered himself to be a bit of a thespian, dressed up as a prisoner and made the whole lesson a complete pain. When it came to me and Nick's turn to go through the procedure the trainer, true to form, started to demonstrate his acting abilities by becoming the most awkward prisoner we could ever have the misfortune to meet. He was really getting into role, becoming very aggressive, shouting and waving his hands about. Wishing to make the situation as real as possible, we warned him not to wave his arms about because we could construe that to mean that he was about to assault us. This did the trick nicely. He exploded at us to try and frighten us so we drew on all our C&R training, landing all over him to give him the 'good news' so he would know exactly what it would be like to actually be a prisoner, rather than play-acting the role. He was always a model prisoner after that.

Radio training was also a pain as most of us knew how to use a radio from our forces' experience. To add insult to injury, the equipment we were expected to use were out-of-date ex-police radios that would have looked odd on the 1960s Z Cars series. We were sent off around the grounds to go through set call signs and to report make-believe incidents. The trainer was a retired prison officer who could obviously talk a very good job and who would never tire of informing us how wonderful he was. So, there we were, out in the pouring rain listening to the radio etiquette being abused by the super screw, whilst being watched by Young Offender Inmates (YOIs) from the local prison. To give the YOIs some unexpected entertainment, we decided to move his car to a different parking space. We then radioed in to say that we had just seen two YOIs take a car that we described as looking like his car and that they had now left the college grounds with the car. Super Screw radioed back to say that he did not find this funny and that we were to make up another incident to radio back to him. It was then that we used army radio procedures and said, "No Bluff, No Bluff, end Ex," and repeated the incident of his car being stolen. He came running out to find his car not where he had parked it and proceeded to run around in circles swearing a lot. We could see that we had a lot to learn from this old-timer.

We were taught all kinds of useful information most of which forms the basic skills of a prison officer, like, for example: performing security checks and search procedures; supervising prisoners; keeping an account of those in your charge and maintaining proper order; supervising visits and carrying out patrol duties; escorting prisoners; assisting in prisoner reviews; advising and counselling prisoners, making sure they have access to professional help if needed; employing authorised physical control and restraint procedures where appropriate; taking care of prisoners' property; being aware of prisoners' rights, dignity and their personal responsibility; providing appropriate care and support for prisoners at risk of self-harm; promoting anti-bullying and suicide prevention policies; taking an active part in rehabilitation programmes, including workshops; assessing and advising prisoners; liaising with other specialist staff, including health and social work professionals; and writing prisoner reports. If it occurs to you that we needed to be prison guards, welfare officers, social workers, life savers and nannies all rolled into one, you would not be too far from the truth about the role of a prison officer.

There were also a lot of correct procedures, mainly around security, that we were not able to carry out because they would slow the prison regime down too much. In such cases, if the shit hit the fan, you would quickly find that you were being blamed for not carrying out the correct procedure as taught by the prison service college.

What was clear is that most of the course was designed to teach us what we should have already known about, what I regard as basic life skills. However, it did become evident that those officers that were most lacking in these skills were the ones most likely to go on to become prison governors. And even at governor level, they still managed to preserve a distinct lack of any basic life or interpersonal skills.

Other than these few incidents and a certain amount of good-humoured horseplay to liven things up at college, it was an exceedingly boring and dull time. We all simply wanted to ensure that we passed the tests at the end of the nine weeks so we could return to our prisons and start to perform the work of real prison officers.

A final irony was not lost on those of us with military backgrounds. Our passing out parade was cancelled as, by this time, the prison service had decided to tone down the discipline side of our training and stop acting like one of the smart, discipline services that we were proud to serve. It was at this time that we were also informed that we would be discouraged from wearing our prison service caps as they may offend the prisoners.

This should have given us a big hint of things to come.

Chapter Two

Bang 'em up

We arrived back at Highdown on the 11 April ready to start work as prison officers. But this time we would be wearing our uniforms, which did not fit and made us all itch (we later discovered that prison officers' shirts were made by prisoners and that no expense was spared on the quality of the materials, in fact hardly any expense whatsoever). The only part of the uniform that most of us did not have on our return was the prison officer's coat, so most of us had to wear our civilian coats to go into the prison. On this particular day the security team had decided to carry out one of their random searches of staff entering the prison.

Security teams inside prisons seem to attract the very worst that we can recruit as prison officers. They tend to walk around the prison as if they own it and they look upon their fellow officers as though they were potential prisoners (which may actually be the case but only in about 1per cent of the prison officer staff team). There was a rule that anyone working for the security department must have served at least one year as a prison officer. However, because Highdown was a new prison and had only been open for about 18 months, the security department was not able to have the pick of the best and most experienced staff. As the security job supposedly had a certain kudos attached to it and because it was virtually 'con free' (work that rarely involves getting too close to a prisoner), it seemed to attract either the budding Rambos or the 'con shy' (officers who are afraid of prisoners; yes there are some).

On this particular morning, the security team had decided that they would not allow any officers to enter the prison wearing civilian coats, in line with Prison Service Order 138.50 sec 2.4 (not actually the real number, but believe it or not, there is a rule that does actually state that we should not take our civilian coats into the prison). I always wondered why this was such a problem, so I decided to ask the senior officer in charge of the search party what the issue was. The reply I got demonstrated that this was certainly not someone who had done well at any charm school: "Don't question my order, just do it, sprog." I realised then that I had no desire to become one of Highdown's elite team in the security department if their senior officer was unable to explain such an important rule as this.

The rationale behind this rule was actually that, way back in the 'good old days', all prisoners used to wear prison issue clothes; brown ones for prisoners on remand and blue for convicted prisoners. Therefore the only people wearing civilian clothing in a prison would either be a visitor or a governor. (There is not much difference between governors and visitors – you don't see either of them that often and neither of them have got a clue.) In those times, the rule made sense, as they would help to prevent prisoners escaping by wearing stolen clothing.

Now, however, all prisoners can wear civilian clothes (except for E list prisoners, who have to wear distinctive coveralls with big yellow patches on them because they have attempted to escape and therefore have to be visibly identifiable and be escorted everywhere they go in the prison by a prison officer). Nowadays, there are also lots of civilian workers: why

49

probation officers have continued with this rule is anyone's guess and why it is only applied to prison officers remains a complete mystery. So, it is no wonder that the best answer I could have got was 'Just do it!'

From my very first day, though, I was getting my card marked as an awkward bugger who questions daft rules and does not comply with the security team motto of '*ab absurdo*' (from 'the absurd'*)*.

Our next stop was to report to the training department to undergo a further one week's induction before we could report to our allocated department. This week seemed to be even more frustrating than the training because we had all thought that, as soon as we got back to the prison, we would be starting work as real prison officers.

The training department was very busy and already they were taking a new batch of recruits through their initial two-week induction before sending them off to the Prison Service College. As we were just newly returned from the college, we were asked to address the class with what they should expect at the college. One of the training staff thought that, as I appeared to have plenty to say for myself, I should finish off with a final address to the class. He told me that I should tell them what a hard time they all would have but how rewarding the training would be, how much they would get from it, how it would turn them into real prison officers and give them skills they would draw on for the rest of their lives. In time-honoured fashion, I decided that it would be best to tell the truth. I told them that the next 9 weeks would indeed be hard – they would be very long and boring and most of the things that they would be taught would be rubbish and be of little use to them in their life as a prison officer – or in any other life, for that matter. I also told them that they would have the opportunity to claim loads of money by way of expenses if they were a driver and were taking others with them in their cars. I also made sure they knew about the daily subs allowance and the fact that all their meals would be provided for. I finished by telling them that they would be staying in a three-star hotel with a swimming pool and a sauna, a state-of-the-art gymnasium and their own bar and passed on a number of tips for ensuring they got the most out of their hotel stay.

The instructor, who had turned a rather worrying shade of red and looked fit to burst, managed to say through gritted teeth, "Thank you for that, Officer Kelly. I will see you later." I had a funny feeling I knew exactly why he wanted to see me later so kept well out of his way.

Because the week's induction was so boring, we spent most of our time drinking tea and chatting, little realising that these would turn out to be the main skills required of a prison officer for the majority of his time on duty.

After our one-week induction programme, we were told to report to the department that we would be working with. I was assigned to houseblock one, the induction houseblock. Like all other houseblocks, houseblock one is made up of three spurs, A, B and C. Each spur (in 1994) held about 50 prisoners and the cells were either a single cell for one prisoner or a double cell for two prisoners.

These prisons were designed as the 'New Gallery' prison, based on the designs of several American prisons. They had workshops, a laundry, kitchen, gymnasium and chapel in a central location with houseblocks surrounding these amenities. Built on the site of a former mental hospital at Banstead, HMP Highdown serves the crown court at Guildford and Croydon as well as the surrounding magistrates' courts. They were designed this way to meet the recommendations of the Woolfe report, as it was believed that holding prisoners in overcrowded conditions not only makes them restless and angry, it is inhumane and can only result in major unrest.

A spur holds prisoners who have jobs as houseblock cleaners, hotplate workers or who do other work around the prison. Most of these prisoners are prisoners who know the system very well and know how to work it to their best advantage. Some of them have either served time before, or are starting out on a long sentence, and are trying to avoid the inevitable of being shipped out to a dispersal prison, where they would be expected to serve the main bulk of their sentence. This spur was usually quiet as most prisoners would just keep their heads down and get on with it.

B spur housed some of the misfits and difficult prisoners from around the prison who had outstayed their welcome and had become very difficult to control. However, in spite of this, they were not yet qualified to be labelled as a 'Seg Rat' (a prisoner who spends most of his time in the segregation unit because he will not comply with any of the rules and has become far too dangerous to keep on the houseblocks).

C spur held the new reception prisoners who were awaiting the compulsory induction programme. The induction programme was designed to inform prisoners of what to expect during their first weeks in prison and to let them know how to access probation staff who assist them with issues such as how to secure their homes whilst in prison. We also show them the prison regime and how to make an 'application'. Applications are how all prisoners apply for any request they may wish to make from asking for a toilet roll to requesting a change of cells. Applications are only taken at a set time during the day and missing the correct application time can cause no end of hassle and frustration for the prisoner. At induction, they also learn about what work they can apply for within the prison and the rates of pay that apply to each.

There are many jobs within the prison that a prisoner can apply for. The most common – and most sought after – jobs are the wing cleaners, orderlies and kitchen workers, which pay around £7 per week. Prisoners are expected to work for about four hours per day for this princely sum. You may wonder why any prisoner would want to scrub floors in a prison for £7 per week. There were also the 'Wombles'. 'Wombles' simply walk around the grounds of the prison and pick up the shed loads of rubbish, furniture, clothing and anything else the prisoners can throw out of their windows. These are prisoners who are supposed to have been security checked to ensure that they could carry out the trusted role of a 'Womble', although most of them hardly ever did their jobs correctly and the only thing I ever saw them do was pass illicit items around the prison faster than any courier company could have, and they probably would have given DHL a run for their money.

Being a prisoner in 1994 was a very boring experience; they were 'banged up' for twenty hours a day, inside a cell of no more than 4 square yards, with only an electric light and, if they were lucky, a book to read. If someone outside loved them enough, then they might also have had a battery powered radio to listen to. One of the main principles of the prison system was to ensure that prisoners complied with the regime and rules and led useful lives whilst in prison. Convicted prisoners were only able to spend a set amount of £10 of their own money and £10 of earnings each week at the 'canteen' (the prison shop, which was available to prisoners once a week). Prisoners could spend up to £20 per week on phone cards for the BT phone on each spur. If, on the other hand, a prisoner did not like the prison issue soap and shampoo they were given each week, their only option was to purchase these items from the 'canteen' so, given all the other things they needed to purchase, you can understand why securing the highest paying job they could was such an attractive option.

It was now time for me to see the houseblock senior officer who gave me my shift pattern and also told me that I would be working on C spur. The wing was run by a principal officer (PO), four senior officers (SO) and 32 prison officers. It was their duty to ensure that the houseblock was kept safe and running 24 hours per day, 7 days per week, every single day of the year. One of the Senior Officers had a duty entitled 'detail SO' and it was his responsibility to ensure that all the shifts were sufficiently staffed to keep the houseblock going.

This was the first time that I had ever worked a shift system. It seemed to have plenty of plus points and very few minus points. I would get to have time off during the week when everyone else was at work and would be expected to work every other weekend, which ensured that, for one weekend in two, I would not have to endure being dragged around the shops. Shifts were spread over a 32-week period and were made up of the following shifts: an E or Early shift from 7am until 12:30pm; an M or Main shift from 7.30am to 5pm; an L or Late shift from 1.30pm to 9pm. Then there was the big, fat A shift – commonly known as the Arsehole shift because it was so long and tiring – from 7am until 9pm and night shifts from 8pm to 8am, which we were expected to do at least once per year.

I was given my shift pattern and told to go to the houseblock manager who wanted to welcome me to the unit. I was feeling quite impressed by the idea of being formally welcomed to the houseblock by its manager until some of the officers in the wing office informed me that the houseblock manager was gay and was always on the lookout for new talent. They went on to tell me that his previous job had been working as a gentleman's tailor. With some degree of trepidation, I went to his office and, with great relief, found no one there. A passing officer told me that he had seen him in the detail office in the admin block so I decided to use the loo first and compose myself somewhat before going back to his office to wait for his return.

When I went into the staff toilets, an officer was already there using one of the traps. He was a small but well-built man with grey hair and, after exchanging the normal pleasantries whilst conducting one's business, the officer said, "So, you must be the new guy."

"Yes," I replied confidently, "and I'm due to see the houseblock manager."

The officer then began, "Oh well, you'd better watch..." but wanting to appear in the know, I cut in.

"Oh, don't bother warning me, the lads in the wing office have already told me that he's a predatory gay. I'm not homophobic, but I tell you what, if I drop my wallet in his office, I'm going to kick it all the way back to my car before I bend down to pick it up." I exchanged a knowing glance and a wry grin with my new-found officer colleague and we both finished off our business.

I then made my way to the houseblock manager's office, only to find that the short, stocky, grey-haired officer was following me. He opened the door, proceeded to put pips on his epilates and, then, turning to face me, invited me to come into his office and sit down.

I was now in a sweat and had turned a very deep shade of red as I realised the full extent of the predicament I was now in. As it turned out, and very fortunately for me indeed, Mike was an extremely nice man who had served over 25 years in the service and was now due to retire in six months. He asked me if

I had been given the story about his previous job and told me that, because he had not worked in the armed services before becoming a prison officer but had instead worked in a department store, he was always given the title of gentleman's tailor. Over the years, the story had become even more embellished and he felt his retirement was coming at just the right time for everyone's sake.

He welcomed me to the houseblock and said that I clearly had a good sense of humour which he was pleased to see because he regarded it as one of the main skills required of a good officer, along with life skills and a hefty dose of common sense. He also warned me that my joke about the wallet could be used against me if it was heard by the new breed of self-righteous governors that the service was starting to employ. Whilst he recognised that most of the gay men he knew would take the joke in the good heart that it was intended, he told me to be careful because there would be plenty of staff who would use any excuse to land a colleague in trouble if it made them look good and gained them brownie points. His advice was very sound and, sadly, I was to come across a number of officers who would do anything to promote themselves even if it was at the expense of their colleagues and, at times, at the expense of their safety. He then told me to get out and report to Senior Officer James Pin.

James turned out to be one of the most knowledgeable senior officers I have ever met and was prepared to do anything for the staff for which he was responsible. He was brave, funny and caring, yet he was the greatest bigot I have ever come across and the most dangerous man you could ever work for. Despite all this, however, he was one of the most enjoyable senior officers you could work with. His character was very hard to describe. Although he was the worst kind of bigot, he never thought he was doing any harm and was always mortified to find out that he had offended anyone. He was from mixed parentage himself and spoke several languages badly! He also talked and worked at top speed and regularly had complaints from his neighbours because he would get his ladders out and clean the windows of his house at 5am, before walking six miles to work. He could drink like a fish and thought that he could sing like Elvis. He was very knowledgeable about most prison service matters and was able to quote any of the rules, although he had trouble trying to follow any of them.

He bent over backwards to help anyone and always seemed to have great fun trying to invent new excuses for the orderly officer (whose job was to ensure sufficient staff were on duty) as to why a member of his team had to go home. On one occasion, Officer Dean had to go home before it got dark as the lights on his car were not working and he needed to get to the garage to get them fixed. On another occasion, Officer Kelly's cat had had a nasty fall and needed to be taken to the vet.

These were all fine except, on more than one occasion, I would be working in the wing office to hear over the radio that a periodical test call would be undertaken to ensure that: 1. everyone who has a radio is alive, 2. the signal is okay; and 3. all is well in the prison. The test call would always start with Alpha 1,2,3,4 to Zulu 1,2,3,4 (the phonetic code of radio users).

On this particular evening, James had allowed more officers to benefit from a 'flyer' (an earlier than normal finish of their working shift) than he should have done and he ended up having to wear three radios (including his own, which had the call sign Alpha 1). I only realised this when the test call from the radio control room (their call sign was HT) went as follows:

HT: "Alpha 1, Alpha 1, test call, over!"

James: "Hello HT. This is Alpha 2. Your signal is good, over!"

HT: "Alpha 2, Alpha 2, test call, over!"

James (in a high voice): "Hello HT. This is Alpha 2. Your signal is good, over!"

HT: "Alpha 3, Alpha 3, test call, over!"

James (in a low, deep voice): "Hello HT. This is Alpha 2. Your signal is good, over!"

This led the control room to believe that we were fully staffed when in fact there was only me, James and a cigarette packet on the houseblock.

Although James was a very generous and knowledgeable man, I always considered him to be a danger to us all. I really do not think that he genuinely understood the risks that he was taking and the danger that he was placing himself and his colleagues in.

Most of my colleagues on houseblock 1 were new with no more than one year's service apiece. In other areas of the prison you would find officers pretending they have been with the service for far more years than they had been. There was an equal mixture of ex-service personnel and civilians, which collectively provided a good diversity of skills. In addition, 25 per cent of the officers working on houseblock 1 were female. This was the first time I'd had a job working with women and I was unsure how I would react as I had assumed that, being a male prison, there were very limited duties that a female officer could perform.

Over the next few months I was to learn how very wrong I had been about the restricted jobs that female officers could carry out. Apart from strip-searching male prisoners, female officers carry out every other task expected of a prison officer, including the Control and Restraint of very violent prisoners.

I also found that that most of our female officers had a lot of respect from the prisoners and, quite surprisingly, the prisoners would be very protective of some of them. This could be for all sorts of reasons: either, quite simply, they fancied them; or they felt protective towards them because, at this time, most prisoners still held the villain's code that you do not hurt a woman, or you would be considered a 'nonce'. Over the years, this very quickly changed, as did prisoners' attitudes towards rapists.

An example of just how good the female officers are was one called Jenny. She was a black cockney girl who was very pretty, always dressed immaculately with a perfectly ironed blouse and prison officer skirt, which came down to her calves, black tights and the kind of highly polished shoes that would make a guardsman proud. She took no shit from anyone, including us. When she was in a bad mood, because of the way she used her bike each month (monthly cycle), we knew that the only way of relieving the tension was to give her chocolate. But, because we would all be too scared to go anywhere near her, the bar of chocolate used to be delivered like a hand grenade being tossed in a room. She would declare us all to be bastards but once she had started to munch her way through the chocolate bar, she would manage a 'thank you'. There was one occasion when she came into the office and was absolutely furious, shouting, "Bastards, dirty, filthy, bastards! They're all fucking filthy bastards."

We were all very concerned and were poised ready to go and terminate the life of whoever had molested Jenny.

"Who? What? Why?" we asked.

"Them," she said, pointing out towards the prisoners on A spur, "They're all fucking dirty, filthy bastards."

"Yes Jenny, but why? What have they done to you?" we asked.

"They've been hanging around at the stairs so that they can get a look up my skirt when I go up the stairs, the dirty, filthy rotten bastards. I don't know what they think they will find up there because all they will see is a black hole."

Jenny meant that they would not see anything as the skirt was black, her tights were black and the skirt had a black sewn in underskirt and they would not have been able to see even the merest glimpse of underwear, let alone anything else. However, the description of her black hole had us all roaring with laughter, which resulted in Jenny kicking the hell out of us, whilst declaring that we, too, were "rotten, dirty, filthy, fucking bastards".

Sadly, though, there were some female officers who gave their sex a bad name by openly flirting with prisoners, or whingeing about whatever job they were told to do, or always seeking to secure a safe job away from prisoners. Male officers were equally as guilty of whingeing and trying to secure con-shy jobs. However, the macho male officer brigade (of which there seemed to be quite a few) relished putting down the good efforts of female prison officers by using stories of the few piss poor ones to tarnish all female officers.

An officer could be selected for a range of duties on houseblock 1. He or she could be the office officer, for example, the person in charge of the wing office. It would be their duty to keep the roll (head count of prisoners on the wing) correct at all times, record it and ensure the safe movement of category 'A' and 'E' list prisoners (category 'A' prisoners being considered the most risky prisoners due to their crimes such as murder and bank robbery). They would allocate cells to new prisoners coming onto the unit and ensure that those that had completed their induction programme were moved on to other houseblocks. The office officer would answer the phone and compile the audit trail of all work performed on the wing. They are also responsible for raising the alarm when an incident occurs on the wing and directing officers sent from other houseblocks to where the incident is so that they can assist their colleagues in dealing with the problem.

Another role was that of general duties officer (GD). The GDs were responsible for checking all the correspondence sent out and received by prisoners, ensuring that prisoners have not received any contraband, like a file in a cake, and such like. GDs were responsible for overseeing the free flow of prisoners; this is when prisoners who have a job in the prison, or who are attending one of the many education courses, are sent off on the secured walkways that are linked to the other units and houseblocks around the prison. They were also responsible for ensuring that the houseblock cleaners and hot-plate workers did their jobs properly as well as escorting the category 'A' and 'E' list prisoners around the prison.

A key role was that of induction officer. It was his duty to run the induction programme and ensure that all new prisoners had been given a full induction into what they can expect during their stay at one of Her Majesty's elite hotels. During the 1990s we used to receive about 90 prisoners per week so this was a pretty busy role.

Yet another responsibility was that of spur officer. Spur officers worked in pairs to control the spur they worked on. Each spur held about 50 prisoners and their movement on and off the spur was controlled by the spur officers. It was their duty to take applications from prisoners, deal with their enquiries and complaints, unlock them and then 'bang them up' at the correct time, ensuring the correct roll of the spur at all times. As you can imagine, the role of the spur officer is one of the most important and dangerous of all the jobs that can be performed in the prison and, to perform this role safely, you need a whole toolkit of different skills to ensure that you do your job well.

I was told to work with an officer on C spur for my first day and, straight away, the hairs on the back of my neck stood up and the butterflies started to get active in my stomach, as I knew that this would make or break me as a prison officer. I knew that prisoners would see that I was brand new and they would home in on me either to see how much they could get away with or to intimidate me, or simply to make fun of me.

I was greeted by Rob, a 'scouser', who had worked at Highdown for a year. He was always looking for other officers to swap shifts with so that he could work very long shifts whilst in London and then have longer periods of time off back home in Liverpool with his family. He had put in for a transfer to a prison nearer home but he would not even be considered until he had passed the obligatory first year's probation. And, even then, there could be a wait of up to two years until a place becomes vacant at a prison of your choice.

True to form, the first words Rob said to me were, "Ay up, our lad, what are you on next week? Watch out for these fuckers as they'll try to pull one over on you. They do that, don't they?"

A prisoner came up to us and interrupted Rob saying, "Guv, can I have…?"

"No," said Rob, "fuck off and play with your cellmate, I'm busy."

The prisoner then turned to me, "Guv, Guv, can I have...?"

Rob then rounded on him and said, "Now, I saw him first, now fuck off and wait your turn."

To this day, I am convinced that, because Rob was a scouser from one of the most violent, crime ridden areas of Liverpool, he suffered from an identity crisis and, at times, thought he was competing with the prisoners, instead of actually looking after them.

As I had expected, I did have lots of prisoners come up to me to test the water. I thought that the best way to play this would be to be straight and honest when asked how long I had been a prison officer. So, when asked, I replied assertively, "All day, mate!" Most of them couldn't quite work that one out and reverted to asking for what I thought were mundane items like soap, toilet paper and application forms.

I then started to go and fetch the very long list of items the prisoners were requesting, slightly concerned that I was going to forget something or get their orders wrong. But, before I could make a move, Rob's voice was in my ear, "Where the fuck do you think you're going?" I told him of my quest and was greeted with: "These fuckers can wait until it's application time, which is when they were opened up this morning at 8am. If they can't get out of bed to make an application for all that crap, then they don't need it, so tough shit. Besides that, if you fuck off from this spur, I'm left on my own and one of these cons might capture me and fuck me."

"He should be so lucky," retorted the prisoners waiting in hope.

As I was quick to learn, there is a clear safety issue as to why there should always be two officers on the spur at any one time and it is simple and straightforward – so that they can watch each other's backs and raise the alarm if they need to.

I then went to sit at the desk located on the 'ones landing' next to Rob and he carried on, "I told you these fuckers will pull one over on you because they do that, don't they? Now, about these shifts that you said you would do for me."

I knew straight away that I had embarked on a very steep learning curve and that it would be in my interests to learn the skills of a spur officer very quickly indeed if I wanted to survive.

By now, it was 8.30am and it was time to feed the prisoners their breakfast. The phrase 'feed the prisoners' was always being challenged by the new breed of 'straight from university and wet behind the ears' governors. They would tell us endlessly that to use the term 'feed the prisoners' was degrading and that we should say that we were serving them their meal. Well, I admit that my understanding of the English language may not be as good as some of these degree-waving, new-breed governors but the process of feeding the prisoners entails us opening the spur gates, standing by them and controlling the number of prisoners that go to collect their food from the hotplate. Six are allowed at the hotplate at any one time, with six being on their way down to the hotplate and a further six coming back from the hotplate. This regime is designed to keep the number of prisoners on the spur collecting their food at any given time to about eighteen. If there were to be an incident, either at the hotplate or on another houseblock (and nine out of ten times, there was), we could easily control these prisoners and get them back onto the spur so that sufficient numbers of staff could respond to the alarm. So, even with my limited knowledge of the English language, that is not, by any stretch of the imagination, serving the prisoners their meal – that is 'feeding the prisoners'.

One of the most common incidents was that a prisoner would not like the food he was being given and would chuck his dolly out of his pram. This would always result in him being 'bent up and taken down the choky' (or as the fresh-out-of-college, oh so politically correct, governors would say: 'restrained using correct C&R techniques and removed to the segregation unit for theirs and others' safety'). Inevitably, that put an end to their feeding time and they would have no dinner at all.

At the hotplate itself, there will be the Principal Officer, a Senior Officer and the General Duties Officer who would be supervising the serving of food to ensure that all prisoners are able to be fed. Again, we were feeding the prisoners and not serving them their meal! As for the term being in any way degrading, our illustrious leaders see fit to overcrowd our prisons by cramming up to four prisoners in a cell that was designed to house only two. Now that's what I call degrading. Then they see fit to hold them in prisons where they spend their time rotting in their cells because there are insufficient viable rehabilitation courses or training programmes to give them some chance of attempting to lead a better life upon their release. Now that's what I call inhuman and pointless. But, according to our illustrious leaders, we should be much more concerned that the term 'feeding the prisoners' could cause offence and be seen to be degrading. An indication of priorities out of kilter with the real world, perhaps?

Once we had finished feeding the prisoners, the morning free flow to education would begin with prisoners leaving the spur to go off along the secure walkway to their appropriate destination. I proceeded to search the prisoners in the fashion that I had been taught at the prison service college only to realise that I was causing some concern to both staff and prisoners. Staff were concerned that, because the regime timetable was so tight, there would not be enough time in the day to search each prisoner correctly. The prisoners were concerned because my searching was so thorough that I was highly likely to find something they would prefer me not to find. But fresh from the prison service college, I carried on searching them in the manner that I had just been taught.

After the free flow had finished, our duties were to 'bang up' the 'new' and the 'work shy', prisoners who were either new and waiting for the induction programme or those who had not found a job and were waiting to be moved to another part of the prison to free up space for the ever-growing waiting list of volunteers on the outside who wanted to come into the prison.

We class them as 'volunteers' because, to earn a place in prison, 95 per cent of prisoners had committed a crime that would warrant a prison sentence of their own free will. The other 5 per cent had either been fitted up by a misguided police officer (who could not find his bum without a search warrant) or they had simply been in the wrong place at the wrong time.

Every prisoner who enters prison must go through an induction programme into prison life and the prison regime, so that they are aware of where everything is and how to access it. They are given a talk on the 'do's and don'ts' of the prison rules, shown a video about the dangers of AIDS in prison and the most likely ways of catching hepatitis from their cellmates. In the early days of life at Highdown, they were even given a guided tour of the prison so they could see the workshops, education centre, gymnasium and chapel. In those days it felt like an introduction to a holiday camp and the tour of the prison serving as a way of ascertaining whether the facilities were to the prisoner's liking or not. The only thing I was missing was my tour umbrella as I was conducting the guided tour.

The term 'workshops' conjures up a rather heart-warming image of prisoners sewing mail bags in happy and pleasant surroundings for the good of the community in which they live. Nothing could be further from the truth, however. In the early days of Highdown, these were more like education units where prisoners could learn a trade that would be useful to them on their release. But this was felt to be too expensive and it was decided they would be used as workshops where prisoners could carry out a host of mindless tasks like: placing a piece of bubble wrap in the bottom of a plastic container that would be used by a supermarket to place fruit in; or assembling headphone sponges onto mini headphone sets destined for the entertainment of airline passengers. We had one prisoner who took great delight in sticking his finger up his bum and then wiping it onto the earpiece. But don't let that put you off enjoying the in-flight entertainment on your next flight as, the chances of ending up with this particular con's handy work would be as high as the chances of winning on one of their in-flight game cards – even if the results are never quite as rewarding as the prisoners' pay.

The education unit is purpose-built with nine classrooms in which prisoners can attend classes to learn English, Maths, Art & Crafts, Pottery, Spanish, Computer Studies and Cookery. Teachers in the education unit were provided by NESCOT (North East Surrey College of Technology). The unit was below the prison library on the ground floor and it was the duty of two prison officers to ensure that the sixty or so prisoners who attended these classes behaved themselves and did not either rob, rape or kill the teachers or make ladders, knives or anything else in the arts and crafts classes that they could use to either attack a prison officer or attempt an escape from the prison. There was a particularly scary moment in the cookery class when I was on duty. The cookery teacher had a habit of treating the prisoners as children and was constantly shouting at them to behave. For most of them this did seem to work as mentally they were very much like children and responded well to this type of control. However, one prisoner took great exception to this and proceeded to shout back at the teacher, offering to cut her throat with the 10-inch chef's knife he had in his hand at the time.

The teacher seemed oblivious to the danger she was in and squared up to the prisoner, continuing to shout at him and telling him that if he persisted in behaving like a child, then she would continue to treat him as such. I decided it was time to hit the alarm button and began to try and calm the prisoner down. At which point, the teacher rounded on me and started to shout at me for having the audacity to interrupt her. Somehow the prisoner and I were suddenly in the same boat and, realising the humiliation we both felt, he was more sympathetic to my request that he handed the knife to me, pleading with me only, "For God's sake, deal with her, Guv." The prisoner was duly escorted back to his cell and, although he faced adjudication the next day, he was not given any extra days on his sentence as he was already serving life for the murder of three people. To this day, the teacher has no idea of how close she came to being his fourth victim.

Plastic bowls, plates and cups are given to the prisoners, because the cost is cheap and they cannot be used as weapons. However back in the '90s we allowed prisoners who were serving long sentences to be able to have their own selection of china crockery sent in, so that they did not have to eat off plastic plates. On more than one occasion I have seen prisoners use these as weapons in a fight.

I recall one officer who was supervising the medication queue when a long serving prisoner who was concerned that he might miss his gymnasium class joined the queue holding his floral china bowl full of Rice Krispies and milk, which he had just collected from the hotplate servery. The officer informed the prisoner that he was not allowed to wait in the medication queue with his breakfast and that he would have to take the breakfast to his cell and then return for any medication. The prisoner protested stating that the PEI's were here to collect him for his gym session and that he would waste too much time going back to his cell with the breakfast and simply wanted to grab his medication and then he was going to put the medication and his breakfast in his cell whilst he then went to the gym.

The officer was insistent and explained to the prisoner that the rules were very clear about collecting medication and that it did not allow for someone to be balancing a bowl of Rice Krispies whilst queuing up to collect medication. The officer explained to the prisoner that he would allow the prisoner to go to the front of the queue to collect his medication once he has taken his breakfast back to his cell and that he would ask the PEI to wait a few moments longer. The prisoner did not like this compromise so he smashed the china bowl across the face of the officer. The alarm was raised and the prisoner was very quickly restrained and taken to the segregation unit. The officer had to go straight to hospital and received 30 stitches to the wound on his face. What bothered the officer more was that he was getting married the next day and he wanted to look his best for the wedding photos.

The prisoner received 28 days added to his sentence, which he had removed when he applied 4 years later for added days to be cancelled, as he had been a good prisoner for the last three years of his sentence. The officer received £500 from the CICA (Criminal Injuries Compensation Authority) which would not have even paid for the wedding photos to be altered.

New prisoners serving their first prison sentence were usually very quiet and confused by the strange world they now found themselves in. They were also the ones who were likely to smell the most because they were too scared to use the showers. They would ask lots of questions and would sometimes be given a bum steer from other prisoners or would have all their tobacco conned out of them by prisoners who preyed on the new intake. It was our job to try and calm them down and give them some lessons in hanging onto their belongings because there were a lot of thieves and con men in prison.

The most argumentative prisoners were those who had served a short sentence before and had returned to prison, only this time with attitude. They were the most likely to get into fights with staff and end up wrapped up for a visit to the Block (or in prison parlance, restrained using correct Control and Restraint methods and removed to the segregation unit). They would consider themselves to be gangsters and have the attitude to match. More often than not, though, they would only succeed in annoying the real gangsters and end up with a condition called 'tuna on the brain'. Prisoners were very adept at naming things along the lines of 'it does what it says on the tin'. So, 'tuna on the brain' involved placing a tin of tuna in a sock, waiting until the victim's back was turned, then swinging the home made cosh and smashing it over the victim's head, rendering the prisoner either unconscious, bleeding profusely or both.

Then there were the 'wannabe lifers' who were serving a sentence of more than six years and who were of the opinion that, because they would not be eligible for parole until they had served two-thirds of their sentence, they could behave as they wished towards staff. They too would adopt this hard man image because they knew that they were destined for what is known as a dispersal prison where real life lifers would be serving their time. As a 'wannabe lifer', they pretend not to care about anyone or anything in the hope of getting themselves a reputation before hitting the dispersal prison, hoping in some perverse way that this would give them some kind of kudos with the real life lifers. They would try and perfect what they believed to be the 'lifer walk', which involved walking down the landings with their head tilted to one side and their shoulders raised as if they had two rolls of carpets under their arms.

There were, of course, the more mature and experienced prisoners, who would simply get on with 'doing their time'. They would keep themselves to themselves and would usually only associate with their own kind. They would steer well clear of trouble as this would have an affect on any parole board they may be applying for. We would only have these prisoners at Highdown if they were staying over whilst being transferred to another prison or if they had been sent to us for accumulated visits. This is where prisoners who are held in many of our far flung gaols are unable to receive visits from their loved ones, and would thus save up their entitlement of one visit per fortnight to have what is known as accumulated visits at a local prison like ours.

When Highdown first opened in 1992, a request was made to have some long-serving prisoners sent to Highdown to help new prisoners and staff bed in. However, some of these prisoners turned out to be those that were a real pain in the arse to the prisons that sent them and they were glad of the opportunity to get rid of them. So, by the time I had joined Highdown, all that was left from this initial intake were the bad and the mad.

Some of these prisoners were housed on houseblock 1 so I got to know a few of them during my first few weeks as a prison officer. One character, known as Shirley, was about 20 stones of muscle, with a shaven head and a very fetching 'mars bar' (scar) down his cheek. If ever a Victorian custom drama film should be made that involves a scene of a convict escaping from Dartmoor, Shirley would fit the bill. He was a very quiet man and had very few associates, although he was always on the lookout for new talent, as he was quite partial to Latin-looking men.

He also had an extreme dislike of 'Bacons' (sex offenders) and if he came across a new intake sex offender, who had refused to 'go on the numbers' (under Prison Rule 43, prisoners can be held separately from the main stream of other prisoners because their offence is likely to endanger their lives), he would choose his moment carefully before delivering the good news to the prisoner in the form of a PP9 battery placed in a sock then smashed over the prisoner's head.

The governors always assumed that we were telling the prisoners who the bacons were. However, we housed two reception orderlies (two prisoners who worked all day and evening in the reception area) on the houseblock and they would get to know everything there is to know about a new intake. They would then either pass on the info through associates they knew who were going through the reception area or would let someone like Shirley know as soon as they returned from their shift. The end result being that any sex offender who was stupid enough to refuse the rule usually ended up being cared for either by our healthcare centre or outside in hospital. What our governors did not realise is that we did not need the extra work that would be created by such an incident and we would do everything we could to convince the bacon to take the rule.

Most of these long-termers were very easy to get along with and you could easily slip into a false sense of security with them, assuming that they really liked you, which would make some officers believe that they had some sort of standing amongst their peers. There was one particular British prisoner, a very violent man who was on remand for the murder of a prison officer in Greece. The murder had happened during an escape he was involved in from a Greek prison whilst serving time for other offences. According to him, the van transporting them to another prison was stopped by an armed gang of friends of two other prisoners in the van and, during the break out, a Greek prison officer had been killed.

The Greek authorities were therefore very keen to receive our prisoner back into their custody. However, he was very reluctant to improve his suntan in Greece as he believed that, as soon as he was back in their hands, he would meet with a very unfortunate accident, which would result in his loved ones cashing in on his life assurance. I have no doubt that, if he were to be returned to Greece, there would be a very real chance that he would either meet with a very unfortunate accident or be shot whilst trying to escape. This is why he was classed as a very dangerous category 'A' prisoner because, in order to stay in this country and therefore remain alive, he would do anything to seriously hurt or kill one of us prison officers, thus ensuring that the British authorities would insist that he serve his sentence with us first.

He had actually made this threat when he was questioned by our police and it amazed me how friendly one particular female prison officer became towards him. Helen had served about 18 months in the service and was from north of the border. She believed that, as she had served such a long time as a prison officer and had such a vast wealth of experience behind her, she knew all there was to know about life in all its guises. It seemed to have escaped her attention that she was extremely lazy and always unable to give constructive advice as she was so convinced that she knew everything and had no need to actually learn the job. She had a total belief that the prisoner was innocent and that we should be mounting a campaign to ensure his safety and freedom. She also did not believe that he would be a danger to any of us and would spend too much time in his cell. It was hardly surprising that this led to a host of rumours about her sexual habits and liaisons, with even prisoners becoming convinced that she was shagging him.

I was astounded that she was never marched straight from the gaol and kicked out of the job, and I wondered how our overzealous security department could be oblivious to her behaviour which was fast becoming common knowledge throughout the prison, not just on our houseblock. It was not until some months later that we discovered that she was providing our security department with all kinds of information, not about the prisoners but about us, the prison officers, most of which was a load of old crap. However, I suppose the security department believed that it was worth keeping her on a leash on the houseblock as at least they would gather what they thought was useful information from the 'hooded claw'.

Eventually the prisoner was moved back to Greece and, I believe, was shot whilst trying to escape from their custody. Perhaps as predictable, Helen ended up pregnant. She transferred to another prison and I am sure that, with her wealth of self-taught knowledge, she will be thinking that she is doing very well in her own little way, still utterly oblivious to the mayhem she is unleashing around her.

There was another senior officer by the name of Barry Smith who had been in the job for over 20 years and had served in the regular army as a grenadier guardsman. He was also the branch chairman of the Prison Officers Association (POA) at Highdown. As a senior officer he was crap and was always shouting at his staff and causing problems, yet as union rep he was one of the best and would never allow our management to place us in danger. Once he was out of uniform, he was also one of the most approachable people you could wish to meet. However, he was a crap SO and, on more than one occasion, he would undermine our authority with the prisoners by overturning our decisions on issues the prisoners had brought to our attention. This meant that prisoners would simply ask to see SO Smith whenever we knocked them back on a request. So, in order to teach Brian a lesson, we allowed all the prisoners who made a request to see him wait outside his office. The queue ended up at about 50 prisoners long and had the desired result. Barry asked us what the fuck we were up to.

He did get the message, however, and never undermined us again. Barry retired from the job at the age of 55 and, sadly, one year later he died from a heat attack. He had a full prison service funeral, which was very well attended and showed the level of respect he had commanded within the service by people who knew him well.

It was then that I discovered that there is a very high mortality rate amongst prison officers once they retire. It is estimated that the average life expectancy of a prison officer who has served over 20 years is about 18 months after retirement. No wonder we have such a good retirement pension, as there are not many of us who get to claim it for very long.

The reason behind this high rate is simply down to the stress that we have to put up with, day in, and day out. There are not many jobs in which you would be expected to fight off a prisoner at least twice a week. In those early days, I resolved that my plan would be to not allow the stress to get to me and, thereby ensure that I left the job in good health, able to enjoy my pension for many years to come.

Being a new prison, there were constantly new staff joining us and eventually we ended up with some very good officers on houseblock 1, who were to become some of the best people I have ever worked with. There were times that I would go home with a pain in my ribs, not because of an attack from a prisoner but because we would be laughing so much during the day. There was one prison officer who had joined the houseblock who was a very fit person, spending all his spare time in the gymnasium. He was asked by one of our senior officers what he did before he joined the prison service and the officer replied that he was a "lifeguard", so the senior officer enquired if he had to sit on a horse outside Buckingham Palace, and the officer said no as he was a lifeguard in a swimming pool. The senior officer said, "Don't bullshit me son, you could not get a horse in a swimming pool."

All cells had to be inspected each day with a process called LBBs (Locks Bolts and Bars). This meant that spur staff would have to inspect every cell every day to ensure that they were in good order and functional for their use. We would enter the cell and insist that the prisoners were out of their beds by announcing, "Hands off cocks and on with socks! We are here for a cell inspection and to see how well you are treating Her Majesty's property." As you entered the cell, which normally housed three prisoners, the smell would hit you hard. You would attempt to breathe through your ears as we asked the prisoners, "You lot must come from one of those three Chinese Cities, either Heaving, Minging or Gopping. By the smell of this cell, I would say that you are from Gopping and that therefore you must be Goppers. This is no way to treat Her Majesty's belongings. Here is some cleaning equipment. Get it clean and make it shine, you Goppers!"

Because of this greeting, we developed a new name for prisoners, Goppers. Many attempts were made to stop us from referring to the prisoners as goppers, however, as the management did not have a clue what this meant. They were even concerned that we referred to them as prisoners, as these were new, enlightened times, when the new breed of prison governors were trying to get us to call prisoners either 'Mr' or use their first name and approach them in a fluffy, friendly way. The new name did not go down at all well. There seemed to be very little attempt to prevent prisoners from calling us all kinds of unsavoury names.

There appeared to be some resentment from the management about the camaraderie that was developing on houseblock 1 and they accused us of being too ready to use C&R on prisoners. However, what they failed to realise was that an induction wing will always have a higher incident rate as most of our 'customers' are fresh from the street. They also failed to see that, compared to other local prisons, we actually had a far lower ratio of incidents on our houseblock.

Because we seemed to be having too much fun and our use of C&R was deemed higher than on any of the other houseblocks, our team was split up and some of us were placed onto different houseblocks and units around the prison. This only served to increase the confidence in the new officers on the other houseblock units. Their intent had clearly been to split up what they believed to be a team of thugs. However, it had the reverse effect by allowing our 'enthusiasm' for the job to brush off onto all the new recruits.

Chapter Three

Okey Dokey, Down the Choky

Prisoner: "Guv, what will I get when I'm dragged in to see the Governor?"

Jeff Kelly: "Well, it depends if you go guilty or not."

Prisoner: "What do you mean?"

Jeff Kelly: "If you plead not guilty and the case goes against you, you will get even more days added to your sentence than if you had simply pleaded guilty in the first place."

Prisoner: "That seems unfair. What if I didn't do it?"

Jeff Kelly: "Did you do it?"

Prisoner: "Yes, I did, but it still seems unfair. How can I make sure that I don't get too many days added?"

Jeff Kelly: "Well, the number one is one of those dodgy handshake lot and, if you give him the secret saying, he is bound by his lodge to be more lenient on you."

Prisoner: "What's the saying, Guv?"

Jeff Kelly: "You must promise not to tell anyone. It is, *if it wasn't for those pesky kids, I would have got away with it.*"

No. 1 Governor: "Bring in the next prisoner. What is your name and number?"

Prisoner: "Smith ER2324, Guv."

No. 1 Governor: "You are charged with attempting to assault a prison officer. How do you plead?"

Prisoner: "I am guilty as hell. If it wasn't for those pesky kids, I would have got away with it."

No. 1 Governor: "Officer Kelly, see me afterwards."

Prisoner Smith was subsequently given ten added days which was about half of what he should have got for that offence. I can only assume that the governor was in a good mood or he, too, was a great fan of Scooby Doo. I never did find out as I avoided seeing the governor afterwards.

The 'Block', the 'Seg', the 'Cooler', the 'Bin', the 'Numbers', the 'Choky' – these are just some of the names that prison segregation units have been called.

Segregation units have been described by some as a prison within a prison. It is rumoured that above the doors of some of the segregation units is Dante's famous words: 'Abandon every hope, all ye who enter.'

Segregation units have the reputation of being brutal places where summary justice is dealt out by oversized officers on steroids. I will not try and deny that there have been some incidents in some segregation units that have indeed lived up to this reputation. In an attempt to dispel the undeserved reputation of Wandsworth prison segregation unit, they changed its name to the Care and Separation Unit. However, at Highdown prison, the No. 1 Governor was keen to make sure that the segregation unit was managed in line with prison rules and that it was run as a centre of excellence.

To be selected to work in the segregation unit, it was not compulsory to be built like a brick shithouse and carry a lobotomy certificate. On the contrary, the work and purpose of the segregation unit is extremely varied and all staff working in these units need to be very experienced prison officers with at least two years of prison service under their belt.

The purpose of a segregation unit is pretty straightforward – it is to house prisoners who are unable to be housed with any other prisoners. A prisoner who is held in the segregation unit is housed there for three main reasons: for their own protection (as other prisoners would like to kill them); for adjudication (they have breached one of the many prison rules and will have a hearing in front of the governor to determine their guilt and the punishment they are to receive); and for punishment in cellular confinement. Only the governor of the prison can order a prisoner to be kept within the segregation unit.

If there is an incident where a prisoner has kicked off and become violent to either prison officers or other prisoners, they are removed to the segregation unit using control and restraint procedures. On arrival, they are strip-searched and placed into a cell. If they are still showing signs of being violent to staff, they are placed in a cell called the special cell.

This cell had only a low level concrete bed, a cardboard potty, a blanket and a non-destructible dressing gown. These cells were designed to withstand a lot of damage and prisoners that were placed in them usually tired themselves out very quickly. They suddenly became very keen to demonstrate that they could behave themselves so that they would be returned to the normal segregation cells.

The normal segregation cells had a bed that was bolted to the floor, a metal sink and a toilet. They were not designed for long stays and there was little room for any personal possessions.

Any prisoners despatched to the segregation unit were usually only there for a very short period of time and those who were there, either as cellular confinement or for 'good order and discipline', or their own protection, had very few home comforts.

There were also prisoners who would come to stay in the segregation unit who had been sent to us on what was known as the 'magic roundabout'. They were the few prisoners who are held in segregation units because they are too dangerous to be kept with other prisoners because they are extremely violent and entirely unpredictable. Some of them have an infamous notoriety like Charlie Bronson. Bronson, whose original name was Michael Peterson, has spent 25 years in prison and is currently serving a life sentence for taking a teacher hostage in Hull prison. He has a larger than life reputation. When I was at the prison college, most of the instructors would have some horror story to tell about him and they managed to create this mythological character that was reputed to be one of the strongest prisoners in the system who hated nonces, governors, female prison officers, male prison officers (who were either scared of him or obstructive to him) and noisy prisoners.

It had been rumoured that he had beaten other prisoners near to death, spent time in Broadmoor prison hospital for the criminally insane and that it took up to three Control and Restraint teams to get him under control. He has repeatedly seized staff and inmates during his years behind bars, and once boasted, "I've had more hostages than Saddam Hussein."

Bronson was jailed in 1974 when he was sentenced to seven years for armed robbery, but he has served further terms for offences inside prison. As he himself once said, "I've ate more porridge than the three bears."

In an incident with three fellow inmates who were on remand for hijacking the Iranian plane at Stanstead Airport,

Bronson barricaded them in a cell for seven hours and made one of them tickle his feet, whilst instructing another to hit him with a metal tray. He had threatened to eat one of the prisoners and demanded a 'Jumbo Jet to land on the exercise field, so that it would crash into the nonce's wing', an axe, sub-machine guns, a cheese sandwich and ice cream. The siege ended after he slashed himself with a razor.

Bronson has attacked prison officers on several occasions and been involved in some twelve prison sieges which resulted in damage totalling £600,000. Bronson has been known to bend cell doors by smashing them with his fists and is considered to be 'probably the most disruptive inmate in the country'.

My first meeting with Bronson happened whilst I was still very new to the prison service and was working on houseblock 1. When he arrived at Highdown he was completely naked other than a body belt (a leather belt that is locked around the waist of a prisoner and has two handcuffs attached either side, so that they are unable to move their arms). He was escorted by officers of the security team who were allergic to either penicillin or steroids and appeared to be trying to impress Bronson by puffing out their sunken chests. Bronson seemed to treat them with indifference and was keenly looking all around him.

He was escorted to the segregation department and was met by one of the segregation senior officers Pete E. Pete was a very experienced senior officer with over 20 years in the job and he had also looked after Bronson in other segregation units. The senior officer welcomed Bronson to Highdown and assured him that all his belongings would be looked after whilst he was there. Pete asked him if he had any questions and Bronson said that he wanted only one bag of possessions which contained a few clothes and toiletries. He also asked if, and when, he could use the gym. Pete agreed that he would be given the bag of possessions as soon as they had been checked by his officers and the question of if, and when, he could use the gym would be determined by the governor. Bronson seemed happy with this and was due to have a visit from friends and family the next day.

By rights, this should have been a very short period of stay for Bronson provided that we did not lie to him or mess with either his mind or his belongings.

The first problem came on the day of his visit, however. Some of his family had to wait a long time because a security principal officer was insisting that more identification was required than what was being shown to him. Bronson started to bang his cell door and make a lot of noise. He was clearly very upset. The call went out to summons the biggest officers in the prison to escort him to his visit once he had calmed down. As I was 6' 3" and 18 stone of controlled fat, I was sent to report to the segregation SO.

When I arrived I was greeted by the very loud banging of a cell door and was amazed to see that the door was shaking with each bang. I also noticed that the concrete that secured the integral hinges was starting to crumble. The senior officer, Pete E, gave us a briefing about the situation and said that we needed to open the cell door and allow Bronson to go to his visit. Pete said that he wanted me to stand by the stairwell that led to the lower level of the unit as Bronson would try and get down there if the pathway was not blocked.

It was at this time that I started to believe everything that anyone had ever told me about Bronson and sheer panic started to set in. I knew that I would get very hurt and I was allergic to pain. Pete started to calm Bronson down and managed to stop him from re-shaping the cell door. Pete said that he was going to escort him to his visit and Bronson reassured him that he would be calm. Pete then gave one final check to make sure that we were all in position and opened the cell door.

Bronson was out of the cell like a ferret, heading straight for me on the stairs. At first I thought of going straight into the foetal position for maximum protection and trying to plead for mercy. However, my body reacted differently and I stood firmly on the stair landing, blocking the route that Bronson appeared to be taking.

Bronson then came right up to my face and said, "Hello Guv, do I know you from somewhere?" I quickly replied, "Do I owe you money?" and he said "No." "Well, in that case," I replied, "you don't know me." He then asked me, "How long have you been in the job?" I said, "All fucking day." With that, he roared with laughter and declared that he liked me.

After Bronson's visit, Pete E said that I had done a very good job and that he would be proud to have me on his team. I said that I would be more proud if I could get a clean pair of pants as I thought I might have soiled the ones I was wearing.

I had not soiled them but the humour was simply my way of dealing with potential violence. An important survival principle that I had learned long before I joined the prison service was that it is very rare for a man to kick the shit out of you while you are making them laugh.

A few days after this, Bronson had been promised by one of our governors that he would arrange for him to use the gym. However, when it was discussed with the security team, it was deemed to be too risky. This really pissed Bronson off and he started to rearrange what little furniture he had that was bolted to the floor. He also made it clear that he wanted to punch the governor for lying to him.

The governor concerned was on duty that evening and came to the Seg to talk to Bronson. The governor was advised that Bronson would attack him. The governor said that, as he had made the mistake of misleading him, he should therefore face him and sort the problem out. The governor was duly punched as soon as we opened Bronson's cell door.

We had a very brief visit from Bronson a few years after this. He was clearly becoming a very demoralised man who had become more disturbed over the years. Not long after his second visit, he was sent to Hull where he took one of the teachers hostage. He received a life sentence for this.

Much has been written about Bronson – and indeed, Bronson has written much about himself, too. I must confess that I know very little about the man and what makes him tick. To me he was just another prisoner and, although he has been very disruptive, he was always predictable which, in a way, made him safe to manage. I am amazed that most prison governors have never managed to achieve this as, in the very brief time that I knew Bronson, it seemed to me that he only requested things that he was entitled to and had a very strong dislike of bullshit and lies.

Another of these 'difficult to handle' prisoners on the prison system's 'merry-go-round' was a prisoner called Prisoner D. When Prisoner D came to stay with us for Christmas, he was very quiet and hardly spoke to any of the staff.

The moment he arrived in the reception area he attempted to assault the officers working there and was taken straight to the special cells. That evening, which was Christmas Eve, the governor decided to move him from the special cell to a normal segregation cell. The senior officer on duty in the segregation unit carried out the order and, as they were moving Prisoner D, he hit the senior officer with such force that the SO was rendered unconscious and was bleeding from a head wound. The other two officers on duty in the Seg raised the alarm via their radios and informed the control room that Prisoner D was armed. The call went out: 'Hello, all station alarm bells, segregation unit, HT out!'

I was working on houseblock 1 this evening and, along with one other officer who was assigned to respond to alarm bells, I made my way at full speed to the segregation unit, about 300 yards and several locked doors away (each Houseblock would assign at least two officers to respond to the alarms). When we arrived, we found that the SO was lying on the floor with a bleeding head wound and one of the segregation officers was nursing a broken jaw. The other officer informed us that Prisoner D was armed. Prisoner D was poised over the SO and appeared to be very aggressive. I have never seen so many officers struggle to get out their staves (truncheons) to give Prisoner D the good news. As it turned out, Prisoner D hit the floor very quickly and defended himself by rolling into the foetal position. Staff then jumped onto Prisoner D to restrain him and the only person to be hit with the staves was a security officer.

Prisoner D was so strong that it took over half an hour to re-locate him back into the special cells and, even though a considerable amount of pain was applied to all the regulated pressure points on his body, none of them seemed to bother him in the slightest.

It was no surprise that, when the nurse turned up at the segregation unit to check on the injuries of both staff and prisoner, he recognised the prisoner as a very difficult mental health patient. I therefore asked the nurse why he was being regarded as a normal prisoner and the nurse said that, as there was such an acute shortage of beds in secure units of mental hospitals, the doctors sign off some patients as sane and therefore they are returned to the prison system.

The senior officer and the segregation officer spent their Christmas in hospital recovering from their injuries. Prisoner D enjoyed his Christmas dinner in the segregation unit blissfully unaware of any problem. I am quite sure that the incompetent doctor who had signed prisoner D as sane had a wonderful and peaceful Christmas.

Both the senior officer and segregation officer returned to work within a few days despite being advised by the hospital to spend at least two weeks recovering. But neither of them wanted to let their colleagues down at the festive season when staffing levels are at their minimum.

The daily routine of the segregation unit is very busy. Mornings are taken up with the adjudication of prisoners who have breached the rules. These breaches of the rules can be something as minor as non-compliance to an order given by an officer to a serious assault of an officer. Most prisoners who are due to face the governor for breaching these rules are taken to the segregation unit by their houseblock staff on the morning of the adjudication, are searched and then placed into a holding cell ready for their adjudication.

On one particular morning, we had a new governor grade that was learning the ropes and part of his induction was to experience and learn how to carry out an adjudication. The senior officer asked me to give this governor a briefing about procedures.

This new governor grade had already gained a reputation of being a self-opinionated twit and had already been very critical about how prison officers performed their duties. Even the other more experienced governors were fed up with his constant sniping. This governor had a bit of a nervous twitch so I thought that I would live up to the preconceived view that he had of us.

I showed the governor into the adjudication room. It was laid out with a desk and chair for the governor at one end. On the desk where the governor was to sit were a set of prison rules and suggested punishments if any of them were to be breached. On the wall behind where the governor sits is a picture of the Queen (it is, after all, Her Majesty's Prison Service). At the other end of the room, facing the governor's desk, is a small table and a chair, which are bolted to the floor (to prevent the prisoner from throwing them at the governor) where the prisoner sits and a chair either side where the escorting officers sit and keep an eye on the prisoner.

I showed the governor the layout of the room and then pointed out the adjudication pen to him. He told me that he had his own pens but I explained that this pen was the official pen and that I needed to instruct him on how he should use it.

I explained the adjudication procedure to him, "We will march the prisoner into the room and we will then come to a halt, turn smartly to our left and give a salute to Her Majesty and the prisoner will give his name and number to you. You will them inform the prisoner that he may sit, at which the prisoner will sit in the chair that is bolted to the floor and place his hands on the table in front of him." The governor asked why the prisoner had to place his hands on the table and I explained that, if the prisoner takes his hands off the table, he is clearly about to attack him or, worse still, he may be about to attack the Queen herself!

I went on: "You, governor, should then read the charge to the prisoner and ask the prisoner how he would like to plead, guilty or not guilty. If he pleads not guilty, you will then drop the adjudication pen and, by the time you have picked it up, we will have shown the prisoner the error of his ways and he will then plead guilty."

I did not give the governor enough time to give me his views on this and quickly made my way to the cell for the first prisoner to face the governor. My colleague and I marched the prisoner into the adjudication room, called the prisoner escort to halt, smartly turned to the left, saluted the Queen, and the prisoner then gave his name and number to the governor.

The governor then invited the prisoner to sit and he read the charge to the prisoner, finishing by asking if he wanted to plead guilty or not guilty. The prisoner said not guilty. We then had to contain ourselves as the governor broke out into uncontrolled twitches that would have made Jack Douglas from *Carry On* fame proud. He could be seen gripping the pen as if his life depended on it. Later that day the number one governor pulled me to one side and warned me to stop winding up his new governor grades.

As the story of Prisoner D demonstrates, the segregation unit can end up acting as an overflow bed unit for the mentally ill and, on one occasion, we ended up playing host to a prisoner who liked to set light to things, namely mental hospitals, so it had become very difficult to get him located into one.

We had had strict instruction that, at no time, must he be given matches or a lighter. One Sunday we had just returned back from the church service with those prisoners that wished to repent their sins (or, in other words, to get drugs passed to them from the other prisoners), when we noticed smoke rising up from the one's landing. An officer who had been on the landing shouted out, "Fire!" and pressed the fire alarm. Another officer, Joe, and I immediately ran to the hose pipe as we were both very keen to play fireman. I beat Joe to the hose and proceeded to the cell door where black smoke was now belching out from the gaps around the door. Another colleague was struggling with an inundation key (this is a key that is designed to undo an access point in the centre of the cell door so we can push the hose through the door and extinguish the fire). The key was not very effective and was being dropped on the floor as the smoke had become very thick and we were all having trouble breathing. Whilst this was going on we could hear the prisoner banging his door.

Joe then warned me that he was going to open the door and, as he did, I let blast with the fire hose to ensure that the flames would be kept away from us. As the door opened, there was the prisoner with a cigarette hanging from his mouth asking us for a light. He was quickly wrapped in a wet blanket, as his clothes were alight, and bundled out to safety. I then proceeded to extinguish the flames whilst the rest of the segregation team evacuated the segregation unit to the fire collection point.

It was at this point that we could hear the whistle tests of the Short Duration Breathing Apparatus (SDBA) that are used by our SDBA teams, a group of staff trained to use the SDBA and rescue prisoners from fires. It was very clear to us that if we had waited for this team to get their act together, the prisoner would have died.

Once we had been relieved by the SDBA team, we went outside to sit down in the fresh air and both then lit a cigarette, which, of course, set us off with a coughing fit. The senior officer of the SDBA team decided to give us a bollocking for what we had done but, this time, Joe beat me to it and told him to fuck off!

We were both given a commendation for our bravery. Although we were both very proud of our commendations and the fact that we had saved the prisoner's life, we could not help but laugh at the fact that we simply wanted to use the fire hose and play at being firemen.

The prisoner with the mental health condition did eventually get a place in a hospital but he was returned to us after he tried to burn it down on the first night he was there.

The way in which we deal with mentally ill people who are housed within prisons is not something any of us should feel proud of. Although there have been some improvements recently with the use of specialist NHS in reach teams, it is still very far from the correct environment in which people with mental health problems should be treated. It is, rightly so, an area of great controversy and needs to be properly debated and sorted out for the sake of everyone who has a mental health issue – and statistics show that one in four of us will have a mental health problem at some point in our lives.

The majority of prisoners who are in prison because of their mental health condition are suffering from Personality Disorder Syndrome. Each of us has a personality or group of characteristics which influence the way we think, feel and behave, and makes us a unique individual. Someone may be described as having a personality disorder if their personal characteristics cause regular and long-term problems in the way they cope with life and interact with other people.

There are many types of personality disorder syndrome and the worst of them is a condition now known as anti-social personality disorder, or psychopathic disorder. This condition can result in sufferers being extremely selfish, impulsive and insensitive to other people's feelings because they feel no guilt or shame about actions which harm others. They are able to commit extreme levels of violence against others and themselves, and very rarely show any warning signs that they are about to explode. I have often become involved in dealing with the violence that these prisoners commit.

On one occasion, a prisoner that had been housed on houseblock two showed signs of obsessive behaviour syndrome, which is a form of personality disorder syndrome. He would place items in his cell in a very particular place and would explode if anyone moved anything. This was clearly not conducive to a prison regime and when prison officers searched his cell, he exploded, screaming and shouting and eventually ended up punching himself. The officers managed to calm him down and the prison nurse was called who suggested that he should stay in the healthcare unit for observations. Whilst he was in the healthcare unit, he had managed to get hold of some razor blades which he hid about his person and used one of them to cut his arms.

The alarm was raised and prison officers and nurses attempted to restrain him whilst they cleaned his wounds and dressed them. He was then searched and placed into a special cell similar to the segregation cell, where he should not be able to hurt himself. An officer assigned to the healthcare unit was carrying out regular checks on the prisoner when he noticed that the prisoner had removed the dressings and cut himself further with yet another razor blade.

This time the cut had severed an artery and blood was now pumping out of his arm. I, and several other officers and nurses, restrained the prisoner, while the nurses dealt with his injuries. This time he had cut himself so badly that the doctor recommended we call an ambulance. When the paramedics arrived, we still had to restrain him whilst they treated him and decided to take him to the local hospital. Whilst he was being treated at the hospital he calmed down enough for the medical teams to sew him back together. He was then returned to the prison.

When we got back to the prison, the doctor was unwilling to have him located in the healthcare unit so the governor agreed to have him placed in the segregation unit and placed on what was called a 15 minute watch. This means that an officer has to make four observations of the prisoner every hour to ensure he is okay.

The prisoner was not happy about being placed in the segregation unit and as soon as he was searched and placed within the cell he started to cut himself. The alarm was raised and the nurse was called. This time we had managed to stop him from cutting himself badly. We searched him again and placed him in one of the special cells. The governor ordered that we use the body belt on him; as described before this belt is locked around the waist and both arms are handcuffed to his side as the cuffs are fixed to the belt. The heating was increased in the cell so that he would not be cold as, by now, he was naked to try and ensure he could not possibly harm himself again. This time the governor placed him on a constant watch, which meant that an officer was tasked to watch the prisoner all the time via observation points in the roof of the special cell.

We had all just started to calm down and I had decided to change my shirt for a third time of it having been soiled with the prisoner's blood, when we heard the officer watching the prisoner call for help. The prisoner had produced yet another razor blade and started to cut open the arteries that had been repaired by the hospital and was cutting open the tops of his legs and groin.

Once again he was restrained, although this time with a lot of difficulty. There was such a lot of blood all over the cell and on the floor. So much blood that you could smell the iron smell that large quantities of blood gives off. The prisoner was struggling all the time and it was becoming very difficult to maintain safe control and restraint holds on him so that the nurse could stop the bleeding. We eventually restrained him sufficiently to allow the nurses and doctor to sew him up.

You must be asking at this point where he is getting the razor blades from, as we had already recovered four blades from him that he had already used and that had not been found when he had been searched before. We knew that the only places that he could be hiding the blades were either up his bum, nose or in his mouth, as he was completely naked.

This time the governor had decided that the prisoner should be placed back in the body belt and three officers were assigned to sit with him so that he would not be able to extract more blades from his orifices to cut himself. This was okay as a temporary measure but was clearly not a practical one that could be sustained.

The rest of us retired to the Seg office and the governor asked for any suggestions as to what to do with him. The doctor was unwilling to use any medication that would sedate him and said that we would have to just keep an eye on him as it was his belief that, when he became too tired, he would calm down. I then suggested that I could possibly negotiate the blades from him as I was a trained hostage negotiator and the process we used in hostage situations might just work in these circumstances. In a way, it was almost as though he were holding himself hostage.

The governor thought that this was a brilliant idea so, with the help of the senior officer known as SO Mutley (because he had a laugh like Mutley dog from the Wacky Races cartoon), we set up the process of negotiating the blades from the prisoner.

I am not going to try and blind you with some bullshit about hostage negotiating as the process is very simple and is just designed to wear the prisoner down to the point that, when you have worn them down, you can then build them back up by giving them some hope and reassurance that they can trust you. It is only then that you can start to steer the prisoner and take control of them as they become more compliant. It takes long hours of building a bond and establishing trust whilst never giving into any of their demands because, when you start the process, the prisoner believes that they are in control and are calling the shots, so the aim is to reverse this.

I managed to get him to remove another five blades that he had hidden up his bum and in his mouth. He was asking me if he could go to the healthcare unit and I was maintaining the governor's position that he would only go to the healthcare unit when it was safe for us to move him there and we could be confident that he would not harm himself further.

I knew that we were just about at the point when, after five hours of negotiating, we could get the other four blades from him that I knew he still had on him, when all of a sudden the healthcare doctor came crashing into the cell, saying that he had come to see how the prisoner was doing. The prisoner said that he was feeling a lot better now and that he was going to be staying in the healthcare soon.

The doctor proceeded to tell him that he would not have him in the healthcare unit and that he should stop this silly nonsense and go back to the houseblock. Well, you can imagine the prisoner was not a happy bunny and, at this point, decided to throw his dolly out of the pram big time. After first retrieving a razor blade, he proceeded to play noughts and crosses on his arm. The doctor ran out of the cell, leaving us to spend another five hours trying to calm the prisoner down and undo the damage that the doctor had done.

SO Mutley informed the doctor that he may need to go home early because, once Officer Kelly had finished, there was a good chance that I would re-arrange his sense of well-being.

The prisoner did eventually calm down, we did get the rest of the blades from him and a note went on his file that extreme care should be taken when searching his cell.

In the prison system you will always find a long-term prisoner who believes that he knows all the rules and has made it his long life challenge to beat the system by using the rules. One such prisoner was sent to us from Wandsworth when they were about to be inspected by Her Majesty's Inspectorate of Prisons. If you have an awkward prisoner and you can unload him onto another prison, there is no better time to do it than just before you have a prison inspection visit.

The prisoner we received from Wandsworth was known as a bit of pain in the arse and considered himself as a barrack room lawyer, regarding all prison officers as thick and easy to manipulate.

On the day that we received him I was on a late shift and, by the time I got to the segregation unit, my colleagues, who had suffered the demands from this prisoner all morning, were well and truly fed up with him. Apparently, the first thing he had demanded was a copy of the prison rules, which he had been quoting at them all morning, demanding this and that. So, when he rang his cell bell, I volunteered to attend and made my way directly to his cell. I opened the inspection flap on the door and noticed that the prisoner was totally immersed in the rule book. I was greeted with, "Guv, are you aware that under prison rule 62.1 subsection (b) paragraph 4, I am entitled…" I cut him short by saying, "Now hold on, fella, you have made a grave mistake as those rules apply to you. I am not a prisoner, I have not read them and I don't care about them." I closed the inspection flap and made my way back to the segregation office.

He then rang his cell bell and asked another officer who I was. He was informed that I was Officer Kelly and that I was his personal officer. The prisoner's shoulders sank as he muttered, "Oh fuck!" It was not true, of course, that the rules did not apply to us as it was our duty to ensure correct abeyance of them and to ensure that prisoners received what they were entitled to and nothing more.

My relationship with this particular prisoner did not improve much when, one evening, when he had been constantly ringing the cell bell and demanding all kinds of different things, I answered his cell bell to a demand from him for a toilet roll. I asked him, "Why?" He said, "Because I want a shit," so I said, "Well, you're in luck as you've just found one!"

It only took about a week for him to realise that you can get far more by asking rather than demanding and that respect is a mutual process. I believe that this prisoner responded well to what we called A&R (attitude realignment).

The segregation was always being used as an overflow for the nonce's unit on houseblock two and you would always find the odd bacon in the unit. Most of them would be very quiet and not cause any problems, enabling us to carry on with our daily routine. There was, however, the odd one who thought he had rights above and beyond the rest of the human race, claiming that they were innocent and that the five-year-old girl or boy had led them on.

There was one that we held in the segregation because he was always trying to rape other prisoners. He was serving a seven year sentence for the false imprisonment of gay men in Brighton and for beating seven bells out of them, before finally raping and robbing them.

He would amuse himself by constantly ringing his cell bell and demanding items that he would never be allowed to have such as a hacksaw. He would try and engage in conversation with the staff so that he could describe his crimes in detail. This prisoner was not very bright and had abused the right to be ugly, so much so that he must have fell out of the ugly tree and hit every branch on the way down.

Every now and then, the governor would risk sending him back to the nonce's wing and, on one occasion, the books were turned on him as he was raped by his two Polish cellmates. When he was returned to us in the segregation unit after that incident, he had earned the nickname of Michael Palin, as he had gone from Pole to Pole.

Another role of the segregation unit was to house prisoners who were on a dirty protest, known as 'shitting up' as the prisoners would defecate on the floor and then spread their faeces all over themselves and the cell.

Our job was to ensure that the prisoners were allowed to take a shower at least once a day and have exercise on the segregation exercise yard. As you can imagine, this was not an easy task to carry out. The smell would hit you before you even set foot in the segregation unit and you were expected to spend your whole shift there, except for lunchtimes. However, by the time you went for lunch, I can assure you that you had lost your appetite as the smell would somehow remain with you.

Before the prisoner would be moved to the shower or exercise yard, we would have to don disposable overalls and a mask, which gave very little protection against the smell. It would simply prevent you from swallowing any shit that may be thrown at you by the prisoner. The prisoner would then be escorted out of the cell and a team of specialist cleaners would clean the cell. The prisoner would be located into another cell whilst the first cell was being cleaned. The prisoner would then 'shit up' all over again and this very smelly 'merry-go-round' would continue until either the prisoner got fed up with it or a stupid governor agreed to his demands.

The only plus side from this would be that some of the prisoners held in segregation were there because they refused to move from one houseblock to another. They would always have the same excuses. "I can't go over to that houseblock because there is someone over there who wants to kill me." We would ask who, as we would move them, but we would never get a name. More often than not, the real reason was because they were too comfortable with their set up on the houseblock, sometimes being involved in the trafficking of drugs on the houseblock and not wanting to miss out on a nice earner or they were genuinely afraid because they owed another dealer money. But, as soon as one of our guests 'shit up', they would very quickly change their minds and move to any houseblock at all.

I hated these dirty protests as they were very disruptive and the smell would stay in your nostrils all day and night and even when you were at home, relaxing from the day's events, you would still smell the smell of someone's shit.

There were some officers who were very good at dealing with the dirty protests. There was one particular officer who had worked in the Northern Ireland prisons where terrorist prisoners would often be on a dirty protest. One of the ways in which they dealt with a dirty protest was, when it came for the daily clean up, the cleaning teams would not clean the cells very well and when the prisoners were placed back into the cells they were placed into the cell of one of the other dirty protesters, rather than being placed back in their own cell. The theory behind this was that you can always put up with the smell of your own shit, but to live with the smell of someone else's is entirely another matter.

On one particular dirty protest, this officer had put some melted chocolate in a jar and, just before he entered the dirty protest cell, he would dip his finger into the chocolate. He would then enter the cell and tell the prisoner that he loves a dirty protest, pretending to wipe his finger on the walls covered in shit and then showing the prisoner the chocolate finger and licking it clean. This would usually be enough to convince the prisoner that the competition for the dirtiest bastard has been won by this officer and they would give up their quest. Even though we all knew that the finger was covered in chocolate, it still made us all feel sick.

There were moments in the afternoons when we were very inactive as we would have completed all the adjudications in the morning and would only have a couple of guests, all of whom would have been watered, fed, cleaned and exercised. All the paperwork would have been completed and the segregation unit cleaned and well stocked with supplies. At such times, we would simply be waiting for a new guest to arrive, wrapped up by staff transferring him from the houseblock to the segregation unit. We would amuse ourselves by playing with a new toy called a 'hands free' speaker phone. This phone had its own outside line and, unlike other phones in the prison, we did not have to go through the prison operator to obtain an outside line. One of our officers, a Brummy called Steve, would call other prisons and we would amuse ourselves by listening to him attempt to sell them double glazing. One day, he even tried to sell them his boots. It was highly entertaining to listen to the bemused staff working in prisons around the country trying their best to politely say 'no' to Steve.

On one of these rare quiet days, I called our own gate lodge and asked what the gate looked liked, explaining that I was a solicitor who had come to see his client but who had been walking around the prison perimeter trying to find the gate. Staff were a bit confused that I had not been able to find the gate and described to me in some detail what the gate looked like. I thanked them and waited a short while before calling them back, pretending that I was out of breath and very annoyed, claiming that I had just walked all around the prison and yet still could not find a gate.

Whilst this was going on we could hear on our radio net that our mobile dog patrol, which had a huge 4x4 vehicle that would drive around the outside perimeter of the prison, announce that they were commencing one of their many patrols. The gate officers were getting a bit fed up with me when I then claimed that I had just nearly been run down by a huge 4x4 vehicle with a mad dog as its passenger. They calmed me down and informed me that this was one of their patrols and asked me to remain where I was and that they would get the patrol to escort me to the gate. We took great delight in listening to them raise the dog patrol over the radio, asking them to go back round the prison to find the lost and confused solicitor. I thought it was probably time to end our bit of fun and called the gate again, saying that it seemed to be an awful lot of security for a category 'C' prison called Downview. Their frustration was audible as they informed me that this was Highdown, a high security prison, and proceeded to give me directions to Downview.

We have had the company of some of the country's nastiest villains but none more so than a bank robber/drug dealer who had stood on one of his rival's neck before blasting him in the head at point blank range with a 9mm pistol. He had become a real problem in the prison system as he would cause much disruption when he was housed with other prisoners. He was known as a bully and thought of himself as a big gangster. Other prisoners were afraid of him and he always seemed to have big supplies of tobacco in his cell, even though he had made no tobacco purchases at the canteen. He would always claim that friends had given him the tobacco and would always have a supply of willing (or very afraid) prisoners to validate this. He also had a reputation of bullying prison officers. He would single out those who appeared easy to bully and would always cadge cigarettes off them and have them run around for him. He would also be very argumentative towards any of the staff on the wing and was known to assault staff at will. He was also known as the ringleader of many of the little riots that we experienced as part of everyday prison life.

Because of his abilities to be such a pain in the arse, he was housed in the segregation unit under 'good order and discipline'. Whilst he was with us, I was assigned as his personal officer. When he noticed that I rolled my own cigarettes, he struck up a conversation about the best type of tobacco and how well I roll my cigarettes. It is my experience that when someone starts to engage in small talk and starts paying you compliments, they either want to fuck you or fleece you. He then asked me for some tobacco until canteen day as he had run out (more like his free supply had been cut off). I asked him if he was sure he would repay me and he promised, "Yes Guv, I'll give double the amount back." So, against the prison rules, I gave him some tobacco. Come canteen day, the routine was that I would escort the canteen officer support grade (OSG) to the prisoner's cell where we would check all items ordered by the prisoner, get him to sign his agreement that all was there and then leave him to enjoy his new supply of sweets and tobacco. However, on this occasion, after we had checked the canteen and the OSG had left the cell, I reminded the prisoner about his deal and picked up the tobacco he owed me. He tried to stop me by grabbing my wrist and was about to punch me, when I punched him, first in the gut and then, introducing my size twelve boot, landing an attack to his groin. The result was that he ended up doubled up on the floor so I helped him to sit up and sat next to him, asking him if he was alright. He said he would be once his balls had come back down and said that I was worse then a 'Whitemore tobacco baron'. He never did ask me for tobacco again.

When an alarm bell sounds from other units, the segregation staff do not respond as they may have to receive a prisoner that is being escorted to the segregation unit. During the early days of Highdown, any prisoner that was restrained with the use of C&R would have been brought down to the segregation unit, whilst still under restraint by three officers, one holding the prisoner's head down to chest level and one on each arm, with a hold that would allow them to apply pain on a pressure point and make life very uncomfortable for the prisoner. When the prisoner arrived at the segregation, they were taken to the strip cell, forced to the floor, stripped of their clothing and left in the cell to contemplate their predicament (cool off). When they had calmed down, they were moved to a normal segregation unit cell, ready for the adjudication the next day.

Some officers escorting the prisoner would reek out some kind of vengeance on the prisoner. One particular Scottish officer had decided to racially abuse and kick the granny out of a prisoner that I was restraining using correct C&R procedures. I told him to stop and one of my colleagues managed to get him out of the strip cell, whilst we continued to deal with the prisoner in the correct fashion. Once the door was locked I heard this Scottish officer mumble that I was a con lover.

This pissed me off, so I grabbed him by his throat and suspended him from the floor while informing him that I was not a con lover, but that their existence paid my mortgage and provided me with a very nice pension. Thugs like him that wanted to put this at risk by kicking the shit out of a con were as bad as they were. I was sure that he had got the message by the way his eyes were bulging and the fact that he was unable to speak.

I do not like violence; however I do understand its use and that to use violence it must be controlled and have a point, otherwise it becomes mindless violence. Because the lives of some of the prisoners are set around a world of violence, they sometimes have to be controlled with the use of violence because it is a language they understand. The Control and Restraint methods are very good and do what it says on the can – it controls and restrains the prisoner. The violence that I had used on the bullying prisoner was because he had initiated an assault on me and my objective was to ensure that, first, I did not get hurt and that, secondly, I gave him a clear and sharp message. We are prison officers and it is our duty to ensure that prisoners are safe and secure under our control; we should not be putting ourselves in a position where we become judge and jury as well as the executioner.

These prisoners have already been judged (or will be) and are serving the sentence given by law. It is officers like the one I described that end up giving us all a reputation as thugs in a uniform. This particular officer has managed to become a governor even though he is still a racist thug. The press are always ready to jump on the very rare incidents where there has been a bad prison officer but, in my experience, 99.9 per cent of prison officers are very brave and hard working. They perform their duties with a high level of professionalism and dedication and I have been proud to serve alongside some of the finest people on this planet. So, when we come across a bad one who either brings in drugs and other contraband or uses their authority to reek out mindless violence in a warped sense of justice, we deal with them because they have no place alongside the fine people who protect the public by looking after society's unwanted.

There are times when, if we had a visitor to the segregation unit with preset conceptions about who we are and who had us already marked as mindless thugs, we would always try and wind them up and send them away with confirmation of their stereotyped beliefs.

As explained, governor grades all have different roles and duties. However, when they are assigned as duty governor for the day, they must visit the segregation unit at least once per day when there has been a prisoner located on the unit, or if there is a problem with a prisoner. Some of the governors are very experienced, having come up through the ranks, and have a very good understanding of the difficulties that can be faced when dealing with potentially violent prisoners. Other less experienced governors, however, who are duty governor for the day, feel they have to try and stamp their authority by pretending they know best and ignoring the advice of the lower ranks.

There are two good examples of how the experience of governors and staff can achieve good outcomes and where some of the less experienced and more arrogant governors can make dangerous situations even more dangerous. The first was when we had a very violent prisoner who had been placed in the strip cell but who had decided that the feng shui of the fixtures and fittings of the strip cell did not meet with his karma and proceeded to rearrange them by smashing the non-destructible light fitting, then ripping out one of the iron bars supporting the frame and smashing the cell door with this five foot iron bar. He had managed to smash the extra thick Perspex inspection window in the cell door and the iron bar was being poked through this hole in an attempt to remove the head of anyone who came near the door.

The duty governor was called and, on this occasion, one of the most experienced governors was on duty, known as Uncle Bob. When he arrived, he found most of us in a very excitable state as we knew that to go in and tackle this prisoner would result in injuries to staff, so testosterone levels were running very high. Uncle Bob very calmly listened to what the situation was and then proceeded to select a C&R team to restrain the prisoner. Other than the shield man at the front of this team, they were either very small or very young female officers. I recognised the fear that was showing in their faces as they flinched with every bang of the door from the iron bar wielded by the prisoner.

The governor first tried to talk to the prisoner, but he was screaming abuse and smashing the door with the bar, so the governor was struggling to gain his attention. Uncle Bob then started to engage in conversation with me and asked me to laugh now and again and nod my head even though the governor was not really saying much but simply wanting to get the prisoner to believe that we were having a conversation about him.

It worked as the prisoner stopped smashing the door and started to shout at the governor, so a two-way conversation could start to take place. Once Uncle Bob had his attention he simply asked what the prisoner's problem was and the prisoner said that he wanted to talk to the governor. Uncle Bob told him that he was not prepared to talk to him if he was continuing to threaten his staff. The prisoner started to calm down, so Uncle Bob said that he was going to open the door and relocate him into another cell as the one he was in was no longer safe. Bob gave an encouraging wink to the C&R team and quietly informed them to stand by unless he either ordered them to go in or he was attacked by the prisoner. Uncle Bob then informed the prisoner that he was about to open the door and told him to stand at the back of the cell. Uncle Bob opened the door and simply told the prisoner to put the iron bar down and to listen to the instructions of the C&R team so that they could relocate him to another cell where he would talk to him and listen to what he wanted to say. The prisoner complied with the order and the incident was resolved very quickly.

The other example was when a fast track governor, who had come to us more or less straight from university, was always trying to tell us how we should be doing our job and yet was always making a pig's ear of her own job. She was in the segregation unit on one of her frequent visits and had asked how long a very violent and dangerous prisoner had been in the segregation unit. She was told that he had come to us from Belmarsh Prison after he had assaulted four members of staff. He had been sent to us with a governor's recommendation stating that he should remain in the segregation unit until a psychiatric report could be done to ascertain whether it would be safe enough to allow him to be placed on the houseblocks with other prisoners.

This particular governor, who seemingly knew better than a governor at Belmarsh, decided to ignore the recommendation, saying that the prisoner should be moved to the houseblocks. When we questioned her decision, she ripped into us and demanded that we do as we were told.

We located the prisoner onto houseblock 1 and, within one hour of locating him there, he had assaulted another prisoner by biting off one of his ears. We are sure that the assault could have been far worse had it not been for the fact that we had warned the staff about the prisoner. Unfortunately, governor grades very rarely get sacked when they fuck up – they either get promoted out of the way or get a sideways move to another prison. This governor was moved to another prison.

In the segregation, we have orderlies who clean the unit, serve meals to the prisoners housed in the Seg and make our tea. Over the time that I spent in the segregation unit, we had a number of very good segregation orderlies. Most of those we selected to be orderlies fitted a profile that meant they were between 30 and 55 years of age, fit, intelligent and knew the prison system better than us. Most of those we selected were some of the hardest and most well-connected criminals who most prisoners would not mess with. As our orderlies, they stayed in their own cells in the segregation overnight and this meant that the other prisoners in the segregation would keep very quite. On one occasion, we were asked to house a particular prisoner and make him segregation orderly because he was not the usual run of the mill prisoner. He was one of the country's most senior gynaecologists and had been invited to stay at one of Her Majesty's finest establishments because he was accused of killing his wife.

The story, according to him, was that his wife was always going out drinking and gallivanting and had returned from an all-night session to find her husband doing some DIY with a 2lb club hammer. On this occasion, she decided that it would be a really good idea to taunt him and, he claims, he lost his temper and gave her the good news with the hammer on her head. He then claimed that panic set in as he thought he had killed his wife so he wrapped her in a big rug or carpet, dragged her upstairs and threw her over the balcony. Well, if the hammer had not killed her, the fall would most certainly have put paid to her. He then phoned the emergency services and claimed that he had found his wife on the patio, dead. It did not take long for the police to get the real story from him, so he was packed off to prison with a manslaughter charge.

When he arrived at Highdown, the doctor in charge of the healthcare unit thought it would be a good idea to have such a learned colleague housed in his healthcare unit as an orderly. It did not take the wife-killing gynaecologist long before he was helping the medical staff in the unit, gaining too much information about prisoners and carrying out far too many duties, way beyond those required of making tea for the staff and keeping the place clean.

What was going on soon became common knowledge so the duty governor had him moved to the segregation unit, asking us to employ him as one of our orderlies. Initially, we were very reluctant, as we could not see what benefit it would serve us having this gynaecologist stay in the Seg, unless he was going to re-paint the segregation through the letterbox. However, he did come and, as it turned out, he became well liked by staff as, not only was he a gynaecologist, but he was also an ex-captain of the parachute regiment (although he was a STAB – a stupid territorial army bastard – he still commanded some respect). He always kept us entertained with his fantastic stories about some of his 'customers' and he did make a good cup of tea.

When he was going through his trial, one of the tabloids ran a story about the alleged crime and the prosecution case, stating that the gynaecologist was a bit of a skinflint and would not spend money on his wife. They gave an example that, on one of her birthdays, he had simply treated her to a burger at McDonalds. This really upset him and he vowed never to buy the paper again because of the lie they had printed. When we asked him why it was such a lie and what had actually happened, he told us that it was not McDonalds he had taken his wife to for her birthday, but Burger King!

He was found guilty of manslaughter and given a six-year sentence, of which he served only three years and eight months in prison. He was struck off from practising as a gynaecologist and made an appeal against the decision, which, I believe, he won, and is still working as a gynaecologist.

The prison rules state that an officer should only spend two years service in the segregation unit. By now, I had served my two years there, my time was up and I was due to be unleashed into a different part of the prison regime.

Chapter Four

Johnny Foreigners

"Now, listen up you goppers, there are only two rules on my landing! Rule number one: Do not do anything that gets me into trouble. Rule number two: Obey all the rules."

Before I was moved off houseblock 1, I attended a new pilot course entitled 'Enhanced Thinking Skills'. This course was designed by Professor Edward de Bono who is regarded by many as the leading authority in the world in the field of creative thinking and the direct teaching of thinking as a skill. He has written 62 books and is the originator of lateral thinking, which treats creativity as the behaviour of information in a self-organising information system – such as the neural networks in the brain. He maintains that, from such a consideration, arise the deliberate and formal tools of lateral thinking, parallel thinking, and so on.

The Enhanced Thinking Skills programme runs for 22 sessions over a 3-month period and is delivered to groups of 8-10 prisoners. The aim of the course is to develop a range of thinking skills that will allow individuals to solve problems more effectively and to achieve their goals in a socially acceptable way.

Psychologists use psychological tests and structured interviews to assess an individual prisoner's needs and to measure change in those prisoners who have been following the programme. Facilitators of this programme are prison officers.

"I knew that," I hear you say, "I was only just talking to Marge at the Co-op about Edward de Bono and we came to the conclusion that he thinks too much."

To put it in layman terms (or, more precisely, prison officer terms): we get to teach the goppers to think of the consequences of kicking the shit out of an old age pensioner for money to buy a wrap of crack and to think about the effect their actions have on others.

I was selected to run the pilot course at Highdown and, although the Prison Service now claims that the course was specially designed for prisoners, the course we were taught to present to the prisoners actually came from a primary school handbook. The psychologists overseeing the course would not select prisoners who were heavy drug users, because they would have difficulty getting through to them, or bank robbers, because the Enhanced Thinking Skills (ETS) programme will simply educate them on how to pull off their next job better and avoid getting caught.

These restrictions have long since left the selection process as the Home Office is keen to prove that prisoners are on rehabilitation programmes that actually work.

I have no doubt that ETS will work with some prisoners. I also know that it will only prevent about 1 per cent from re-offending and that will be because they do not want to end up in prison again being taught how to think by a hairy arsed screw.

Houseblock 3 was designated as the houseblock where the Enhanced Thinking Skills programme would be run from. And so, I was assigned to this houseblock.

Once all the classrooms had been set up on the houseblock, we were able to start the Enhanced Thinking Skills course and the psychology department selected our first 22 prisoners. My co-tutor was Dave, who was a very experienced prison officer and had a great sense of humour; he was small in stature but was as voracious as a pit bull when attacked by prisoners. As this was the first morning of our new class, we had decided to get in early to ensure that everything was ready (and that we had enough time to rob the main education block of anything that we would find useful).

Whilst setting up, we were discussing how difficult it would be for us to break the ice with the class and to get them out of the prison officer/prisoner relationship and into a tutor/prisoner relationship. Suddenly, we heard a commotion coming from the houseblock, which was disturbing the beauty sleep of the rest of the inmates.

Off we went to the wing office where the duty orderly officer and his crew of three officers were discussing how to deal with a very violent prisoner. This particular individual had decided to practise some Feng-Shui on his cell by smashing the sink and toilet and flooding the landing before the officer support grade (OSG) realised that he could turn the water supply off from outside the cell.

The orderly officer was suggesting that they should wait until there were sufficient officers on duty on houseblock 3 and then organise a planned intervention (C&R take out) to remove him to the segregation unit.

The only flaw we could see in this plan was that there were never enough prison officers on duty. We could see that we would be waiting all morning for this orderly officer to make a decision and do something, and we knew that this would put our chances of running our first class right out of the window.

The orderly officer was a fast track university graduate who had very little experience of prisons or violence. Although, to be fair to him, he did realise his limitations in this respect and was always open to suggestions from more experienced officers, which gave him a lot of kudos amongst us.

So, I offered our services to the orderly officer, suggesting that I call the segregation unit to ensure that they had enough officers on duty to receive a prisoner. I then went on to propose that, with us two plus the three officers he had with him, we could safely move the prisoner to the segregation unit. He agreed readily to this plan of action and allowed me to go down and talk to the prisoner to calm him down, since I knew the prisoner and felt this would help to gain his cooperation.

On the way to the cell, my fellow tutor, Dave, asked what the plan was so I said, "It's simple, just follow my lead." I opened the cell door, the prisoner moved towards me, I gave him the good news and then wrapped him up. The other officers assisted and he was placed safely into the segregation unit without any further disruption to the houseblock or the prison.

I am not suggesting that the orderly officer's overcautious approach was wrong, it's just that sometimes a bit of common sense and straightforward prison officer work can be the best way to operate. Quite apart from any other consideration, I also did not want our first class to be cancelled. As the other prisoners could all hear what was going on, they too were appreciative of the quick resolve of the incident as it prevented any disruption to their day, particularly since this prisoner had woken them all from their beauty sleep. It also gave the prisoners who were attending the class something to talk about – so our problem of how to break the ice was resolved too.

The class was made up of 16 very different characters and we thought it would be impossible to get through to even half of them. It was very difficult at first and we had some resentment from a couple of prisoners but, even they, after a couple of lessons, soon began to get involved.

As I have mentioned before, the course is designed to make the student examine the way they think, demonstrating this through a set of scenarios, exercises and games.

One of the games is charades and I asked for a volunteer from the class to start us off. A small, odd-looking prisoner, who had not participated much during the sessions, volunteered, and I was pleased to see that he was prepared to be the first to start the game off.

I handed him the card that gave him the character he had to mime to the rest of the class. He promptly extended one arm out at right angles to his body and, with his right hand in a loose fist, proceeded to move it very fast over his groin area.

At first, there was some bemusement amongst his fellow students until they all began to laugh uncontrollably and, before long, both students and tutors were in tears with laughter. Finally, one student managed to take a guess at what he was portraying and declared that he was wanking. But this only resulted in the small, odd prisoner moving his fist even faster with a look of sheer determination on his face. This, in turn, only increased the laughter from all of us but none more so than from me as I knew that the card had asked him to portray Keith Richards of the Rolling Stones.

The object of this lesson was to demonstrate that we can get the wrong idea from someone's interpretation and our small, odd prisoner had demonstrated this point very well.

I was pleased with how successful the classes were and I enjoyed tutoring them. However, the prison governors expected us to still cover our evening duties even though, after running a class all day, we were shattered when it came to working the evening. In the end, we decided to give up tutoring as most of the classes were being cancelled at the last minute due to the shortage of prison officers.

The other main function of this houseblock was to house the Foreign Nationals who were held in our prison. Because Highdown prison's catchment area included Gatwick Airport, we seemed to have quite a few foreign prisoners, most of whom were in because they did not pack their own suitcase and some rotter had placed drugs in their case. The moral of many of their stories was that, if you are a poor, foreign national planning on flying into London on a flight that would cost more than your year's wages, paid for by someone you have never met before provided that you take a few things for them in your suitcase, just say no!

Failing this, when you arrive at Gatwick and the Customs and Excise ask, "Is this your luggage and did you pack your own bags?" you should respond indignantly, "No, I have never seen this suitcase before" and then start shouting, "Where is my lizard skin suitcase?" It may not work but it's worth a last ditch attempt as you are about to spend the next ten years at one of Her Majesty's establishments and your only tour of London will be via the prison wagon taking you to court.

There are many ways that drugs are smuggled to our shores. By far the most common is via our not so secure seaports, although there are still quite a few kilos of all kinds of drugs arriving via our airports and it is this route of smuggling that uses what is known as a 'donkey'. The methods used are varied although the four most common are:

> hidden in the luggage;
>
> hidden on the body strapped to the person (this works well with pregnant smugglers;)
>
> hidden in the body, method one, where the drugs are placed into condoms and swallowed prior to the journey and retrieved when they have a poo in the next day or two; and
>
> hidden in the body, method two, where the drugs are wrapped in clingfilm and are shoved up their anus or, if they have one, vagina.

As you can imagine, there are many dangers associated with the last two methods. I have spent many hours on an escort bed watch with a prisoner who has had these drugs burst from the confines of their packaging inside his body. Most prisoners, who are unfortunate to have this happen, die.

The foreign nationals that we held came from four main areas: Africa, the Caribbean, South America and East Europe. 90 per cent were inside due to drug smuggling. The Africans, Caribbeans and South Americans were usually caught whilst smuggling drugs in via the airports and the Eastern Europeans were here for driving truckloads of the stuff across from France, along with the human smuggling of illegal economical immigrants. To demonstrate how poor some of these wretches were, they were delighted to be able to earn £10 per week in the prison. This was four times the amount they could earn back in their own country and they were able to send some of this money back home to their families.

When you understand how poor some of them are, you can begin to understand why they take the risk of being caught. The worst that can happen to them when they are caught is that they will spend up to ten years in a prison, where they will be fed and clothed, carry out a menial job for four hours per day and earn more money than they could usually earn back home. However, the negative side of this incarceration is that they are deprived of being able to see their families, as it is impossible for them to visit. With some of the Colombian prisoners, the chances are that they were forced to carry out the role of a 'donkey' as they were usually given the choice that, if they refused, they would be shot but only after watching their families being killed in the most gruesome manner you could imagine. I will never forget hearing a pompous judge preside over the case of one of these reluctant Colombian drug smugglers. When it came to the defence lawyer putting across the mitigations of the horrific description of their client's plight and the fact that two of his children had been raped and then shot by the drug baron's henchman, the judge dismissed this as "no excuse". I was pleased, however, to see that the English lessons I had been giving the prisoner were paying off because, when the judge asked the prisoner if he had anything to say before he handed out the sentence, the prisoner informed the judge that he was a "wanker".

Sundays were always a good day to work in prison, as there was very little to do other than sit around and talk to prisoners and colleagues. We, of course, still had our usual security checks to perform, there were the Sunday papers to read and the day would be broken up by a visit to the British Legion for a liquid lunch.

Now, before I get you screaming, "I told you! They're all a bunch of drunken yobs in a uniform, who get pissed every lunchtime and return back to the gaol and beat the living daylights out of any poor wretched prisoner they may bump into," let me reassure you that it doesn't actually work like that. For most of us, the ability to be able to relax in the safe confines of the local British legion on a Sunday lunch was a nice way to unwind during a long shift. And for most of us who did use this facility, we did so in an adult and responsible way. However, there were those who did indeed participate in drinking a little too much at lunchtimes. They would return back to the prison and would suddenly become brave towards prisoners, whereas when they were compos mentis, they would never have dared challenged them. Most of us were responsible adults, though, more than capable of ensuring that we did not drink too much and never allowing alcohol to change the way we treated the prisoners.

Of course, a Sunday would not be a Sunday without the church services.

There were two services each Sunday, starting with the Catholic service at 9am and this would be followed by the Church of England service, which would start at 10.15am.

Both services were always very well attended by prisoners who either were going to the service because they believed in their faith or, more often than not, because they needed to meet someone from another houseblock, so that they could pass on or collect contraband.

Our ever vigilant, brave men and women of the security department would be on full alert, with their overzealous leaders having planned a carefully orchestrated trap for those would-be smugglers that would dare to defile the sacred ground of the church by peddling the devil's drugs.

The security department works on a security intelligence system that, if used correctly, should throw up possible risks to the security of the prison. This is achieved by gathering all information and feeding it into a computer that will then highlight where and what the risk may be.

The main source of information for this system comes from an SIR (security information report), a report that can be written by any member of staff who works within the prison. SIRs are for reporting information about prisoners or staff that any staff member might feel should be passed onto the security department.

On the face of it, the system is very good and is usually guaranteed to have the warning signs flagged up by the computer in about 30 per cent of the serious incidents that occur in the prison. I am quite sure, however, that whoever designed the system did not factor the human element into the equation.

There are all kinds of people who work in a prison and they are exactly like any other workforce. How often have you been entertained by the shop floor or office gossip? Every workforce has its gossips and most also have jealous, nasty people who take great pleasure in telling tales on their work colleagues.

Well, imagine giving these sort of people the opportunity to write this down as a report, add to that the possibility of submitting the report anonymously, and the sky can be the limit for their vindictive tittle-tattle.

The other side of the human equation that this system has not taken into account is the kind of person who wants to work in the dark, windowless rooms of the security department, believing that they are capable of running entire empires. In my experience, I have found that most principal officers in charge of security departments are very unhappy men who, struggling with their sexuality, try to address their inadequacies by purchasing black combat trousers, black magnum assault boots and black polo shirts for their crack troops. The only item missing is the 'Sig Runes' SS unit insignia.

Security departments would even employ prisoners to give them information about staff. I had one prisoner approach me to tell me that he had received a visit from the 'black turds' (I am sure that the security PO would prefer a better nickname from the prisoners) asking him if he would like to become an informer against staff in return for tobacco and sweets. I could see a great source of entertainment in feeding the security department full of crap and, at the same time, enabling a prisoner who did not have much money to get extra tobacco and sweets.

Meanwhile, back to the church service.

I was given the duty of escorting foreign nationals from houseblock 3 to the church service. At this particular time, most of the foreign nationals were African and were very religious so they thoroughly enjoyed attending church and would sing their hearts out. On this particular occasion, I had about 40 prisoners that I had to try to keep all together so that we arrived at the chapel at the same time, as I would have to report my numbers to the officer checking them into the chapel.

This task was presenting quite a problem to me as I was having trouble being heard by the prisoners. They were all very excited and some had already started to practise their singing skills, so I resorted to a good, old, tried and tested method of shouting orders at them in good military fashion. "Right you bunch of noisy fuckers, shut up and listen!" I screamed.

The group fell silent.

"You will not be going anywhere this morning if you continue to make such an awful noise. I want you formed up in three columns and you are going to march to the chapel."

There was a little mumbling and shuffling but, amazingly, the group formed themselves into three columns and their spokesman had his hand up, asking if they could still sing whilst marching. I agreed.

"Now, listen up, we will march to the chapel and we will show the rest of the prison how well we can do this, by the left, quick march."

The foreign nationals set off as a well-disciplined group and started to break into *Onwards Christian Soldiers* as soon as we left the houseblock.

The effect was amazing. All the other prisoners were dumb struck and the duty governor could not believe what he was seeing but, best yet, was to see the faces of the crack security department troops who had been lying in wait to search a few prisoners from my houseblock.

The queue stretched all the way back to the houseblock and the noise from complaining prisoners, impromptu choirs and an irate security PO was deafening.

The church service was delayed, which upset the chaplain, and the Sunday lunch was served late. The duty governor was not a happy bunny that day.

Most of the foreign national prisoners were very easy to manage and, as long as you understood that the majority of them could be very vocal and emotive, they were not a difficult bunch of cons.

Before I was moved to houseblock 3, I attended an alarm bell that had sounded on the houseblock. On arrival, I found two officers struggling to encourage a foreign national prisoner to leave the foreign national spur and the prisoner was attempting to headbutt them. I was amazed to see that other officers from the houseblock were simply standing by and watching what was going on.

I could also see that the situation was potentially about to take a turn for the worse. It appeared that other foreign nationals were attempting to harass the two officers to let the prisoner go back to his cell. So, without any further thought, I stepped forward and grabbed the prisoner's head and brought him smartly to the floor in an approved Home Office Control and Restraint method.

The prisoner became very vocal and started screaming like a stuck pig. With this, the rest of the prisoners on the spur also became very volatile and I started to have visions of what it must have been like at the battle of Isandhlwana, where the Zulus decided to destroy a British force of more than 4,000 men. We quickly moved the prisoner from the spur and other officers, who had responded to the alarm bell, helped put the irate foreign national prisoners behind their cell doors. When we had finished, the senior officer decided to give me a bollocking as he claimed that he had had it all under control, although the two officers who had been struggling with the prisoner and in danger of being headbutted by him, were clearly of a different opinion and grateful for my help.

On another occasion, I was asked to escort a prisoner back to his cell after the SO had given him some bad news about his entitlement to canteen as the prisoner had no money. The prisoner became very volatile and started to kick over the dustbins on the spur, so I quickly restrained him by wrapping my arms around his waist and pinning his arms by his side. I was assisted by two other officers and, as we brought him safely to the floor, he suddenly became very quiet and loose. At this point, we discovered that he had fainted and shit himself, which ended up all over us.

Therefore, the two most important rules to remember when dealing with foreign national prisoners are: first, do not use Control and Restraint methods on one when all the others are out of their cells and, second, do not restrain emotive foreign prisoners until they have had a chance to go to the loo first.

On another occasion, we were supervising prisoners on the exercise yard when we noticed thick black smoke starting to emerge from one of the cell windows on the foreign nationals spur.

I quickly made my way back into the houseblock and raised the alarm with my fellow colleagues inside. An officer called Dave, another called Trigger (because he looked like a horse) and I proceeded to the cell with the fire hose to attempt to rescue the prisoner who we knew was still in the cell.

We quickly got the cell door open and, through the thick black smoke, we could just make out the legs of a prisoner, so Dave grabbed them and started pulling with all his might. However, the bunk bed appeared to be moving as well. We then discovered that the prisoner was attached to the bunk bed with a home-made tourniquet rope around his neck. We managed to cut the rope from his neck and Dave gave the prisoner Cardio-Pulmonary Resuscitation to re-start his breathing and, despite us laughing our bollocks off because we had inadvertently almost aided his suicide attempt, we did manage to save his life in the end.

The prisoner was a foreign national Arab who was in fear of being deported back home as he was under a death threat. The pressure must have become too much and he had decided to end his life by hanging himself after setting light to the cell. He was released from Highdown two weeks after the incident as the Home Office had decided to grant him asylum in this country and he went back to work as a waiter in the West End of London. We received a very moving thank you letter from him and his wife for saving his life. What Dave forgot to tell us was that it was him who had given the prisoner the matches.

We were always getting new principal officers and they seemed always to be posted to houseblock 3. On one occasion, we ended up with a new principal officer from Downview who was on the 'accelerated promotion scheme' and who believed that, because her father was a prison governor, it went without saying that she would make a good governor too. Now, I considered myself to be a good plasterer, but you would certainly not want my son to skim your walls. There is a great deal to learn before you can become either a good plasterer or a good governor.

Unfortunately for her, her name rhymed with smelly gash. She was always giving us words of advice about how to perform our duties and had a very annoying habit of treating us like school children. She would get us all to gather round in the wing office and share some wonderful piece of advice that we should 'take on board'. On one such occasion, she told us that we should take great care when opening a cell door and that we should ensure that we check the prisoner through the inspection flap first before opening the door. We should all then ensure that we release the door lock so that the door bolt is locked rigid so that the door cannot be shut behind us in the cell. So one of our team, a very funny Brummie lad called Steve, responded earnestly, "I see, you would like us to check the flaps before we shoot our bolts?" which caused us great merriment before we stepped onto the spurs to get on with the day's work. In spite of her extensive experience gained in the few months that she had been on the job, I am sure that she neither recognised nor understood the sexual connotations to this comment.

Another time she had been told by one of the prisoners on 'C' spur that they were going to have a riot if they were kept banged up during what was their association time. There had been a lot of cancelled association time due to the extreme shortage of prison officers and the increased overcrowding. We therefore operated a rota for which spur would be allowed out to associate. For some reason, 'C' spur believed that they were being banged up more than the other spurs on the wing. So this prisoner had asked to see the principal officer to warn her that, unless they were given more association, there was a strong chance that there could be a riot.

Without checking any of the facts, or talking to those of us who worked on the spur and had already dealt with the prisoners' moaning about the amount of bang up, she quickly informed the security department (who specialise in panic) and the orderly officer. Although the orderly officer was 23 and had ten minutes more experience in the job than smelly gash, she looked like a little boy of no more than twelve years old and we often wondered whether her mother knew where she was. They then informed the duty governor who knew more about bird watching than prisons, before starting to get the prison ready for a riot.

They were about to call in riot teams and inform head office when the principal officer decided she should inform us. At this stage, we did not have a clue about the panic she had started and the actions that were about to unfold at her command. She informed us smugly, "We will not be opening up the prisoners yet. I have it on very reliable information that, when we open up 'C' spur, we will have a riot on our hands as the prisoners are upset." She paused for a moment before finishing with, "What's that noise? Why are those prisoners out of their cells?"

If she had told us earlier, then we might have been able to prevent her from making a complete fool of herself. She still insisted, however, on telling us to keep away from the spurs until help had arrived and then went to her office. I went onto my spur and got together the most influential prisoners on the wing and said, "Right you fuckers, what's all this bollocks about you wanting a fucking riot? I thought I had explained the situation this morning and you were all going to write and complain to the governor about your problem?" They then explained to me, "Prisoner Smith had decided to tell the PO that we were going to kick off if we get banged up again tonight, which is bollocks, Guv. We are going to write to the governor and complain as you suggested. The last thing we want is a riot, as we always lose."

I reported this to the principal officer, who then decided that she would give me a lecture about following orders. As I couldn't be arsed to listen to the pronouncements of a twelve-year-old, I left the office just as the riot team and the governor arrived on the spur to find a very embarrassed looking PO.

The prisoners did write and complain to the governor who, in time-honoured fashion, ignored them. About a month after this, there was a sit down protest on the exercise yard. The one thing I have learned over the years is to know when there is danger and when prisoners are about to riot. Any officer worth his or her salt will know when this is about to happen. At the time of this so-called threat, 'C' spur was the induction spur and new prisoners were housed there. Nearly 95 per cent of the prisoners on the spur were on remand, with about 50 per cent of them hoping that, when they get sentenced, they will be either time served whilst on remand or set free. It doesn't take much to work out that the last thing that these prisoners would do is to riot and face a possible ten year sentence for their efforts.

Riots do, of course, happen in prisons and when they do they are the scariest incident you could ever not wish to be involved in. They normally start over the kind of incident mentioned above. I have found that the key element to a riot seems to involve the wrong kind of prisoner who has a bad influence over the other prisoners on the wing. A typical type of prisoner that will influence others to riot are those serving above ten years and who are at the beginning of their sentence. They have the right hump with authority, and all it stands for, because they see us as the enemy and the cause of all their problems. They are full of hate and, given half the chance, will strike out at staff or other prisoners to gain some kind of hard man reputation. They will work away at other prisoners and eventually the riot will explode.

If you are lucky, you will get a warning from a prisoner who will simply tell you to get off the wing now! Most staff will pay attention to this and get off the wing and try to warn and help other officers to get to safety before the wing explodes. An explosion is the best way to describe what happens as the noise level becomes deafening and any small object that can be thrown at an officer is thrown (these are usually pool balls). The prisoners will then smash and destroy anything they can, furniture, bedding, toilets, sinks and plumbing. They build barricades at the entrance to the spurs and then some of the experienced rioters try to block the emergency access doors located on the spurs of modern prisons. The prisoners shout encouragement to other wings to join in, although by this time the officers will have shut down the whole prison. Fires will break out from the piles of broken furniture and bedding and prisoners will wear makeshift masks to prevent the smoke from choking them and to try to hide their faces from us.

In the meantime, officers will have been organised to ensure that the rest of the prison is safe. Governors will have declared an Operation Tornado, the code name given for these emergencies, and informed the area and head office, who organise the provision of prison staff who are trained in riot control. By the time that officers are ready to implement a plan to retake the wing, the whole wing will be in complete devastation with anything that can be smashed, burned or unbolted being used to form a barricade. Some prisoners will have made makeshift weapons of knives, spears and clubs. Others will have rigged up barricades at the entrance to their cells and others will be trying to hide, scared of upsetting the ringleader and of the impending doom of a fully trained Control and Restraint riot team storming the wing.

Retaking the wing is carried out with the utmost military precision. Prisoners will usually put up a horrendous fight that will almost always result in officers being hurt. However, we will always remain disciplined and professional and will always regain control of the wing.

A prison riot at Lincoln Prison that caused almost £3m of damage and left one inmate dead was sparked by a row over sandwiches. The destruction at Lincoln Prison in October 2002 was the worst disturbance at a British jail for eleven years. Prisoners seized control of the jail for eight hours during the riot. Sex offenders were forced to barricade themselves in their cells as the mob ran wild after prison officers were forced to leave the building. Some 168 prison riot officers were brought in from jails up to 150 miles away before they could retake control of the jail. One prisoner died after taking an overdose of drugs looted from the pharmacy, while another 35 people needed hospital treatment.

But meanwhile back at Highdown after our would-be riot, life on the spur was returning to normal with my dulcet tones ringing out across the landings, "Now listen up you goppers, this evening has been very memorable and enlightening, and as your association time now draws to a close, I would like to share with you a quote from Shakespeare– *Good night, good night! parting is such sweet sorrow,* however in this case it is a fucking blessing; now bang up."

Chapter Five

Jailhouse Rock

I was assisting with the free flow on the walkways, ensuring that prisoners went to the correct areas of either education or workshops and not to healthcare to scrounge some more drugs from the nurses, when one of the young, pretty, psychology students working at the prison asked me if it was correct that I could play a guitar. I noticed that one of my colleagues was giving me the nod to just play along, so I did, and said that I had dabbled a bit with the odd guitar or two. She said, "Wonderful! Would you be interested in helping out with a music project we're working on?"

I was about to turn her down when she told me that I would not be expected to play, unless I wanted to, as they had some professional musicians coming in to teach prisoners how to set up a band and play in a concert, but they did need a prison officer to assist them, as there was the obvious matter of organising security and liaising with the various disciplines in the prison so that the project would work.

The truth was that I had never played a guitar in my life, other than an air guitar, and I did not have any musical ability whatsoever, other than a belief that I could sing. I was the only one, however, who was of this opinion. I later found out that the pretty, young, psychology student had been asking most of my colleagues and they thought that they would volunteer my services by telling her that I was an ace guitar player.

As I did not want to disappoint the pretty, young, psychology student, I decided that I would volunteer, coming clean on the fact that, after such a long time, I might be a bit rusty on the guitar. She was delighted and, before long, the number one governor had agreed to my duties being adjusted so that I could work on this project.

The deal was that a group of musicians, called the *Rockshop*, would be coming into prison to lead this project. *Rockshop* is headed by Herbie Flowers of the band *Sky* fame. He had also played on some of the very best David Bowie tracks, my hero, on Lou Reed's *Walk on the Wild Side* and on some of Mark Bolan's tracks. To his shame, however, he is also responsible for the Clive Dunn hit *Grandad* but I did not let that put me off my excitement of working with such an icon of the '70s.

Herbie and his team usually work with children. Their format is to go into a school for a week and help children form into bands and either create their own score or cover other tunes. They then practise and finally stage a concert for the rest of the school.

This was to be somewhat different. It would be the first time that Herbie had tried to run a 'Rockshop' in a prison, trying to get hardened prisoners to conform and produce similar results to those he had achieved. As if that wasn't a challenge enough, he would have no more than two days to form the groups and get them to practise before staging three concerts in one day. Little was Herbie to know that the prisoners were just as difficult as the children he had already worked with but probably less dangerous.

My first task was to get 25 prisoners to volunteer for the 'Rockshop' so I put a notice up on all the houseblock spurs to see what response I would get. The only houseblock that I did not recruit from was the nonce's wing. When I was asked by the head of probation why I had left them out, I chose not to give him a reason and treated the question with the contempt it deserved. I was staggered by the response. I managed to get over 50 prisoners to volunteer, which meant I could do some informal vetting of the candidates, based on criteria known only to me. I decided to eliminate any category 'A' or escapee prisoners, psychopathic murderers and nonces. I was also able to choose some prisoners who I knew to be very good musicians and, by the time I had finished, I had 30 prisoners ready for the 'Rockshop'.

You are probably wondering why I had picked 30 and not 25 as instructed. I knew that there would be some movement of prisoners and I knew that Sod's Law would ensure that some of my prisoners would be expected to transfer to another prison before I could try to get a hold on them. I also knew that one of the officers who worked in the OCA department (Observation, Categorisation and Allocations) did not like me and would make it his mission to try and scupper the show. As it turned out, I was spot on with my estimation and my group was whittled away to 25 before any one of them could pick up an air guitar let alone get their hands on a microphone. I also knew that, to try to maintain the discipline of 25 very excited prisoners for three days would be an impossible task, so I set about getting two volunteers to help me. I was lucky to get two very good officers, Cathy and Martin, who, although very reluctant at first, soon became dedicated to the task which I knew they would, which is why I picked them.

My first problem was to get the governor to ensure that I would receive the help and cooperation that I would need from all departments in the prison. I knew, however, that my main stumbling block would be the security department. This was one of the reasons why I picked Martin as he worked with the security department and I knew that he would be able to influence his other colleagues to get some cooperation from them. I also anticipated the security department's response to the news that they were about to end up with eight civi musicians who, in their eyes, would all be on drugs and, worse still, most likely to be communists to boot.

So I made sure that the group knew that they would all need at least three forms of identification and arranged for the main bulk of the group's instruments to be delivered to the prison the day before. In this way, the security department could carry out a thorough search to ensure that there were no drugs or guns being smuggled in by this band of Che Guevaras. Although the drug dog did get very excited by the smell of most of the equipment and a close search was carried out, the dog handler was a very experienced officer and knew that, at some time, most of the equipment would have come into contact with one drug or another during its travels amongst the different venues where they had been played and he was therefore not too concerned.

My next task was to find a venue that could be used for the band to practise and then a place to stage the concert. I knew that the education block was not being used on weekends and it was, therefore, easy to get the governor's permission to use this facility. Even though the Head of Education was a bit put out by our intrusion, the governor's word proved to be final.

I thought the hardest thing to organise would be sorting out the venue for the concert as the most suitable place was the chapel. For some reason, the chapel was hardly ever used on a Monday and as the concert was to be staged on a Monday, the chapel seemed the ideal location. However, I thought that my biggest problem would be to convince the chaplain to agree as I knew that, when it came to the authority of who was in charge of the chapel, my money was on the chaplain. However, I need not have worried. As it turned out, the chaplain was a great fan of Herbie Flowers and was very excited about him coming to the prison and so was more than happy to help out in any way he could.

Next I had to ensure that the kitchens were aware that 25 prisoners and eight guests would need to have food delivered to the education block over the weekend and on the Monday of the concert itself. Again, I was very fortunate. The head chef on duty for the weekend happened to be a good friend of mine, Ewan, who promised to make sure that there would be a good supply of food for everyone. He even went as far as saying that there would be enough food for the officers, too, as we would not be able to take a break and go to the canteen ourselves. This was very noble of him because, if the governors had found out that officers were eating prison food, we would have been disciplined. I will never forget a memo that went to all units on Christmas Day from the duty governor reminding staff that it was an offence to eat from the hotplate and any officer caught eating prisoners' food would be disciplined. Bearing in mind that our canteen was closed on Christmas Day, we responded by wishing him a very Merry Christmas himself and I am pleased to report that he is no longer with the prison service but is now fucking up the Home Office Immigration Department.

All that was now left for me to do was to ensure that I could find at least two officers from each houseblock to make sure that the prisoners who had been selected were up and ready to move each morning. Again, my luck was in as I knew most of the officers and, because I was well thought of by colleagues, they were very happy to work with me to ensure the project was a success.

The big day arrived and I was at the prison early to ensure that everything was in place. I was also waiting for the first 'security department generated problem' to occur and, on cue, this happened as soon as the musicians started to turn up. Some had only brought their passports with them and the security rule book states that any guest that enters the prison must have two forms of identification with them. As I had anticipated, the security department were taking great delight in making a meal of this. I managed to contact the duty governor of the day who, to my delight, overrode their nonsense and agreed to let the musicians in. You would have thought that a passport would be the best form of identification and it certainly is for our immigration colleagues. However, for our security department colleagues, if the musicians had presented a bus pass and a bogus utility bill, they would have had no problems in letting them into the prison.

It was great fun meeting all the musicians and to see them all looking very nervous about entering a prison. They were still somewhat confused by the greeting from the security department who were wearing their best storm trooper outfits and searching each musician with a thoroughness that the prison service college would be proud of. But eventually they were inside the prison and being reunited with their instruments which I had arranged to have delivered to the education block, as there were enough guitars, drums and other instruments for at least seven bands.

Before we could make a start, I needed to brief the musicians about the do's and don'ts of the prison rules that would apply to them while they were in the prison. I also needed to warn them that some of the prisoners were highly likely to ask them for a spare cigarette, which would quickly develop into them being asked to bring something in for them like a pack of cigarettes, and then on to a request for drugs or other illicit items. The musicians were confused by this as they could not see how a simple act of kindness, such as letting a prisoner have a cigarette, could lead to drug smuggling. I explained that most requests for a cigarette were simply that, a request for a cigarette. However, there would be those prisoners who were very aware that the very act of giving them a cigarette was a breach of the prison rules and although this would not warrant a prison sentence, it could lead to a criminal conviction. Some prisoners would then use this knowledge to their advantage by upping the ante on their request of contraband, by reminding you that you had already breached the rules and that you would be in trouble if they were to inform one of the officers. Put quite simply, there are some prisoners who would be very much up to a spot of blackmail to get what they want.

The musicians also needed to be aware of what to do in the event of an alarm bell sounding in the education block and evacuation procedures in the event of a fire. I told them that they should make sure that they were not blocking any doors or passageways, to ensure that their visitors badge were clearly displayed and to follow the officers' instructions. Most of what I had to tell them was basic common sense and the best advice I gave them was, when in doubt, ask one of us or just follow our instructions in the event of an emergency.

All the basic stuff was clear to them and there were no questions about procedures. However, they were much more interested in the kind of prisoners that they would be dealing with. They wanted to know whether they were dangerous, whether they would harm them and what they were in for. I simply said that the prisoners had been selected because they were very keen to either show off their musical talents or to have three days of fun and total escapism from the prison sentence they were serving. I also suggested that their crime was irrelevant in terms of the Rockshop and the contact they would have with them. I illustrated the dilemma of knowing their crimes by asking if any of them had been burgled recently and one musician said he had been six months ago. I then asked how he would feel if the prisoner he was trying to teach to play guitar turned out to be the very burglar who had trashed his home. Would he start to treat the prisoner differently, I asked. Most prisoners do not want to discuss what they are in for, although there will always be some who have no problems whatsoever in telling anyone who will listen what a big gangster they think they are, as if it were something to be proud of. I pointed out that there would be a complete cross-section of prisoners, from petty thieves to murderers, amongst the 25 prisoners selected and reassured them that, once they get to know the prisoners as individuals, they would find them no different from any other person they might meet in the pub.

The prisoners arrived from the houseblock and sat down in the seats provided for them while Herbie Flowers introduced himself and his Rockshop. He explained what they were hoping to achieve and then went through a few example songs, which instantly had the prisoners totally enthralled and willing to listen to anything he had to tell them. I remember thinking that Herbie Flowers must have some special way with goppers to get them to behave so well on a first meeting but he broke into my fantasy by whispering to me how amazing the power of music can be even in the most unlikely places.

Herbie quickly got the prisoners arranged into groups, asking them to start practising with whatever instrument took their fancy. The prisoners were just like kids in a sweet shop and were all over the instruments in seconds. In next to no time the noise was horrendous. Someone on the walkway above the education block was so concerned by the din that they pressed the alarm bell, fearing the worse.

In the meantime, we were trying to calm the prisoners down and regain something resembling order and discipline. We were oblivious to the alarm response that their noise had created because we could not hear our radios above the din. Suddenly the doors to the education block burst open and in poured about 20 prison officers ready to deal with the alarm response. The first person they came across was one of the guest musicians, who was standing by the entrance door at the time, and they started to restrain him, taking him to be one of the goppers. We quickly jumped in between the would-be Control and Restraint team and the musician, explaining, with some embarrassment, that this was not a prisoner. When the orderly officer in charge of the alarm response team arrived we finally managed to explain the situation and restore some degree of calm. What concerned me most, however, was that we were unable to hear our radios, a real health and safety issue, so we made sure that we got hold of some ear piece extensions from our friends back in the security department. The musician, although unharmed, was visibly shaken by the incident and it took him about two hours before he could calm down and stop shaking enough to pick up an instrument and play.

Eventually some calm returned and the musicians moved in amongst the different groups that were forming. They started to participate with the prisoners, helping them to understand and play the instruments, and before long most of the groups seemed to be working well together.

There was one group of prisoners, though, who were struggling to make any kind of coherent sound and Hebbie approached me, saying that he had been told I could play bass guitar. I felt very anxious, and rightly so, because the very next question from Herbie was whether I might like to play bass with the group of prisoners who clearly could not play any instrument whatsoever. I knew there was no way out of this one other than to come clean. So I quickly informed Herbie that I couldn't imagine who had told him of my musical talents as I was probably less talented musically than the group we were observing. Herbie was clearly a man on a mission as this did not faze him at all as he was clear he could quickly teach me enough to sound good. There was to be no escape for me! Herbie let me use his own bass guitar, the very one that he had used on most of the recordings of some of my favourite records: Dave Bowie's *Space Oddity*, T. Rex's, *I Love to Boogie* and Lou Reed's *Walk On The Wild Side*. Although Herbie had made it sound so easy, it was a real struggle to learn the few chords he showed me but I eventually managed to get some kind of coherent sound from the guitar that vaguely resembled a tune.

I could not get too carried away with my new-found talent, however. I still had to make sure that all was well in the education block. When I wandered around, I was very impressed that, within just a matter of hours, the prisoners were playing some very impressive music, with help from the musicians. Herbie then called us all back into the largest of the rooms to explain what they were aiming to achieve; that they will be staging three shows on Monday for the rest of the prison and that each group will perform two songs. Individual groups, he told them, could decide what they would like to play, whether it be a cover version, or their own song, as he was aware that some of the prisoners had already written their own songs. The groups then went back to their classes and started in earnest to discuss and agree what they would be playing at the concert on Monday.

During the day we had visits from various duty governors and prison officers, all of whom found some excuse to pop their heads into the education block to try to disguise the fact that they were simply inquisitive to find out what we were up to. One group of prisoners seemed to cause some concern to our visitors. This was a group of Jamaican Yardies who were playing some kind of Jamaican gangster rap that was loud and very threatening. To anyone listening outside, they would be forgiven for thinking that there was a major argument going on rather than a song being sung. We did manage to get the group to calm it down a bit but Herbie was must reluctant to dampen what he saw as enthusiasm.

Quite surprisingly, there were some really talented prisoners amongst the groups. One of them was a prisoner called Neil who could play a guitar very well and had compiled his own song. The song was about how his life of crime, drugs and booze had messed up his family's life. It was very good and the group was keen to perform the song at the concert. The other song they had chosen was an Oasis number, *Some Might Say*, and although it sounded rather odd being sung by a cockney voice, it was still performed very well indeed.

Another group who were doing well was being led by a young man who clearly had a lot of talent. He had obviously been schooled in music because, not only was his voice pitch perfect, but he could also play an instrument really well. It turned out that this young man had been a member of an up and coming boy band and had made the mistake of trying to live up to the drugs part of the '60's adage 'Sex, Drugs and Rock 'n' Roll' and ended up cutting short what would have been a very promising career. He was good, and would prove to be a great asset to the concert.

There was also an older group of Jamaicans, led by a man know as The Colonel. He was reputed as being a Mr Big of the Jamaican drug smuggling world and there was a lot of respect towards him from the other Jamaicans in the prison. He was always very polite to prison officers and gave us the impression that he was a very devoted Christian, although he clearly had some standing amongst the Jamaican criminal fraternity and was not someone to upset. As it turned out, he loved his music and had a very good singing voice. He had chosen to sing two of Bob Marley's hits and was able to sing them so perfectly that you would have believed it was the real thing.

The group that I had attached myself to were still having difficulties and I did not seem able to improve their musical skills as I had forgotten most of what Herbie had taught me earlier in the day. To say we were struggling is an understatement. Out of the four of us non-musical misfits, only the drummer could actually play the drums, but the problem was that he was as mad as a box of frogs and resembled the mad drummer 'Animal' from the Muppets. Herbie decided to have two of his musicians play along with us so that there would be some hope of a recognisable tune emerging from our tone deaf troupe. We did eventually manage to come up with two songs, *Wild Thing* by the Trogs and I *love to Boogie* by Marc Bolan T.Rex, although it was hard to distinguish which song was which.

It was Sunday afternoon before we knew it and the final rehearsals had taken place ready for the three concerts that would be staged on Monday. Houseblocks 1 and 4 would be first to see the show at 10am, then a show at 12.30pm for staff, followed by the healthcare unit and houseblocks 2 and 3 at 3.30pm. The head of probation and re-offending complained, however, that we were leaving out the prisoners who were separated under rule 45 (Sex Offenders and others), so we had to ensure an extra show at 2pm for them. The news did not go down at all well with the Rockshop prisoners as they were not prepared to perform for 'Bacons' (Bacon bonce= nonce).

142

I reported this back to the do-gooder who had decided that life should be fair for these creatures but he was adamant that we must stage a show for them or there would be no shows at all. As it was his budget that was paying for the Rockshop, and given that the number one governor would not want to be reported to the Home Office for discrimination against 'Bacons', I was left with no choice other than to convince the prisoners to comply.

This was no easy task. Even though I managed to persuade them to go ahead with a performance for the bacons, there was one prisoner who admitted to me that he would rather kill them than perform for them, so we agreed a compromise arrangement involving him not playing in that particular show.

I must admit that even I was impressed with the cooperation from the prisoners. They clearly understood the difficult position I was in and I was taken aback by the fact that they were only prepared to do this out of loyalty to me and respect for the way in which we had worked together over the weekend. In fact, over the two days of practice, I had got to know the 25 prisoners very well and, although I had always kept a prison officer/prisoner divide, I did see them as a group that I was proud of and I was impressed by their loyalty and commitment and, at times, their humanity. The musicians from Herbie Flowers' Rockshop asked me what all the fuss was about and I explained about the bacons. It was harder to convince them to carry on with the show than it was the prisoners.

Monday morning arrived and I was in work early along with my two very helpful officers, Cathy and Martin. We made sure that everything was in place in the chapel and, as soon as Herbie Flowers' Rockshop musicians arrived, we helped set up all the equipment ready for the show. The 25 prisoners were collected and brought to the chapel and I have never seen a more nervous group of villains. Herbie was again fantastic and managed to calm them all down and gave them all a pep talk. He told them how much his team had enjoyed the last two days and how much they were looking forward to ensuring that the concert went well.

It was odd to see some of the country's hardest villains suffering from pre-show nerves, until I realised that I was also nervous about performing in front of all the prisoners, particularly as I was the lead singer of our group and we were the first group on.

The chapel filled up with our first audience and the time for the first concert to begin had arrived. As I took my place on the stage with the rest of my group, there were some boos coming from the audience as some of the prisoners clearly did not want to be entertained by a screw. Herbie then introduced the Rockshop and Neil, one of the prisoners of the Rockshop players, had been asked to say a few words about how the Highdown Rockshop was put together. He had wonderful praise for Herbie Flowers and his musicians and then, to my embarrassment, he want on to say what a privilege it had been to put the concert together and that this would not have happened if it had not been for the hard work that Officer Kelly and his two colleagues had put in. He ended by telling the audience that they had better give me a warmer welcome than the one they had just given or else!

With that done, our band struck up and I suddenly remembered that I was not watching the show but performing in it and that I had better quickly start to play the chords that I had been taught by Herbie for the *Wild Thing*. The cheers from the crowd were great and it made the hairs on the back of my neck stand up, I was so scared though that the adrenalin was flowing through me so fast it was making me dizzy. Somehow, I managed to remember to start singing at the correct time and, when it came to the instrumental part that was greatly aided by the two Rockshop musicians, I performed a little dance routine that had the crowd roaring with laughter and applause. At the end of the first song, we were given a standing ovation from the prisoners before going straight into our second song, which was received just as well.

As our set had broken the ice, the next group up were spot on time and were a much more polished act than ours. It was great to see how nervous our security department friends became when the Jamaican gangster group played their two rap songs with the whole chapel audience joining in. They looked as though they were about to become the first victims in a full-blown riot. The do-gooders and governors who were watching looked perplexed, some tried in vain to tap their feet to the beat, and all were clearly very unsure about how to respond.

However, it all soon settled down when the Colonel and his group took their place on stage and he enthralled the whole audience with his rendition of *Redemption Song*, followed by a great version of *One Love*. If it was not for the fact that he already makes huge amounts of money via the illegal enterprises he conducts, he would have a great career mapped out covering Bob Marley songs.

As I expected, Neil and his group went down very well, especially his own song called *Drink and Drugs Free*. And, I was right, it did sound odd having a cockney sing an Oasis number, although he did it very well. The rest of the groups were just as fantastic and every one of them deserved the rapture of applause they received from the audience.

The only show that was different was the one that they performed for the 'bacons'. It was very clear that their hearts were not in it and the songs were played with no feeling. I even found myself being flatter than I was before and did not bother entertaining the 'bacons' with my little dance routine during the instrumental part of the song. Feelings were running so high amongst some of the prisoners that a couple of them were reduced to tears in trying to contain the disgust they felt towards the bacons.

The show in the afternoon went just as well and finally, like all good things, the concert came to an end. The prisoners were absolutely knackered, but they were all still buzzing with excitement. However, they did manage to contain themselves and remain quiet while their spokesman, Neil, thanked Herbie and his team for all they had done. The musicians, in turn, thanked the prisoners as they had enjoyed an experience that they would never forget. Finally, Neil again embarrassed the hell out of Cathy, Martin and I by thanking us for making it all possible and giving them the best day of their lives.

Because of its success, the Rockshop was repeated the following two years but, sadly, after that the prison service became so totally driven by bogus performance targets that such an event just did not feature in anyone's targets so it got dropped. Each Rockshop was just as good as the other and, when I was asked what I had gained from the experience, I summed it up by saying, "A shed load of TOIL hours, very sore feet and the biggest smile that stayed with me for a very long time."

Chapter Six

Hostage

"Right now, fucking listen up you slags. I want a helicopter and a cheese roll and a cup of tea, or I will cut this nonce's cock off."

Other than a riot, the most feared incident that can happen in prison is a hostage situation.

There are different types of hostage scenarios but the three main ones are: a static hostage incident, where a prisoner (perpetrator) takes a person (victim) hostage within an area that he is controlling and is refusing to allow the person to leave his control; a mobile hostage incident, when a hostage situation is on the move with the perpetrator usually holding a weapon to the victim and threatening to harm them if he is not allowed to continue to wander, normally in the direction of the main gate; and a self-hostage situation which involves a prisoner threatening to harm himself, having set up the means to do so, such as setting up a makeshift noose, tying it around his neck and threatening to throw himself from a height sufficient to give his neck the good news.

Put simply, a hostage situation is when a prisoner uses the threat of harm on others, or himself, unless their demands are met. Some hostage incidents are spontaneous and the perpetrator has put very little thought into what it is they are trying to achieve. These are usually easy to resolve because, once the perpetrator's anger has subsided and they have not harmed the hostages, they are usually very willing to be talked out of the mess they have created. This still needs to be conducted in a controlled manner, however, because they will still be concerned about the repercussions of having committed yet another criminal act and may panic and go back to square one. Hostage incidents that are planned are usually the most difficult to manage and can take a long time to resolve peacefully as the perpetrator is usually prepared for a long siege. It is not uncommon for the perpetrator's mood to swing up and down as the incident progresses. They become frustrated over their lack of success and increasingly desperate which is a very dangerous and volatile situation. Then there are those, thankfully, very rare, hostage incidents which are carried out by either psychopaths or terrorists. Neither play by the rules and the terrorist hostage taker may even have had training in how to use the incident to their best advantage.

The hostage negotiator's top priority is to do everything within his or her power to prevent harm from coming to anyone. The hostages will be very scared and, at times, will become angry towards the negotiator because they will be wondering why we are not resolving the situation, and freeing them, by giving into what they see as simple demands from the perpetrator. This can result in what has become known as the Stockholm syndrome, a psychological response sometimes seen in an abducted hostage, in which the hostage shows signs of loyalty to the hostage taker, regardless of the danger in which they have been placed by the hostage taker. Stockholm syndrome is also sometimes referred to in other situations with similar tensions, such as in cases of domestic violence, rape and child abuse. The syndrome is named after the 1973 Norrmalmstorg robbery of *Kreditbanken* at Norrmalmstorg, Stockholm, Sweden, in which bank robbers held bank employees hostage for five days. In this case, the victims became emotionally attached to their perpetrators, and even defended them after they were freed from their six-day ordeal. The criminologist and psychiatrist Nils Bejerot, who assisted the police during the robbery, and referred to the syndrome in a news broadcast, coined the term 'Stockholm syndrome'.

When incidents like a riot or a hostage situation occur in prison, the prison service does not phone Bruce Willis, the A team, the police, or even Arnold Schwarzenegger, to resolve the incident, instead they have to rely on people like myself who, although I may not have the physique of Arnie, I certainly have the commitment to do the best job I can. However, there was one riot in Peterhead Prison's D-wing which resulted in prisoners taking over the building and taking a prison officer, 56-year-old Jackie Stuart, hostage. The hostage takers were lifers, in prison for violent crimes. It was thought that they had nothing to lose and would not hesitate to make good on their threats to kill their hostage, whom they had now taken up to the rafters of the Scottish prison. Feeling unable to intervene without putting their colleague's life at risk, the prison authorities called for help from the SAS. It was a controversial request. Sending in UK Special Forces to deal with a domestic criminal situation would set a dangerous precedent, and several politicians were against it. At first, an SAS officer was sent to Peterhead in a purely advisory role. As a stalemate ensued at the prison, the call was eventually put out to send in the SAS to rescue Jackie Stuart and end the siege. The SAS accomplished this with great panache in the way that only the SAS can achieve.

Even the prison service recognised that they could not rely on the skills of the SAS whenever they faced a hostage situation. They therefore decided to ensure that they had sufficiently trained staff to intervene, negotiate and bring such incidents to a successful conclusion.

When I was about to finish my probationary period I witnessed a hostage situation on houseblock 1 where I was working. We had all just arrived back from lunch and one of the prisoners started banging his cell door. We responded and were about to crack open the door and give the fellow a thorough telling off, when we noticed that he had a home-made knife up against the throat of the prisoner that was sharing his cell.

We backed off and one of our team, Roy, who was a very experienced officer, told us to leave this to him and to raise the alarm and inform the orderly office. We did exactly as he said and, before too long, a team of negotiators and a Control and Restraint team had been put together to deal with the situation. Within about two hours Roy, and his fellow negotiators, had managed to resolve the incident peacefully without anyone getting hurt. All that was required was a clean pair of trousers for the victim.

There was always a queue of macho Arnold Schwarzenegger wannabes waiting to join the C&R advance team. This is a specialist Control and Restraint team, set up in all prisons, and their primary task is to deal with incidents of concerted indiscipline, riots and hostage situations. They all work as prison officers in various departments around the prison and have their own riot kit, which consists of flame resistant overalls, protective padded gloves, knee/shin protectors, PR-24 side-handled baton, riot helmet and visor and toe protector boots. They must be prepared to respond to a call 24 hours a day. When they are called out, they collect their equipment from their prison and are then briefed as to where and what the incident is.

Sometimes the incident can be at another prison or they could simply be called out to be on standby at another prison. Most of the women and men of the C&R advance teams are very brave and dedicated officers, who get pissed off hearing on the news, after a prison riot that they have helped quell, reports that police riot squads had been the ones in the prison dealing with the prisoners. So I want to put the record absolutely straight that, whenever you hear that a prison or detention centre has erupted into a riot, it will be the women and men of Her Majesty's Prison Service who deal with the problem, not the police or the army or the SAS. And if you see police vans outside the prison, they are there to ensure the safety of the public outside the prison walls, and not the prison staff inside the prison. It is also worth pointing out here that, during the early days of the private prisons, our teams were constantly being called out to quell riots because they lacked the manpower and experience to ensure that prisoners were kept in a safe and secure manner.

You may be wondering why you don't hear about these riots if there are so many of them. The answer is quite simple. A gagging order is placed on the press so that they cannot report on the incidents. The only time these riots become public are when they are too close to a town not to be seen by the public. One of the reasons given by the Home Office for these reporting restrictions is because they believe that, if prisoners at other prisons get to hear about the unrest at another prison, they may start a sympathy riot. I think the more accurate reason is that the Home Office does not want the public to hear how understaffed our prisons are and that overcrowding is causing many of these concerted acts of indiscipline.

The selection of officers who had applied to be a member of the Control & Restraint advance teams at Highdown were instructors who were either physical training instructors (PEIs) or gym queens (fit, muscle bound, guys who pose a lot in front of gym mirrors). As I was not keen on having communal showers with guys who like the look of a well-toned male body, I was never going to be selected for the team.

So, I decided that I would apply to be a hostage negotiator. Not only had I been impressed with the skill and calmness with which my colleague, Roy, had dealt with the first hostage situation that I had witnessed, I was equally taken by the fact that he had managed to piss off the testosterone-filled few within the C&R advance team that had simply wanted to go crashing through the doors, hitting anything that moved.

The psychology team at the prison carried out the selection process for the hostage negotiation team as they needed to be confident that you were of sound mind and could be trusted. This is prompted by the fact that it is hard to imagine why anyone would want to volunteer to stand at a cell door, be screamed at and hurled abuse at for hours on end and run the risk of being taken hostage for all your efforts.

Somehow, I managed to hide the fact that I was clearly well away with the fairies and convinced them that I may be an asset to the hostage negotiating team, so I was packed off to HMYOI (Her Majesty's Young Offender Institute) Dover to be trained as a hostage negotiator. HMYOI Dover dates back as far as the Napoleon days, with an old, disused segregation unit in the bowels of the old prison that is very damp, cold and smelly, yet ideal for the training of hostage negotiators.

There were about ten of us from different prisons around the country and we were briefed by our two tutors who were both experienced hostage negotiators. They informed us that, although they would be showing us some fundamental procedures for conducting negotiations and sharing some of the do's and don'ts of hostage negotiation, they were really simply there to put us through a series of scenarios to test whether we had the ability to be hostage negotiators. They told us that there would be no shame in failing this course, as it was vital that they be convinced that we would be able to rise to the challenge, and nobody was sent to negotiate who wasn't up to the job, which could result in someone's life being on the line.

I was of the view that, although I needed to ensure that I learned as much as possible, I could not imagine that a couple of prison officers (who we had not seen yet) would convince me that the hostage scenarios we would be using as role plays would be in any way life like. My giddy aunts, was I wrong, or what!

We were divided into negotiating teams and given numbers from one to three; I was number one. They then told us that a noise had been reported coming from the cells below and that we needed to investigate it. As we approached the area, we could hear the most horrendous banging coming from the area of the cells. All of a sudden, a hooded prisoner came out of the cell with a knife up against the throat of a civi woman. Just as we had noticed that there was blood trickling out from a wound on her neck, another hooded prisoner rushed out of the cell and threw a club hammer straight at my head, which I only just managed to avoid.

They shot back in the cell, screamed at us to "fuck off", told us they were going to fuck the girl and started banging and making the horrendous noise again.

We decided to take their advice and re-group (fuck off) and re-think our approach (let them fuck the civi woman in the hope that they might calm down). It was at this point that some of us, myself included, had to give ourselves a reality check as this scenario seemed very, very real indeed. Adrenaline was pumping round our bodies and our hearts were pounding.

Thankfully for the civi woman, our situation did improve. Without explaining the techniques in every detail, as I am sure that any would-be hostage perpetrator would keep this chapter in their possession, just in case they decided to practise their hobby of hostage taking, we started to enter into dialogue with the two prisoners. Although, to begin with, most of the dialogue seemed to consist of them insulting us and us trying not to show that we were about to run away from the door screaming, "I have failed" or "I need a clean pair of pants."

These training sessions always followed more or less the same format. Information is passed back to a gold commander who is always an awkward fucker who never makes your life easier by either revealing information to you or making you feel confident that you are doing well. Instead, the awkward fucker will come up with some daft question like what political party the perpetrator votes for and then expect us to go and find out. At the time, I believed that this part of the scenario was over the top and that, in a real life hostage situation, the gold commander would be very switched on and in control. But like hell are they! Role plays involving governors could not have been more accurate.

The three days training were very tiring and, by the end of the programme, I was absolutely shattered. The tutors gave us all an individual debrief and told us whether we had passed or failed. I was amazed to learn that I had passed and even more amazed to hear the tutor tell me that I was one of the best he had come across in a long time. Although I did admit to him that I hated every moment of the course and had been on the verge of jacking it in at every moment, I couldn't help but feel rather proud and his words puffed me up like a peacock. As it turned out, only four of us were selected, which made me realise just how tough this course actually was.

So there I was, a fully fledged prison service hostage negotiator. I was now listed on the service's books and was ready to be called upon at any time of the day or night. Mixed in with all this excitement, though, I couldn't help feeling that I was not looking forward to the real event and was beginning to wonder what I had got myself into.

I did not have long to wait, however, until I was involved in my first incident. I was working on houseblock 3 one morning, waiting for the all clear to open up the prisoners for their breakfast, when we heard a call for a recount of the prisoners. As this was before the unlock of the morning, this was not the normal procedure and had us all speculating about what might be the problem. My brain was just trying to put two and two together when the phone rang in the office and I was told to report to the command suite, which is located well out of harm's way near the security department.

When I arrived, I found two other officers there whom I knew were hostage negotiators and we were then briefed by one of the principal officers in the command suite. The suite was manned by about eight staff of varying ranks from senior officer to a governor grade called Dick, who was to live up to his name in every respect. We were told that a prisoner on houseblock 4 had decided that he did not want to go to court that morning and was threatening to harm his cellmate who was in the cell with him.

The PO said that he wanted me to do the talking and that the other two officers were there to support me and communicate back. We grabbed whatever equipment we needed and made our way to the incident, escorted by a senior officer. I began by talking with the prisoner to ascertain if we might be able to resolve the situation peacefully without the intervention of a C&R team, which was already getting kitted up and positioned so that they could storm the cell if that became necessary.

When we arrived, I found that there was also a female officer there called Angie who was trying to keep the prisoner calm. The prisoner was just screaming at her to fuck off and telling her to get the governor. When she saw me approach the door, she immediately handed over the task of dealing with the prisoner, went straight to the lower office and promptly burst into tears. I felt like joining her. The thought of trying out my new-found skill in a real life hostage situation was filling me with dread.

When I got to the door, I was surprised to see a prisoner who I knew and who I got along with quite well. Although not one of the brightest in the bunch, he was always very polite to me. The cell was in a bit of a mess as he had decided to remove the sink and toilet and had then tried to rearrange the beds into a kind of support for the door. Others, however, were to refer to this as a barricade.

As soon as he recognised me he was very apologetic about what he had done and wanted to know if he was in trouble. I assured him that worse things happen at sea and that we deal with these kinds of things all the time. I also suggested that it might be nice if he were to stop sitting on top of his cellmate and refrain from poking him with the table leg. He complied with my request and let the very scared and bemused cellmate sit in the other corner away from him.

He then started to tell me that he wanted to speak to the governor, as he was sure that only he could help him. I told him that I doubted if the governor could help him as the governor on duty was Dick. Even the dumbest prisoner knew what a complete cock he was. Realising that he stood no chance of help from Dick, he asked if I could help him. I told him that I would try but I would have to know what the problem was. He explained that he could not travel to court in a sweat box (cellular vehicles are used for transporting prisoners to court in which the prisoner is locked into small individual cells inside the vehicle) as he was claustrophobic. I asked him why he hadn't explained this to someone already, such as someone from healthcare. Apparently he had told the night duty nurse from healthcare who had simply told him to grow up. I then wondered why he had decided to trash the cell and start hurting his cellmate. He explained that, after the nurse had told him to grow up, his cellmate had started to tease him and, when he had used the en suite lavatory in the cell, his nice cellmate had pinned a bed to the door and trapped him in the loo. So, he concluded, he just lost it and went berserk.

By now, his predicament had begun to dawn on him. He started pleading with me, saying he did not know what to do, that he must be in a lot of trouble now and begged me to help him. I reassured him that I would be able to sort things out but that I first needed to make sure that no further harm would come to his very helpful cellmate. I went on to tell him that he must do exactly as I say if he wanted to get out of the cell and the mess he was in.

I then asked my colleagues, who were very close by, to feed back all the details of the situation to the command suite, but told them that the bit about Dick the governor was a little trick of mine to get the trust of the prisoner and that they didn't need to feed that back to the command suite. It would remain a secret weapon in the toolkit of the experienced hostage negotiator!

It then came back to us from command suite that they were not yet ready for a surrender and that we would have to keep him talking. I could hardly believe what I was hearing, and it was at this point that I realised just how accurate the training scenarios had been concerning commanders and their inability to get anything like their act together.

So we then embarked on what was to be the hardest part of this hostage situation, trying to keep the perpetrator calm while prolonging the hostage situation, even though he was ready to surrender, until the command suite had got its act together sufficiently so that they were ready for us to bring the hostage taker in.

We did eventually get both prisoners safely out of the cell and, after a short stay in the segregation unit, the hostage taker was eventually taken to court via taxi. I am sure that the victim learned an easy lesson the hard way that day: don't tease a prisoner who you are sharing a cell with.

During my time as a hostage negotiator, I attended dozens of incidents, most at Highdown Prison but a few at other prisons. Generally, I worked with a close colleague of mine called John who had a great sense of humour and we found that we worked off each other well and therefore made a very good team. We were often called upon to help teach the hostage negotiator courses and had the opportunity to play the part of prisoners during the scenarios. In the end, though, we had to give this up as we started to really enjoy pretending to be a prisoner and frightening the shit out of prison officers.

We would often be called out during the middle of the night to attend all kinds of hostage incidents. One of these incidents had escalated into a copycat situation. A prisoner in the cell opposite to where the original hostage incident was taking place decided to smash up his cell and declare that he was taking his cellmate hostage and would cut him up unless he got transferred to another prison.

The original perpetrator from the first incident, cell b-21, simply wanted more medication and, although he was not threatening his cellmate, he had refused to pull down a makeshift barricade from the door unless we had the medication for him.

John and I were the first negotiators at the prison that night as it was 2 o'clock in the morning. A very good duty governor, who I had worked with when he was an officer and who was known to us as Dib Dob, asked us to make an assessment of the situation as he suspected that the second incident was simply a prisoner fucking about.

As soon as we arrived at the scene, John went to the copycat incident and I went to the real one. I managed to calm the prisoner down by assuring him that we would help him as, by now, he was very scared; although not, I suspect, as scared as his cellmate who was looking a whiter shade of pale.

John had managed to get a good look at what the situation was in the copycat incident and confirmed that it all looked very stage-managed and, although some prison property was broken in the cell, not one item of any of the prisoner's property appeared to be damaged. John also knew these prisoners and knew that they were always taking the piss out of staff. One, in particular, had been wrapped up (had Control and Restraint techniques used on him to prevent him from hitting staff) more times than a Bernard Mathews' turkey. This prisoner was taking great pleasure in being very abusive towards us and was attempting to wind up the other prisoners.

Before long, we had all the negotiators in place along with four advanced Control and Restraint teams who were more than chewing at the bit to get stuck in. Despite the distraction from the pretend copycat hostage taker, who was constantly trying to worry and bother the real hostage taker and original perpetrator, we did manage to talk him into surrendering and brought the situation to a safe conclusion, to the great relief of the cellmate who, by this time, needed a whole new set of underwear.

When we went to the cell of the pretend copycat hostage incident, the so-called perpetrator and his two cellmates had pulled down the barricade they had neatly placed at the door and declared that they were all prepared to come out. As John uttered the words, "Like fuck you are," he moved swiftly to one side to allow nine prison officers in full riot gear to go crashing through the cell door and wrap up every prisoner in the cell. Even as the final C&R wrist locks were being placed on them, they were already grassing each other up for whose idea it was to fuck us about.

A very common type of incident is the so-called self-hostage one, whereby a prisoner threatens to harm himself unless his demands are met, or he requires an audience for his act of attempted suicide. They can also simply be a cry for help. Whatever the motivation of the prisoner, these incidents cause major disruption and the prisoner in question needs trained negotiators to try to talk him out of his plans to self-harm.

I was just coming to the end of a very long 'A' shift when I was asked to report to the command suite. By now you will have realised that the only time I get invited to the command suite is when the shit has hit the fan and they need me to start shovelling. When I arrived, I was met by the duty governor who informed me that a prisoner on houseblock 2 had climbed to the top of the spur bars, which is about 35 feet high, had tied a noose around his neck and was threatening to jump off and hang himself. As if the situation were not dramatic enough, he had decided to add further tension by slashing one of his wrists.

I knew from experience that, although this suicide attempt was likely to be very real and could easily end in tragedy, there must be something that this guy wanted or he would have jumped by now.

Soon after I was briefed, I was pleased to see my mate John turn up. I filled him in on the complexity and sensitivities of what we were facing. He paused for a moment to take in all I had told him and to consider the severity of the situation, before pronouncing, "Right then, let's go and find out what this stupid fucker wants."

When we arrived at the scene we found that an ex-negotiator called Helen was talking to the prisoner. The reason why she was no longer a negotiator was because she had been promoted to senior negotiator and the criteria to be a negotiator is that you should not hold any kind of rank above your other colleagues as this may encourage the perpetrators to talk only to you, believing that you had higher authority because of your rank. Helen had been on a rest day and had been called in because the call out list in the control room had not been updated. She was very smartly dressed in her twin set and pearls, as she had been to watch the trooping of the colour up in London.

The prisoner was perched on the bars, running from the floor to the roof, at the highest drop point that can be reached which was about 35 feet. He had a noose around his neck and the other end was securely fixed to the bars. He had also slashed his wrist and, although there appeared to be a fair bit of blood from the wound, it had stopped bleeding as Helen had managed to get him to wrap a towel around it to apply pressure.

We decided that John should take over from Helen as he knew the prisoner better than me and there was more chance that he could establish a good rapport with him. When John took over Helen was very willing to back off and went to the command suite for a de-brief. As soon as she had disappeared, the prisoner asked John, "Who the fuck was that guv? I was getting so fed up with the posh bitch, I was going to jump just to get away from her."

John then tried to establish what the problem was and why he was doing this. He discovered that the prisoner wanted to have a video camera to film his suicide as he wanted to make a statement for the press. The prisoner was not making a lot of sense as to why he wanted to take his own life and we could see that his mood was deteriorating as our line of questioning continued. We decided we had better change tactics. I joined John on the landing near the prisoner so that we could start a three-way conversation that was more light-hearted, hoping to try to lift his mood. The banter between me and John soon had the prisoner laughing, although we were very aware that he clearly had a troubled mind and that he could still harm himself at any moment.

He was constantly asking who else was with us. We had paramedics on stand-by and this worried us because, if he believed that we had shed loads of help on hand, we thought he would be more likely to jump, although he probably hoped that the medics would quickly react and save him and he would then receive all the attention he was so desperately seeking. We knew, however, that not only did we not yet have all we needed in place, he had chosen a very difficult place for us to prevent fatal harm coming to him if he did decide to jump.

The purpose behind our negotiation was to try to establish calm, find out what the problem was and try to talk him into coming down and letting staff in healthcare help him. However, as we know by experience, these situations do not always go to plan. We therefore also have a specialised intervention team, similar to the advance C&R teams, whose purpose is to prevent prisoners from being able to kill themselves. Another of our objectives is therefore to stall for time while this team gets into place with all their equipment, in case he does decide to jump.

I was impressed with the governor this time, as he had remembered to arrange food to be sent to us. The only flaw in this, however, was that the specialist suicide intervention team had eaten it all before John and I could get a look in. Also, by this time, a hostage negotiator coordinator had arrived. This was a new concept to our team as they were psychologists who were trained to help and advise the negotiators and the governors. However, most of them appeared to be about twelve years of age and looked like they should be at home in bed with teddy.

By now, we had been negotiating for four hours and we were all getting very tired, none more so than the prisoner whose mood was now turning to despair and gloom. He was also running out of tobacco and had announced to us that he was sorry to do this to us as he regarded us as the two best officers in the prison service (we would not argue with that, although there are shed loads who would), but that, as soon as he had finished his last cigarette, he was going to jump.

I had already managed to have a quiet word with John and we had agreed what we would do to try to save him if he jumped. I had also managed to pass back the news to the psychologist hostage negotiator coordinator, who was flirting with some of the C&R team. She dismissed my warning by informing me, "They all say that. He won't jump yet."

I wandered over to the team leader of the suicide intervention team and advised them that, in my opinion, we were nearing the end of the road and we probably had no more than two minutes before he jumped. He quickly signalled to his team to very quietly get into place and to wait for his command.

I went back to John and the prisoner and he was now not far from finishing his cigarette, I could tell that John had moved on to very desperate measures by now, as he had offered the prisoner one of his own cigarettes (I had only ever seen John cadge cigarettes from others and I had never witnessed him actually giving any out). All this was to no avail, however, as the prisoner apologised to us and then jumped from the bars.

Adrenaline then kicked in, my heart was racing, I could feel my whole body tense but I knew I had to remain calm and focus on what I had to do to ensure that we did all we could to save his life. I went into overdrive, shouting the command word to the intervention team and, with John, rushed in towards the prisoner, even as his body was still falling. I managed to grab him around his chest to prevent the final noose from breaking his neck and John had grabbed his legs to prevent him from kicking loose. The intervention team were with us within a split second and were starting to take over the support of the prisoner. He was cut loose from the noose, and restrained by the team as they searched him and removed two home-made knives. The medics on stand by then checked him over and he was moved to a secure cell in the hospital wing. During this time, he was talking to John and I and apologising for what he had done and for what he had put us through. Although he had given us a very difficult task and stretched our hostage negotiating skills to the limit, there was something very sad and pathetic about this guy who, when all was said and done, was clearly suffering from a lot of problems and just needed a helping hand and someone to talk to.

John and I were both on a high. As far as we were concerned, this was another job well done. We gave a brief report at the hot debrief (that occurs immediately after the incident) and a very detailed report at the cold debrief (that happens about a week after the incident so that all parties involved can give a clear report without the emotion of the incident). I had mentioned that, in my opinion, this prisoner was attempting to make a statement on camera so that he could then commit suicide.

Sadly, however, the prisoner was found hanged in HMP Frankland, Durham in October 2002, not long after our incident. After a five-week inquest into his death, jurors found that a series of failures had contributed to his death.

I do know that officers at Frankland had desperately tried to save the prisoner but they were too late. It is my experience that, if a prisoner is determined to take their own life, they will, and there is very little anyone can do to prevent them from succeeding in their sad quest one day.

With this case, though, I am confused as to why the governors of our prisons always think they know best and make decisions without gaining sufficient knowledge from the prison officers who work day in and day out with these prisoners. I was surprised to find out that the governor of Frankland prison had allowed the prisoner to be filmed by an outside film crew the day before he had committed suicide.

There are some prisoners who make a habit of taking hostages as some form of perverse entertainment, or they simply do it because they can. These are the ones who are fully aware that they never achieve anything from the activity as they have been there before.

One prisoner who falls within this category is Charlie Bronson.

Charles Bronson is a serial hostage-taker and, during his 30 years in jail, he has taken hostages on 10 different occasions – one of whom he threatened to eat. On one occasion, Bronson had taken hostage two Iraqi men accused of the Stansted hijacking and another inmate hostage at Belmarsh prison in London. He insisted his hostages call him 'General' and told negotiators he would eat one of his victims unless his demands were met.

At one stage, Bronson demanded that one of the Iraqis hit him "very hard" over the head with a metal tray. When the hostage refused, the 18-stone strongman slashed his own shoulder six times with a razor blade. He later told staff, "I'm going to start snapping necks – I'm the number one hostage taker." He demanded a getaway helicopter to take him to Cuba, two Uzi sub-machine guns, 5,000 rounds of ammunition and an axe. He later reduced his demands to a cheese sandwich and a cup of tea.

He was given seven years added to his sentence for his efforts. In court, he said he was "as guilty as Adolf Hitler". He said, "I was on a mission of madness, but now I'm on a mission of peace and all I want to do now is get home and have a pint with my son."

My encounter with Bronson was brief but it is my opinion that he is an intelligent and talented man. Due to him being as mad as a big box of frogs, however, he is bloody dangerous and has progressively become madder during his incarceration. Where Bronson is concerned, the prison service has failed in its purpose and the psychiatrists and doctors who have stated that he is sane need to find a job that they know something about.

I have attended many hostage incidents and I still believe that the most frightening and nerve-wracking situations are when I have had to attend refresher courses each year and go through the scenarios. Although the real incidents can be very dangerous, they are also very exciting and rewarding. There is no better feeling than working with a good team of hostage negotiators and intervention teams, who know what they are doing and do it well, and gaining a successful result through our combined efforts.

Chapter Seven

High Days and Holidays

"Good morning!"

"Good morning, Guv, and Merry Christmas!"

"Merry Christmas to you as well Smith!"

"Has Santa left anything in the stocking that I left hanging outside the door, Guv?"

"No, Smith, and he has nicked your stocking."

"Oh, he's a bastard, Guv! That fucking Santa has never given me any presents. Do you know when I was a kid, if I never woke up with a hard on, on Christmas Day, I would have had nothing to play with."

"That's enough about your smutty love life. Now, hands off cocks and on with socks, Christmas Day breakfast will be ready in 10 minutes."

Christmas Day in prison is not like any other day in the calendar. It can be very sad for those who are missing their family, especially those with children. There are long periods of boredom, and the usual crap on television that is no distraction from the misery of being in prison on Christmas Day. You cannot even get a newspaper to read as none are printed on Christmas Day. And it's even worse for the prisoners.

The build up for Christmas usually starts with the carving up of the duty roster for the two-week period over Christmas. No one is allowed to pre-book any leave as the senior officer in charge of organising the roster is usually very careful to ensure fair play so that everyone has a chance of some quality time off with their families. You will usually get the chance to choose which of the two weeks you would prefer, Christmas or New Year week. I always picked New Year week because I found that Christmas Day can be a drag. If I had volunteered to work part of a shift on Christmas Day, I usually got to pick the morning shift, which meant that I was still able to get home by the afternoon to enjoy a Christmas dinner with the family and would still have New Year's Eve off so that I could party.

The next build up for Christmas is the double canteen day. This is where prisoners are allowed to spend two weeks' allowance in the week before Christmas, because the prison canteen is closed during the Christmas week itself. It always amazed me how excited prisoners could get simply because they were allowed to have two weeks' worth of canteen. Although this sounds a fairly straightforward process, there were always problems, particularly if some prisoners were not able to get their money sent in via the post in time, or if it was delayed in the post because of all the extra Christmas mail. It is very difficult, at the best of times, to explain to a prisoner who has not received his money on time that he will have to wait two weeks before he can buy any tobacco. But, at Christmas, it is downright dangerous. You will always find officers trying to convince canteen staff to allow them to canteen the prisoner as soon as his money arrives rather than making them wait until the next official canteen day. Then, of course, by the start of the second week their canteen supply of sweets and tobacco will have run out far too soon and they will have to wait until after the New Year to purchase from the canteen again.

The next big event is the arrival of the Christmas trees. The governor has a small fund set aside from the budget to purchase Christmas trees and we usually end up with one in the visitors' centre outside the prison, one in the entrance lobby of the gate house and one on each residential unit in the prison. There would always be volunteers from amongst the officers to decorate the tree with the stash of Christmas decorations held on each houseblock. The tree would usually be erected on the lower level, near the hot plate or the lower office, and they would normally remain there unmolested until the festive season was over. There was one year, however, when one of the prisoners wanted to test if the decorations were flameproof by lighting them. They weren't! The decorations and the tree went up in flames and the prisoner received an early Christmas present from some of the other prisoners, although I don't think that a black eye would have been on his Christmas wish list to Santa.

At one Christmas time, we had a very good saxophone player who had decided to join us for the festive season. In fact, because he had been caught at Gatwick with two kilos of cocaine, it was to be the first of many Christmases in prison for him. He had managed to get permission to have the saxophone brought in and kept in his possession as long as he did not piss off the rest of the wing by playing late at night. As it was very novel to have this kind of instrument in the prison, we asked him to stand by the tree when the meals were served on Christmas Day and play a number of festive tunes, which went down well with both prisoners and staff. This resulted in some confusion for our newly arrived clients from the detox wing, however, who thought they were somewhere on a London underground station and started begging for their next fix.

Then there are the Christmas Eve visits. Because there are no visits on Christmas Day, Boxing Day or New Year's Day, we are usually cram packed with visitors every day of the week before Christmas with the busiest day being Christmas Eve. The noise levels are horrendous – and must be almost beyond health and safety regulation levels – as there are excited children everywhere, already wound up by promises of the latest playstation. Wives and girlfriends would be all dolled up, trying to make the best impression to their loved ones who are incarcerated and separated from their families by those big, horrible, nasty screws. The really sad part is that we would always have a bumper find of drugs on visitors trying to smuggle them in to give the prisoner a bit of festive high.

And then the big day itself arrives. I would always try to arrive early so that I could ensure that the poor bastard working the night patrol on my houseblock can get away early. There was hardly a soul on the roads as I drove in and the gate staff would greet me wearing silly Santa hats at some ungodly hour of Christmas Day morning. I would make my way to the houseblock to find a very happy night patrol who knew he could now go home and spend Christmas Day with his family.

The houseblock would be very quiet, whereas on any other day you would normally have several cell bells sounding from prisoners. They would have heard that there had been a change over of staff from nights to days and therefore they had someone else to whom they could ask their question. No matter that they would have already asked the question and would have either been told the answer already, or told to wait until they were unlocked or, more often than not, got an answer that they did not like so they thought they would try asking the question to someone else in the hope of getting a different and better answer.

However, Christmas morning was different and was always very quiet.

Soon the rest of the daytime staff would drift in, some may be wearing silly Santa hats or reindeer antlers, others might be wearing a Christmas tie or brightly coloured Christmas socks. I always kept to my regulation uniform. I was never that great about Christmas and I did not want prisoners to think that I might be an easy target to try and con something from me, particularly when I was wearing some silly Santa hat or reindeer antlers with flashing things hanging off me. Bah humbug Kelly! It is one thing to be taken as a fool and conned by a prisoner but quite another to actually look like one as well.

Once we were all in position, we would start to open up the prisoners for what would be a very long day indeed. Once they had been opened up most of they would emerge from their cells and greet their fellow prisoners with a festive, "Merry Christmas brov, another one up the judge's bum." Some would simply lie in their cells as they would rather forget that they were spending Christmas in prison. However, most just get on with it. As one prisoner put it, "If you can't do the time, don't do the crime."

There is also usually a rush for the phones and 99 per cent of the prisoners will form an orderly queue, with the remainder trying to bully their way to the front of the queue which is a hangover from their school days when they bullied their way to the front of the dinner queue. Some behaviour just never changes. We would then get the hotplate workers out. They don't even get a rest on Christmas Day, but it is regarded as one of the best jobs in the prison, and they will get the best food and all the extras they want once the houseblock has been fed. Their first task is to fetch the Christmas Day breakfast from the kitchens which consists of cereal, scrambled egg, tinned tomatoes, grilled sausage, bacon, mushrooms, toast/marmalade and a beverage pack of tea and coffee. You would be hard pushed to get a better breakfast at a motorway service station.

One of the toughest tasks on Christmas Day is to try to encourage prisoners to participate in competitions on the pool table or table tennis table, or play with the many board games that are provided for their entertainment and delight on all the spurs. Most just want to return back to their cells to watch television or, before they had their own TV in their cell, they would have gone and sat in front of the television in the spurs' TV room. These were reminiscent of what were known as day rooms in hospitals but without the chance of catching MRSA or any other kind of hospital superbug.

The Christmas church service could always be relied upon to provide one of the highlights of the day. We would ensure that the prisoners were dispatched to these services as quickly as possible because we needed to have them back on time so that we could serve them lunch. The Christmas service was always very popular and usually attended by the local good and the pious 'god-botherers', along with a gospel choir. It was interesting to see that some of them felt pity for the prisoners and others simply looked like frightened rabbits caught in headlights, but they all demonstrated the good old Christian belief of forgiveness and goodwill to all men. This was short lived one year, however, when a church orderly robbed some of their belongings from the chaplain's office where they had left their coats.

Lunchtime becomes a very complicated balancing act requiring the skills of a contortionist and a juggler at the same time. On many an occasion I have seen prisoners lose there entire dinner on the floor. The problem is that we issue them with a standard 10-inch diameter plastic plate and a small dessert bowl. Then, on Christmas Day, we expect them to collect the following in one trip and one trip only to the hotplate: salmon fillet with parsley butter, roast turkey, bacon roll, Yorkshire puddings, chestnut and sausage meat stuffing, roast potatoes, Brussels sprouts, baby carrots, gravy, cranberry sauce, bread and butter, Christmas pudding with vanilla sauce, Christmas cake and mince pies.

For our entertainment on Christmas Day, we then challenge them to balance all of these items whilst also collecting their free £2 phone card. Some had this down to such a fine art that, to our amazement, they were also able to grab hold of some toiletries from the stores while they were on route.

Once they had returned to their cells and we had managed to get the phones switched off so that we could 'bang 'em up', we would submit the role count as soon as humanly possible and then either go off for something to eat ourselves or, for those lucky enough to be on an early shift, back home for a proper Christmas lunch.

After lunch, though, would be the challenging task of opening the cell doors and getting the prisoners out on association. The challenge was in getting prisoners out of their cells while trying to hold our breath to avoid the stench of the overcooked Brussels sprouts that, by now, would have fermented, the gastric effect of this having taken a serious toll on the quality of air in the cells. Most of the prisoners would be in a very lethargic mood. They were most likely to either resume their place in the queue to try to phone their families or, a few of our more overenthusiastic prisoners would continue competing in the games and competitions that would have been organised for them by the officers.

It will be at this point that you will start to get the most stupid amongst our prison population coming up and complaining about some medical problem: stomach ache, headache, toothache or bollock ache. Unless it is something that can be dealt with by a paracetamol or they have stopped breathing, they will have no chance of any medical attention at 4pm on a boring Christmas Day. The prisoners, by this time, will have started to get bored and most will have drifted back to their cells to watch the Christmas Day blockbuster on television.

The duty governors would, by now, have made their rounds of the prison units to ensure that officers have not stolen any of the prisoners' food or decided to keep them all banged up, whilst they get their heads down (now, that would be a good idea). Then it is 4.30pm and time to serve the evening meal. We get another chance to see the magical balancing of food act as the prisoners collect: a mixed salad, salmon steaks, ham, corned beef, tomatoes, cheese and onion quiche, potato salad, mixed salad rice with nuts and raisins, Christmas cake, mince pie and custard, four slices of bread, a packet of biscuits and a beverage kit.

We will then prise off any remaining prisoner from the phone queue and bang them up again for the evening so that we (other than the poor bastard who has drawn the short straw to cover the evening patrol) can all go home to our families to enjoy a warmed up Christmas dinner and listen to Aunty Liz break wind whilst playing charades. ("Is it a film? I know, it's got to be *Gone with the Wind*!")

Then it's back to the prison first thing in the morning, because it's Boxing Day. Now most of you will associate Boxing Day with a traditional sporting day and a chance to blow the cobwebs away with a brisk walk in the park. Well, it's kind of similar in prison. Prisoners are unlocked so that they can get their breakfast and there will always be the odd stupid one who will come out of his cell with an application form in his hand, wanting something or other. They will be told by one of the prison officers that, because we are the only stupid bastards actually working in the prison on Boxing Day, there are no education, medical or governing staff to process their application and that they will have to wait until the following week when things return to relative normality.

After their stroll to the hot plate to collect breakfast, prisoners are then locked up again so that we can get the cleaners out to clean up the mess from the day before. When the area is clean, we hand out free newspapers to the cells designated to receive one that day. Each houseblock of about 180 prisoners will have 15 free newspapers that are given out to prisoners on a cell rotation system. However, if a prisoner wishes to purchase a newspaper, they need to pre-order them the week before and then we, in our multifaceted role as prison officer come postman, provide a door-to-door service and deliver them directly to the prisoner's cell. Once newspapers have been delivered, the prisoners are unlocked again for association, making phone calls and organising their day's viewing and gambling on the day's sporting events. They will also get their own chance to 'blow the cobwebs away' with a little walk around the exercise yard. It is usually around this time that we get to witness the true meaning of Boxing Day at the prison as there will always be the opportunity for a fight between prisoners to settle a score with someone who has failed to pay up against a bet of some kind or who has robbed one of them or smoked all their tobacco. These types of disagreements are very common in prison on Boxing Day. And, because the segregation unit is very likely to be busy at this time of year, violent prisoners are normally placed in the segregation unit's strip cells, more commonly known as the 'Box', to calm down. So, from our perspective, we understand only too well why it is called Boxing Day!

The following days seem like endless Sundays without the church service to break up the boredom and monotony. There is no education or workshops and prisoners become increasingly frustrated with not being able to process most of their applications because administration staff are on holiday. But then comes New Year's Eve.

New Year's Eve in prison is strangely exciting for some prisoners, as a lot of them will have saved either some drugs or 'hooch'. I am sure that will all have heard of 'hooch' – an illegal alcohol brew that is made up in prison. The ingredients can differ from prison to prison but the most popular variety is the rotten fruit type. The prisoner initiating the 'hooch' production and his friends, who want to contribute to the brew session, will start to save fruit. They will then place the fruit in a position that will allow it to over ripen to the point where it will be nearly rotten. They will then try to acquire a bucket and a clean dustbin bag – there was one incident where the whole wing had contributed to the brew session and had managed to lay their hands on a dustbin. The rotting fruit then gets placed in the bag which goes into the bucket along with lots of water to begin its process of fermentation.

Their next task is to find somewhere warm and safe to store this fermenting mass. Often this will be either in their cells by the hot pipe (a very large pipe that runs through the cells and serves as a radiator to keep the cells warm) or in a store cupboard. More often than not, store cupboards were the preferred choice as the 'hooch' could be well hidden amongst the cleaning equipment. They also had the added advantage that the smelly buckets and cleaning chemicals often prevented discovery by masking the rotting smell of fruit and a further advantage in that, if the 'hooch' was discovered, it was unlikely that the prisoner behind the production would be identified as it would be hard to establish for sure who had placed what where.

The final trick would be to add sugar to the mixture to speed up the fermentation and bread to help with the yeast effect that is needed.

A good brew should take about a month and our task was to watch out for who was collecting fruit and sugar and keep track on their movements. The best way that I found of finding the supply of hooch was to observe the reaction of the cleaners when I turned up with tins of paint to decorate the store cupboards and assign one of them to the task. I would then ask them in which order they wanted to start painting the store cupboards and, inevitably, the cupboard that was to be painted last would be the one with the hooch.

Prisoners are very adept when it comes to ensuring that their hooch supplies remain undiscovered. When the hooch has had long enough to brew, or on occasions such as New Year's Eve, they distribute the hooch amongst themselves in fruit juice bottles and place them in their cells ready for the evening.

Come late evening on New Year's Eve, the prison will be in patrol state with officers on fire watch. On the stroke of midnight, the whole prison erupts in the most horrendous din of every prisoner's boot and fist banging and kicking the cell doors, along with their screams and shouts. Then the fires will start by way of the prisoner's very own personal bonfires or firework displays. If you are lucky, it will simply be newspaper that is set alight and thrown out of the windows, although prisoners have been known to set light to bedding, prison clothing, pillows or anything else that is flammable and will fit through the windows, so that the blazing items fall on the ground outside their cells. For prisoners on the ground floor, they discover this is not the best time to have a cell at ground level as the smoke can be very bad and, in the case of pillows on fire, fumes from the burning foam can be deadly. Prison officers who had been on fire watch come into their own, extinguishing all they come across with fire extinguishers, before returning to look out for further fire-related incidents during the rest of the night.

Easter was another long, tedious and laborious holiday that seemed like a week of Sundays. Unlike Christmas, prisoners would not receive a double hit of canteen, as the canteen would be open on the normal days except for Good Friday and Easter Monday. Extra church services are laid on over the period to celebrate Good Friday but there are no visits on Good Friday or the Monday. Education and workshops are closed for about a week, which gives us some very bored prisoners to play with. It would be rare to see any special food laid on over the Easter period, so there is little to distract prisoners from becoming so bored that, to relieve the monotony and create some interest, they start fighting with each other – or us. There was once an officer who thought it would be funny to spread a rumour that, as it was Good Friday the next day, the kitchen would be closed and the governor has decided to allow the prisoners to order a pizza from a Pizza Hut takeaway menu that he had placed on each spur. I was amazed at how many of the prisoners fell for this one and actually placed their order for a pizza. However, come lunchtime on Good Friday, we had to make the officer apologise to all the bitterly disappointed prisoners, some of whom were in tears because they were not going to get stuck into a stuffed crust meat special.

It can be so boring over the Easter period that even I have resorted to silly games with the prisoners. On one occasion, I hid three Cadbury's cream eggs on the spur where I was working, drew up a clue sheet for the treasure hunt and handed them out to any prisoners that wanted to play. To my surprise, every single prisoner took part in the treasure hunt and although there was a rather heated altercation between two prisoners regarding who had found one of the eggs first, the Easter egg hunt expedition went down very well and kept both prisoners and officers alike amused for a couple of hours.

Other occasions that can cause a break in the normal prison routine are great sporting events like the World Cup. The World Cup always used to give us real problems in the days when prisoners did not have televisions in their cells, as the only place to watch the matches were in the television rooms that were on each landing. It would always become a problem when there was an interesting football match on in the evening which was due to end prior to bang up or when the match had gone into extra time with a possible penalty shootout. To prise the prisoners out of these rooms so that we could bang them up was always near impossible and filled with danger from the risk of assaults on staff. Prisoners would plead, beg, and, in some cases threaten, to try and watch the end of the match. I always found that the best way to deal with these fraught moments was to be very direct and straight with the prisoners. I would inform them that I would be locking the television rooms at the correct time and that, if they wished to hear the rest of the match, they had best get back to their cells to ensure that their radios were tuned in to the correct station. There would, inevitably, be some prisoners who had only just arrived a few days before hand and who would claim, quite legitimately, not to have a radio. I only encountered this problem once before making sure that I always had a supply of old radios that I could loan out on such occasions.

There was only one occasion when I was actually attacked for turning the television off during a match. All the other prisoners had left the television room as ordered and there was just one prisoner remaining so I told him to hurry up to his cell and listen to the match on the radio. As I turned the television off, he sprang up and punched me straight on the jaw, breaking one of my teeth. I was on my own as the other officer was trying to get the prisoners out of the television room on the landing above me. I managed to stop the prisoner from hitting me again by punching him square in the face, causing him to collapse immediately onto the floor. Thankfully, the alarm bell had already been sounded by a prison officer who had been coming onto the spur to help with the bang up. The next day the prisoner was brought up in front of the duty governor, an accelerated promotion type, straight from some University of Tree Hugging and La La Land, with a degree in How to be a Cock. The governor noticed that the prisoner had two black eyes and a very swollen, but not broken, nose from my single punch to his face. When the duty governor asked me how hard I had hit the prisoner, I replied, "Hard enough to stop him from hitting me again" and thought, "You cock!" The governor dismissed the case and decided to lecture me instead on how I should have allowed the prisoner to finish watching the television. As I said, clearly a duty governor from La La Land with his head up his arse.

We were always amazed by how much time, money and effort would be put in by our management to keep prisoners amused during these high days and holidays, with the actual task of keeping these goppers entertained always falling on us. I always believed that it would be interesting to organise an Olympic Games for prisoners. Events might differ somewhat from the real Olympics and instead of long jump, for example, you could have 'jump the dock'. We could construct a makeshift court dock, raised to different levels for the prisoners to jump. There could also be the 100-metre sprint with a twist as, instead of the normal pacers we see at races, the prisoner could be chased by one of the prison attack dogs to encourage greater speeds. Then, of course, there could be the 1,000 metre hurdles – but this time over razor wire. The fencing competition could take on an entirely different meaning – gone would be the swords and visors and in would come the stolen goods. Pole vaulting would, of course, have to be banned as it would pose too great a risk to security but the Prison Olympics ceremony could still end in the traditional Pentathlon of five sports – but, in our games, it would also include the most favourite sport amongst prisoners of getting their drugs smuggled into prison with an extra award being made for the most innovative place to hide a drug when getting it through prison security.

Chapter Eight

Courts and Escorts

When I first joined the prison service, we did our own escorting and transporting of prisoners, along with the staffing of all courts within the country. One of the departments we used to have at Highdown was the courts, escorts and visits department. This group tended to attract those prison officers who were either not fully fit to be on the wings, who were nearing retirement, or who were not wanted by any of the other managers in the prison. You will not be surprised to learn that I found myself with this group because of the latter reason.

If you were part of the court escort staff, you would have to get to the prison for around 06.30am and, along with your colleagues, go round the different residential units gathering up those prisoners who were on your list to appear in the court you were allocated to serve. They would be moved to the reception area, where they would be strip-searched by their escorting staff (on the premise that, if your life depended on making sure that the prisoner was searched properly, you would be better off doing it yourself). They would then be processed through the reception area, ensuring that we had the right prisoners in the right vans at the right time for the right courts.

It was very rare for a prisoner to refuse to go to court as there was always sufficient numbers of staff on duty to 'deal' with any refusals. Most prisoners would have been warned by other inmates (certainly those who had already been foolhardy enough to try to refuse a court appearance) that they would only end up in the segregation unit to reflect on their decision. Given that the vans had a tight timetable to get all the prisoners to court on time, their period of reflection never needed to last very long – and, before they knew it, they would be back at reception, this time as keen as mustard to board the van.

Prisoners would be loaded on to the prison cellular vans or mini buses depending on their security risk. If they were transported by minibus they would be double handcuffed in pairs. This involved handcuffing their hands together using heavy duty handcuffs with positive locking and unlocking, which incorporates a 10-disc Ava mechanism designed specifically for use in custodial environments. These things weigh about two pounds in weight and would, I imagine, be near impossible to break off. The prisoner would then be handcuffed to another prisoner, so that if one of them wanted to pick his nose, the other prisoner could help, although it was very rare for any of them to attempt to scratch their arses.

If a prisoner was to be placed into a cellular van, he would have his hands cuffed together as above and would then be handcuffed to a prison officer who would escort him to the van. These would be conveniently parked outside the reception building and, once inside the cell within the van, the cuff linking him to the officer would be removed.

The whole process was over very quickly and with minimum fuss. The vans would make their way to one of the various courts that our prison served. In my case, I worked at Guildford court for a short while. We always managed to be one of the first vans out of the gate and on our way to court because Bill, one of our experienced prison officers, would be at the court before us preparing the kind of fried breakfast that enabled me to maintain the wonderful physique that would challenge even the most experienced physical education instructor. It wasn't just the thought of breakfast that spurred us on. We did not want to spend too long on the van with these prisoners as the 'eau de con' would be so pungent as to be an assault on the most hardened officers' nostrils.

At court, we would place the prisoners into holding cells and sort out the running order for the day. When a prisoner was required to appear before the judge or the magistrate, we would use a simple ratchet cuff and escort him into the dock. Depending on the security risk of the prisoner, we would normally have just two officers in the dock to ensure that the 'gopper' did not decide to jump the dock and try to escape. Surprisingly enough, some actually did try this trick. During the time that we held responsibility for the courts served by Highdown, there had been several attempts to escape from either the court itself or during the escort but, thankfully, none were successful.

. The normal method for an escape attempt from a court would be the good old 'jump the dock' trick. This should never, however, be confused with any type of strange West Country water sport, although there are some similarities as strong legs and good training are required for both. As you will have seen on television, the docks are just above waist height and about 12 inches in width and rounded, so as to prevent the would-be 'dock jumper' from gaining enough purchase to launch himself up and over the dock. They are also usually raised from the rest of the court floor to ensure that any potential 'dock jumper' does not have a soft landing.

The average court case is very, very boring. The hardest task for the prison officers, seated in the dock with the prisoner and having probably just eaten a very healthy full English breakfast, is to stay sufficiently alert to record any directions or orders the judge may make concerning the prisoner, be mindful of when the judge is leaving or entering the room, as they like us to give them a little curtsy, and stay awake long enough to prevent the prisoner from attempting his bid for freedom by becoming an Iron Monger and making a bolt for the door.

One of my best jumpers was a prisoner we had from Iran, who had to have a team of interpreters in the court as he was unable to speak English. As court cases are very, very boring at the best of times, this one was made even more boring because everything had to be relayed back to him in Arabic.

The case went on for five days and, on the fifth day, it looked very likely that the prisoner was going to get an invite to spend the next ten years of his life learning English at Her Majesty's pleasure. When, all of a sudden, he was on his feet and had launched himself up and over the dock. Before I could make any rational assessment of the situation, my body decided to leap into action and follow him over the dock.

I landed directly on top of him, bringing the full weight of the law to bear down on him, in my particular case, 18 stones worth of law, to pin him to the floor. I was surprised to hear protests in Arabic coming from the female interpreter but even more surprised to hear the prisoner screaming back, "I can't get up because I have a fat bastard screw on top of me." What really surprised me, though, was that my fall had clearly and suddenly enabled me to understand Arabic. I soon found out, however, that this was neither some inexplicable freak of nature nor a divine intervention in miraculously improving my linguistic abilities. It turned out that the prisoner could speak better

English than me and that, when he had jumped the dock, he had landed on top of the interpreter and I, in turn, had landed on top of them both.

As we held category 'A' prisoners at Highdown, we were responsible for escorting them to whichever court they were being tried at. More often than not, it was the Central Criminal Court in London at Justice Hall, more commonly known as the Old Bailey.

Justice Hall, or the Sessions House, was also called the Old Bailey, after the street in which it was located, just off Newgate. The Old Bailey is England's most important Crown Court. It can try crimes from any part of the country and was originally established as a Session House in 1539 but was rebuilt in 1774. The Old Bailey became known as the Central Criminal Court. The building was demolished in 1902 and today the Old Bailey stands on the site of Newgate Prison.

Above the door of the court, which opened on 27th February 1907, is the motto: 'Defend the Children of the Poor & Punish the Wrongdoer.' On top of the dome is the world-renowned golden statue of Justice, clasping the famous sword and scales, but not blindfolded like its American counterpart. One of our more philosophical prisoners once pointed out that the statue actually represents injustice, because if you do not have enough money to put in the scales, then you will get a hefty whack around the head with the sword.

The Old Bailey has a special area for category 'A' prisoners which is rumoured to be haunted because a small group of cells in this section of the building are never used. These are the cells where prisoners who had been condemned to hang were housed before being transported back to their prisons to await their fate. All cells at the Old Bailey have a cell bell that prisoners can press for urgent matters and we will respond – although we do advise prisoners not to misuse the bell. These old cells where the condemned were kept also had cell bells although they were supposed to have been disconnected. The rumour was that you would sometimes hear the bells ringing out from the condemned cells. Now, I do not believe in ghosts, but I did hear the cell bell go off once and when I went to check the condemned cells, it was colder than a witch's left tit.

I don't know if I have told you this before but court cases are very, very boring and, on more than one occasion, I have found myself having the greatest of battles…to stay awake! You would use whatever method you could to try and keep yourself alert and, at the very least, appearing to be interested in the proceedings. Some of us would read while others would chew gum (although this was not allowed and the judge can get really pissed off with people eating in court). But there was also the old tried and tested method of holding a pen between the finger and thumb of both hands and, if your body was about to sink into a nice little slumber, the pen would drop and, in principle, wake you up. On one occasion, I did not have a pen with me so I tried desperately to follow the case in an effort to stay awake. At this particular trial, however, the prosecuting barrister had such a droning, monotonous voice and the ability to dribble on for hours, that despite all my best efforts, I left this world and was transported off to slumber land. Suddenly, I was woken up by the category 'A' prisoner digging me in the ribs and warning me that I was snoring fit to drive the cows home. The judge had apparently been glaring at me so I had no option but to wipe the dribble from my chin, stand alert and look around the courtroom as if nothing had happened, only to discover that, by now, the judge himself and two of the jurors had nodded off and were taking turns to drive the cows home.

We have had to take some pretty awful things, some that would not even qualify as pond life, to the Old Bailey to be tried.

One of them was a particularly disgusting individual who had enticed a twelve-year-old girl back to his flat in Croydon, then sexually assaulted and raped her, before knocking her over the head and putting her in a suitcase to take to his girlfriend's house for more abuse of the poor child. Somehow, the girl managed to survive this appalling ordeal and the police managed to arrest the disgusting thing very quickly. During the build up to his defence at the Old Bailey, he decided to sack his defence lawyer (no doubt to the lawyer's great relief) and proceeded to carry out his own defence which he did in real piss poor style. He succeeded in upsetting the judge on more than one occasion, and it was clear that he had lost all patience with the thing from quite an early stage. Indeed, he was probably wishing he still had a black cap to wear when he gave this particular 'gopper' his just desserts as the Black Cap was worn by a judge when passing a sentence of death.

The trial seemed to be drifting on forever and the thing was very demanding of what he called 'his rights', frequently trying to shout the judge down, which is not one of the best defence tactics. The judge finally ordered him to be quiet and we were poised waiting for the nod from the judge when, all of a sudden, the thing stood up, brandished a small razor blade and started to cut his own stomach open. We did not wait for the nod from the judge. We simply piled into the prisoner who resisted us fiercely, trying to cut us with the blade as well. According to a member of the prosecution team, all that could be seen were arms, fists and elbows thrashing about until we managed to wrap him up, remove him from the dock and get him back down to the cells for medical treatment.

As the blade was very small, he had only managed to scratch the surface of his skin and his wound needed no more than a wipe with an antiseptic wipe. The next time we attended court with the thing, we ensured, as far as we could, that he had no blades on him. We did stop short, however, of ensuring that he had not hidden anything up his bum. We were not going to take any chances with him and explained our rules of engagement for when he was in the dock – namely that there would be an officer on either side of him, his hands would have to be in view at all times and, at the slightest hint of anything suspicious, he would be wrapped up and removed back to the cells immediately.

When the prisoner entered the dock he asked the judge if he could make a statement of complaint. The judge groaned before responding, "If you really must." The thing then went on to say that the prison officers in the dock with him had beaten him up and threatened him with torture if he was not quiet, finishing up with accusing us of acting worse than the Gestapo. The courtroom erupted into laughter and applause. The judge called for silence before stating that he did not believe a word of what the thing had said. He went on to say that he had had a good view of the incident that had occurred in the dock and he thought that the prison officers had acted with complete professionalism. He ended by pronouncing that he was proud to have us in his courtroom, to the sound of further applause throughout the court

The thing was eventually found guilty and sent down for twelve years, not in any way long enough in my opinion.

Some of our court escorts were to small-town magistrates. On one occasion, I was told that I must take a prisoner to a magistrate court on the south coast. I protested because I was only on an early shift and believed that the case would make me late back to the prison. More importantly, however, being late back would mean that I would miss out on a piss up that had been arranged with some of my mates for that evening. The PO reassured me, "Don't worry! This one is a 'show and blow'. They just want him for a quick remand hearing and you'll be back in the gaol before lunch." I did not want to argue with him as he was a good P.O. and had done many a favour for me in the past and so off I went to court.

Only two officers were used for these types of escort. The officer with the longest service would be the officer in charge of the escort and the other officer would be handcuffed to the prisoner who was double cuffed. We would use a local taxi firm and the two prison officers and a prisoner, who would be seated between the two officers, would all cram into the back of a Ford Escort and spend the next hour or so on their way to court.

When we arrived, we made our way to the court cells only to learn that the magistrate was late and we would have to wait. This really pissed me off because I knew that this one would now drag on past my finish time. What was even more annoying was that the prisoner's brief wasn't even expecting him to be present today as the hearing was just a formality. I took the opportunity to lie like a cheap rug and suggested that we could take the prisoner back as we had another urgent job on that afternoon. The brief said no. Now that the prisoner was here, he would like to see him later. Eventually the magistrate was ready and we took the prisoner into the court, handcuffed to the other officer. The brief was horrified that we still had the prisoner handcuffed and requested, via the magistrate, that we remove the cuffs immediately.

Now, I knew that a judge was all powerful in a court and that, if he ordered you to take the handcuffs off a prisoner and give him the keys to the prison van so that he could drive himself home, you had better obey him, or else you would find yourself on a contempt of court charge. A magistrate, on the other hand, is a very different breed and although they wield power within the confines of their courtroom, they do not have the right to go against the security advice of the officer in charge of the escort, which was none other than my good self!

The magistrate's courthouse was undergoing some refurbishment; there was scaffolding up all over the place and some of the windows were not secured. I also knew that the past record and security report concerning our prisoner was not good and that he had previously tried to jump a dock on another sentence. I therefore informed the magistrate that I would not be relieving the prisoner of his cuffs and went forward to explain. As this particular magistrate did not have much of a concept of security, he was fairly pissed off that I had declined to release the cuffs. He looked as though someone had declared him God, but then forgotten to inform the rest of the world.

The case was adjourned and the magistrate complained like an old granny to the governor, who in turn warned me not to piss off magistrates in the future. I did, however, get back in time for my piss up so it all turned out right in the end.

However, one by one, our courts fell prey to the wonderful Private Finance Initiative, which started the programme of privatisation of the prison service. The union tried to put up a good fight but we had just gone through a major recruitment drive and there were a lot of new staff who were not willing to rock the boat when they had only just started out on their new careers. On top of that, did I tell you that courts are very, very boring? Their 'boringness' and the new recruits' lack of willingness to rock the boat meant there was no appetite for a fight over this except from the Prison Officers Association who tried to rally support to stop what they knew would be the start of a bitter battle. It is also worth noting that, to ensure that we could not put up a fair fight, the government introduced section 127 of the Criminal Justice and Public Order Act 1994 ('the 1994 Act') which provides that a person owes a duty to the

Secretary of State not to induce prison officers, custody officers and prison custody officers to withhold their services or to commit a breach of discipline. In plain English, they made it illegal for us to take industrial action.

Escorts were not always as boring as courts. Sometimes there would even be the chance of seeing other prisons when we took a prisoner to another prison on a 'shit bag exchange'. This is where we swap one nasty prisoner for another nasty prisoner. This is done either because, by moving the prisoner to another gaol, he just may calm down or because there is a game of 'governor's poker' being played out. This involves one governor calling another governor's bluff into accepting a one-for-one swap, only to find out that they have ended up with an even worse shit bag than the one they managed to palm off onto the other governor.

Then there was the Feltham Meat Market where we would load up a coach load of prisoners to be transferred to other prisons to serve their sentence and deliver them to an exchange point, which was at Feltham prison. Here, the prisoners would be herded into pens (sorry, placed into holding cells), which would have the name of the prison they were to be sent to. This was always a great fun day out for the officers as you would get to meet a lot of old mates who had transferred to another prison to work. Much of the day would be spent reminiscing about the good old days and, even though I had only been in the job five minutes compared with some of the others, I was always amazed at how many officers I knew from other establishments.

Escorts to hospital also provided some light relief. For most people, a trip to the hospital is not normally an experience that they enjoy as it usually involves a long wait, followed by some discomfort, and maybe even pain, for themselves or a loved one. A trip to the hospital with a prisoner who is double handcuffed to a great big hairy-arsed screw, on the other hand, usually provides much more entertainment and a much shorter wait. We can reduce the waiting time even further, especially if when asked what the prisoner is in for, we tell a little porky that the prisoner is a mass murderer or worse. As for the pain and discomfort that the prisoner may have gone through as a result of our little revelations, I have to be honest and say that I really did not mind how painful it got for him. Indeed, in some cases, I would have liked to have had recommend the highest levels of discomfort and pain possible but, sadly, that's not how it works.

These escorts are also usually carried out by two officers, again using the services of the local taxi company, so we all get to cram into the back seat of a Ford Escort, only this time the prisoner may be nursing some kind of injury.

On one occasion, such an escort did not go to plan. I had to take a particularly nasty piece of poo, who liked to rape very old women after he had battered them and then robbed them. He had been caught masturbating over a woman who was unconscious in a theatre recovery room of a hospital. The security report was therefore very clear and entirely unambiguous: DO NOT TAKE THE CUFFS OFF. The reason this thing had to go to hospital was because he had a broken arm (which he had got from a community beating on the nonce's wing) and there were surgical pins that had to be removed. The doctor asked if it would be okay to remove the cuffs and I said no as he was likely to attempt to escape and harm someone. The doctor agreed to carry out the removal of the pins whilst the other officer was handcuffed to the prisoner.

This particular officer was very new to the job and had only just got back from training college. We were asked to put gowns on in the interest of hygiene and as they started to lay out the surgical equipment that would be used in this straightforward procedure, I heard a thud and found that our new recruit had fainted. So we had to take the handcuffs off the prisoner and place them on me whilst they carried out the minor surgery procedure and the new officer received medical treatment for a bump on the head. I do not know what hurt the new recruit most – the bump on the head or the embarrassment when I had to arrange for another officer to come out to assist in bringing the prisoner back to the prison.

You may think that it is a bit over the top to have a prisoner double handcuffed to a prison officer when they are being escorted to a hospital. However, you would be astonished by the number of prisoners who would be limping with some dreadful condition and yet, as soon as we take the handcuffs off for treatment, they make such a rapid recovery that they could qualify for the London marathon and scarper off at a speed that would leave Linford Christie standing. During my time at Highdown, there were at least three attempts to do a runner. As the pursuing staff managed to catch all the prisoners, I was always surprised that the prison service was not better represented in the London Marathon or the Olympics for their undoubted running skills – although this could have been more to do with their fear of dismissal for having let a prisoner escape.

Another different form of escort involves transferring prisoners to secure mental hospitals. There was one very strange prisoner that comes to mind, who was in Highdown for the murder of his neighbour. He lived in a house that was divided into bed-sit type rooms. He had always had a fascination with death and had decided that he would kill a female neighbour of his, so he crept into her room whilst she was sound asleep and battered her over the head with a hammer. Whilst she was still alive, he proceeded to cut her open so that he could reach inside her body and hold her heart as she died. He then cut her body up and dumped it in a pond.

Thankfully, he was very quickly caught and, even though he would not speak about the case and refused to cooperate at all with the police, it was established during his trial that he was as mad a very large box of frogs and the DNA evidence was conclusive. He was sent to us at Highdown until a place could be found at one of our most secure mental hospitals. During his time with us, the psychiatrist found that there were sets of numbers that were likely to send him over the top and that we should avoid using these numbers at all costs. One of these numbers was twelve.

A space was found for him at Rampton High Security Hospital, which is in Nottinghamshire, and a transfer to this hospital was arranged. These escorts are normally carried out by two officers, depending on the security risk of the prisoner, and the transport is usually our own prison minibus, driven by an officer support grade. As the prisoner is being transported under the Mental Health Act, the prisoner is not to be handcuffed unless this has been agreed by the governor. At this time, we had a governor who was so indecisive that he would never agree – or disagree – to anything; he was probably the most non-committal governor we have ever had. I was given the task of being the officer in charge of this escort and, after having read the security file of this prisoner, I requested that we use handcuffs. True to form, the governor was not sure whether he could allow this. I then requested that another officer be placed on the escort with us, which would increase our numbers to three, and that we should all carry a set of ratchet cuffs (these were the old style police ratchet handcuffs). To this day, I do not know how I managed it, but I actually got the governor to make a decision and agree that, in the event that we felt that an escape was likely, we could use the ratchet cuffs. The prisoner was then thoroughly strip-searched and brought around to the reception area to be checked out. The governor then left the reception and went back to his office. It was at that point that I made a tactical, operational decision that there was sufficient risk of the prisoner escaping that the ratchet cuffs should be applied.

Everything was going well on the way up to Rampton and the prisoner was in good spirits. Indeed, so chatty was he that he decided to let us be the first people in the world to hear his confession, in every gory detail, of what he did and why. As he came to the end of his confession, the van swerved and the officer support grade who was driving called out, "Did you see that lunatic in the BMW cut us up?" With chilling calm and precision timing, our prisoner retorted, "I am the only lunatic that cuts people up." I checked the cuffs just to make sure they were still secure.

When we got to the hospital, the staff were really good and seemed to take everything in their stride, whereas we were like a bunch of scared rabbits who could not wait to get rid of the prisoner and return to our nice, safe, calm, cosy prison. Oh, by the way, they put him in cell twelve.

There were some opportunities to get a bit of a nice number on the escorts, though. One of these would be a trip to one of the prisons on the Isle of Wight if we had to return a prisoner there or collect one from the island. There are three prisons on the Island: the one that everyone knows, Parkhurst, which was then a high security prison; Camphill, a category 'C' training prison; and Albany, a dispersal category 'B' prison, which mostly housed nonces.

The one we were going to was Parkurst, to drop off a 'return shit bag' who we had taken off their hands to give them a rest. Normally these trips would result in a one-for-one exchange to make sure we had a prisoner in the van for the trip back to Highdown and weren't returning empty. However, the senior officer in charge of the escort had arranged this trip and he wanted to be able to simply drop off the prisoner and have a bit of time catching up on the good old days with friends of his who worked on the Island. So he picked two officers who he knew he could trust to carry out the escort, which were Higgins and I.

We always use the prison van for these types of escort so there was an officer support grade as well as the three of us. The ferry was booked for the outward journey for 10am and, according to the senior officer, we would be unable to get a ferry back until 5pm due to it being the busy holiday season of the month of February. For our mind, the holiday season was a long way off and, even then, the ferries are only full of Corkheads on their way home and not coming back to the mainland. Corkheads is the name given to Isle of Wighters and there are many variations as to why they are called this. In my view, the most plausible one being that, when they are thrown into the water, they tend to float like corks (because you can always tell a Corkhead by their webbed hands and feet from in-breeding).

So off we went to the Isle of Wight. The journey across was very pleasant and uneventful and we arrived at Parkhurst prison for about 11.15am. We simply dropped the prisoner into the segregation unit and went straight to the Parkhurst clubhouse, where our senior officer had some urgent business to attend to.

We left the club at about 4.30pm and we were very, very happy. We caught the ferry back across to the mainland on time and Higgins and I decided that we would hold a snoring competition on the floor of the prison van. Suddenly the senior officer's phone rang and we could hear our senior officer pleading with someone to use someone else, but without much luck. The van came to a halt in a lay-by on the A3 next to a snack wagon. Our senior officer informed us that, because the Guildford court van had broken down, we had been tasked to pick up five prisoners from the court and take them back to

Highdown. So there we were, all trying to take on board coffee from the snack wagon to sober us up. We picked up the prisoners at Guildford and it was the fastest that prisoners had ever been loaded onto a prison van by two very dishevelled looking prison officers who, by the smell coming from us, were not to be messed with. We got the prisoners back to Highdown and even managed to get them all singing a jolly little song along the way.

On other occasions, we have to escort a prisoner to the funeral of a close relative. First of all, though, a prisoner must apply to attend the service. The best way this can be done is through the chaplaincy who carries out checks to ensure that there is indeed a funeral taking place and then our escort department makes the necessary arrangements for the escort.

Again, two officers are needed for these escorts and normally we are asked to wear a civilian jacket or coat over our uniforms so as not to make it too obvious what we are and what we are doing. I don't suppose that the bereaved prisoner being handcuffed to a 6' 6" screw who is built like a brick shit house, but not as pretty, would give the game away ever so slightly. Even Reggie Kray managed to have one of the biggest prison officers attached to him when he attended his mother's funeral, as being about six feet tall, the prison officer he was attached to was not far off 7 feet tall. If you believe all the hype that he got better treatment inside and that he controlled the screws, how comes he went to the service and the burial, the whole time handcuffed to a man who appeared to be the biggest prison officer in Britain?

I always tried to avoid these escorts because, as soon as you get in the van, the prisoner will start asking if you could take the handcuff off that is holding his two hands together so that it does not look too obvious and distressing for his relatives. Some officers make an informed judgement and release this handcuff, although the prisoner still remains handcuffed to the officer. The most daunting funeral escorts are those which involve prisoners who are travellers or gypsies as you are at extreme risk of being mobbed and told to take the cuffs off the prisoner under health and safety regulations – that is, your health and safety. So if you were given the task of being on one of these escorts, you had to hope that the security department had found sufficient intelligence that it would be too risky to attend. In my experience, you simply phone the local police where the funeral is going to be held and ask them if they would be able to provide back up. You know that they will inevitably respond that they are going to keep well away whilst proclaiming that we must be "fucking mad" if we are going to take the prisoner anywhere near there. Armed with this comprehensive and robust intelligence information, you have every right to refuse to attend and the governor has little choice but to cancel the escort.

And then, of course, there were the bed watches. These were when the prisoner had to go to an outside hospital for treatment and had to stay overnight or longer in hospital. We mainly used Epsom General Hospital and the nursing staff were very used to us turning up with a prisoner. They would usually provide a private room so that we did not disturb patients on the ward.

The prisoner would be transported to and from the hospital whilst doubled cuffed, although, of course, if their injuries were of a nature that prevented this, the governor and doctor would sign the part of the escort form concerning the use of handcuffs and the governor would make a decision on what restraints should or should not be used. However, once we are all settled into the hospital and the prisoner is tucked up in bed wearing his prison issue 'jim-jams' that are at least three sizes too small, he will be restrained using a handcuff called a closeting chain.

This is a six-foot chain with a single standard handcuff attached to each end of the chain. The original use for this type of restraint was so that if a prisoner needed to use a lavatory whilst he was being escorted out of the prison, the officers could attach a closeting chain to him, take the other handcuffs off and attach the other end to the escorting officer, thus allowing the prisoner to use the lavatory whilst still remaining handcuffed. Although, it has to be said, if the prisoner had eaten an extra portion of prison curry the day before, this experience may not be too pleasant for the officer who is attached to the other end of the chain and trying to breathe out of his ears.

It became common to use these chains when the prisoner was tucked up in bed. Although there was one particular prisoner who had been 'jugged'; this is a quaint practice which involves another prisoner throwing boiling hot water into the face of a fellow prisoner. The injuries can be very distressing and painful and can result in the skin on the face of the victim peeling off. This is especially so when they have used a good quantity of sugar whilst they were boiling the water as this helps to raise its temperature, causing it to become thicker and thereby sticking to the face more readily. This particular prisoner who had been 'jugged' was very charming to the nursing staff and they were always insisting that we take the handcuffs off as he had told them how much they were hurting him. The nurses also said they wanted to be able to treat the patient without us being in the room as there may be a risk of infection to the prisoner.

It was interesting to see just how dramatically the attitude of the nurses changed when someone explained that the reason this particular prisoner was serving time was because he had brutally raped two nurses.

Sometimes bed watches can be seen as very easy work. One, in particular, comes to mind where one of our trusted orderlies had to go into hospital for a small operation. He had been with us for about four months pending his trial for holding wealthy Chinese restaurateurs hostage until they gave him the combinations to the safe. I can assure you that their methods of persuasion were very brutal and they had an unenviable reputation for being highly dangerous in their hometown of Liverpool.

The operation was booked at the local hospital and the escort was arranged as normal. I and another officer were chosen as we knew the prisoner well and had a good rapport with him. When we arrived at the hospital, we found armed police there. We thought that there must be something going on until we discovered that the armed police were there because of our prisoner, and because he had a reputation for escaping from custody, usually with the assistance of an armed gang. I decided that I would visit our security department when we got back to the prison to thank them for the security briefing they did not give us.

As it turned out, the last thing on our prisoner's mind was escape. On one occasion, he even had a call from his family who were coming up to see him to ask what he would like them to bring him in to eat. Perhaps not surprisingly, he wanted a Chinese takeaway, and even asked us if we would like some as well. His family turned up with a massive selection of Chinese food and there we all were, having a grand banquet in a private room in Epsom hospital with armed police twitching each time a door opened. I couldn't help but wonder whether they had actually paid for the Chinese meal, considering why he was in prison in the first place.

Chapter Nine

Visits

Prisoners can get whatever drugs they want in prison. There are four main ways that they are brought into prison.

The first is via a member of staff who has either been enticed or bribed into bringing them in or has decided that they could make a nice little earner. Normally, they bring drugs in either hidden on them or, like one prison officer I heard of, hidden in the sports bag of another officer who had no idea that they were there.

The second is that a prisoner who knows that he is going to receive a custodial sentence at court will hide drugs on them, so that they can either use them themselves or sell them on to other prisoners. The favourite hiding place for these drugs is up their bums, known as 'plugged' (how they can bear to have a quantity of anything stuffed up their back sides is beyond me; one thing is for sure, my arse is exit only).

The third way is via the wall; we never cease to be amazed by the amount of contraband that is thrown over the prison wall. Once on the prison side, it is picked up by trusted prisoners who work within the prison grounds either clearing rubbish or gardening. One of our dog patrol officers was hit on the head by a hefty package containing booze, drugs and money when he was patrolling the prison wall.

The fourth way, which is the most used, is via the visits. So, if a prison is so secure, how do they get the drugs in via a visit?

When the visitor arrives at the visitors' centre outside the prison gates, they have a chance to hide or 'plug' the contraband in an orifice of their choice, when they visit the lavatory. They are then escorted over to the prison where they will undergo a rub down search, before being escorted to the Visits Hall waiting area, which is located by the Visits Hall in the prison.

The security department usually patrols this area and if they believe that a visitor is suspicious, they will pull them aside and escort them to a room, where they will conduct a more thorough search, which can involve a strip-search. All prison officers have the power of a constable whilst serving as a prison officer but if the visitor declines this search, they will be refused entry to the Visits Hall to see the prisoner. If the security officers believe that they are sure that the visitor is concealing drugs, they can arrest them and call the police who will then take them off to the police station, where they will be strip-searched.

Sometimes a drug dog will be used and the visitors would be expected to line up before they enter the Visits Hall, so that the dog can pass by them to sniff out any drugs. If the dog 'knocks' (indicates to its handler that they smell drugs, usually by sitting by the visitor) the visitor will be taken to a room where they will be asked to comply with a strip-search, or they will be refused entry or arrested.

Once the visitor is in the hall and they have managed to smuggle in the contraband past the checks, they will go straight to the prisoner who will be seated at a low table on a chair that is bolted to the floor. This is a measure to prevent them from using the furniture as weapons when a fight breaks out. There are now several opportunities where the drugs may be passed to the prisoner.

The first of these opportunities is as soon as they kiss; known in prison parlance, not surprisingly, as the 'kiss-pass'. Some smugglers will have been to the visitors' lavatories before they enter the Visits Hall to retrieve the contraband from their orifice of choice. They then place it in their mouth (it is normally at this point that the smuggler wishes they had chosen a better orifice) ready to pass to the prisoner as soon as they kiss.

The prisoner will do one of two things; he will either swallow the item and wait until he has had a good poo the next day to retrieve it, or 'plug it' up his arse. If he decides to plug it, visitor and prisoner alike will start to scan the hall to see if any officer is looking at them. As soon as the coast is clear, the prisoner will carefully spit the item into the palm of his hand, whilst pretending to take a sip of tea. Once he has the item in his hand he will again have to make sure the coast is clear for the main move of plugging. This used to be made easier in the good old days when prisoners were allowed to wear nice stretchable tracksuit as they would simply lean back in their chair and lift the right cheek of their arse and very quickly place the item of contraband straight up their chocolate star fish, rusty sheriff's badge. Once lodged in his poo pie tunnel, he will then practise external sphincter muscle control to reverse the normal function of their tom thumb, which is to extradite poo and not be used as a store cupboard. Nowadays prisoners are not allowed to wear tracksuits and must wear trousers or jeans, although this still has not stopped them from plugging. There is clearly no end to the machinations that they can put their bodies through and some would be gold medallists if there were ever an Olympic contortionist team.

You will not be surprised to learn that there is a search area for the purpose of searching prisoners on their way back from visits. They make their way down to the visits area along the upper walkway and the search area is located above the Visits Hall. It is a room within a corridor that leads to stairs that then lead unto the Visits Hall. Two officers man this area and their job is to 'rub down search' all prisoners that go down for a visit and return back up to go back to their houseblocks. Some of them will receive a strip-search especially if it suspected that they are hiding something. The golden rule is simple: nothing must go down with the prisoner and nothing must come back with him.

There are some rare methods of concealment that have been used from time to time and one is that they will place the contraband under their foreskin or prepuce. As with plugging, the prisoner checks to see who is watching and, as soon as they believe that the coast is clear, they simply place the item in their underpants. For this particular practice, it is important that they choose their underpants carefully as boxer shorts will allow the item to simply drop out when they get up to walk and they risk either losing the item on the floor or being discovered by an officer. The pants that are best suited are briefs, so that the elastic around the leg opening holds the contraband securely in position.

As the prisoner makes his way back to the search area, two officers will be waiting to search him but he can always find an opportunity to either 'plug' the item or hide it under his foreskin before he undergoes a search. The only key requisite item that will be needed by a prisoner is a foreskin, so this method may rule out believers of certain faiths.

Another, slightly more rare, variation to these 'plugging' methods, is that some prisoners have been known to make a small pouch that they tie to the base of their penis so that it hangs down behind the testicles. They can then simply pop the contraband into the pouch. This is an ideal method for the 'foreskin deficient' and for those prisoners who believe that a rectum is exit only.

Failing the 'kiss-pass' method, there is the 'bag of crisps surprise'. The visitor goes straight for the visits canteen inside the Visits Hall. Visitors are allowed to bring in loose change so that they can buy lots of sweeties for the prisoner and then have the dubious pleasure of watching them stuff as much chocolate into their mouths before the end of the visit. The visitor purchases just one packet of crisps and two drinks, opens the packet of crisps whilst the drinks are being prepared and then carefully checks that no officer is watching them as they place the contraband in the crisp packet. They take the drinks and opened packet of crisps to the table and have a very quick 'hello' kiss before sitting down. It is at this point that they both start to scan the hall to ensure that they are not being watched. As soon as they believe that the coast is clear, the visitor offers a crisp to the prisoner who takes a crisp, along with the contraband. Both the crisp and the contraband go into his mouth (at this time, he will not know if the strange taste is the choice of crisps or the visitor's orifice), before making an informed choice as to whether it is to be plugged or swallowed, depending on whether officers have already spotted him and are closing in, or whether or not he is prepared to draw any more attention to himself than necessary.

All contraband that is passed in these ways is wrapped in Clingfilm and sometimes also placed into a plastic bag or condom, in the hope that, if they have to swallow the drugs, they will have been wrapped well enough not to burst within their stomachs.

The most sickening method that I have ever seen was when a prisoner had got his wife to bring the drugs in stuffed into the knickers of his four-year-old daughter. Thankfully, he was charged under prison rules, his wife was arrested and handed over to the police and social services were informed about the child.

Several officers patrol the Visits Hall and are constantly on the lookout for anything suspicious. The security team may also grace the hall with their presence from time to time and will stand well away from prisoners, communicating into their specially adapted microphones and earpieces, whilst dressed in their sinister looking black commando type uniforms. To assist them, they have a CCTV Dome camera system that is monitored and, when they have a suspect, they communicate their find to the security officers in the hall who then move straight to the prisoner. As they approach the prisoner, they will warm him not to move and to keep his hands away from his body. If the prisoner ignores these instructions and tries to get the contraband to swallow it, they will be very quickly restrained from doing so by the use of Home Office approved Control and Restraint methods (that is, jumped on by three heavy screws, one of whom may have his hand halfway down the prisoner's throat to try to retrieve the drugs).

As soon as this happens, everyone in the Visits Hall looks on; half of them will be jeering and shouting at the staff, and it is likely that the prisoner's partner may have to be restrained because she has kicked off and is trying to help her boyfriend/husband. The other half will be quickly shoving everything they can up their bums, down their throats or attaching it to their cocks. Sometimes an incident may be staged so that the mass swap of drugs can be done while the focus of the officers is on the incident. The most common of these types of decoy incidents is when a woman suddenly jumps up and starts screaming at her husband/boyfriend accusing him of all kinds of interesting things.

When a prisoner is stopped from swallowing or plugging, they are removed to the segregation unit to await an adjudication hearing in front of the governor; the wife/girlfriend is handed over to the police and charged with trying to smuggle drugs into a prison and may eventually find herself in prison, too.

Prisoners take the risk of being caught because, more often than not, they can make a lot of money from the drugs that they smuggle in. Some smugglers do not even use the drugs themselves, they either sell them on or they have been intimidated by the 'wing thug' to bring them in. Most, though, are drug users and will risk anything to get a fix, having little or no regard for their family or loved ones who they put under pressure to carry out the deed.

Most social visits, however, pass off without incident and some prisoners have even been keen to introduce their families to me. Prisoners are allowed up to three adults to visit them at any one time. There are no restrictions as to the amount of children that can visit, however, and although some facilities are provided for them, there are very few within the Visits Hall itself and kids would clearly be out of control, running about the hall screaming their heads off. Considering that the majority of prisoners in the hall are only spending a short sentence in prison, I could never understand why they would have their whole litter come up and visit them. And, frankly, when you see the way in which these kids behave, you know that it will not be too long before they too are serving time at Her Majesty's Pleasure. "Don't knock it!" an old experienced and philosophical hand once told me, "They keep us in work and help pay the mortgage."

Every now and then something would happen in the Visits Hall that would break the monotony of trying to convince prisoners to control their children or they would have their visit terminated. I've known of cases where we've had to stop a prisoner and partner from shagging each other, sometimes in front of their own children. I have even seen another prisoner get up, punch and knock spark out another prisoner and his girlfriend who were getting a bit too amorous on the table next to him. He had, apparently, already warned them once, telling them that he did not want his children to witness such debauchery. They had chosen to ignore him, so he simply went over to them, pulled them apart and punched the prisoner square on the jaw, knocking him spark out on the floor. The girlfriend then kicked off and he hit her too so she ended up lying unconscious next to her boyfriend.

On one occasion, I was the officer in charge of allocating which table the prisoners would sit at. They were waiting at their designated table while the visitors were let into the hall to sit with them. I had just seated this particular prisoner when he came back over to my desk and asked who was visiting him. I said I did not know, so he then went back but looked very nervous. His wife then came into the hall, walked straight up to him and laid into him with punches and kicks. We quickly separated them but the prisoner was already in need of treatment to what looked like a broken nose. She had hardly spoken a word but as we escorted her back out of the prison she suddenly attacked another woman who was waiting to come into the prison. It turned out that the prisoner had inadvertently sent out two visiting orders, one to his wife and the other to his girlfriend; and they wonder why they get caught when they commit crimes.

In the Visits Hall there is a corridor leading off to eight self-contained visiting rooms. These are for what is known as legal visits. Social visits at Highdown occurred only in the afternoons between 2pm and 4.30pm, whereas legal visits could be in the morning, the afternoon or sometimes in the evening, so that barristers who are at court during the day can see their clients afterwards in the evening.

Although they are called legal visits, they include a multitude of different disciplines, as well as the solicitors and barristers who are visiting their clients. The police would sometimes pop in to either get a prisoner to grass up someone or to do a deal on 'clear ups'.

Burglary clear ups are a straightforward piece of police work; where they have a prisoner who has been caught robbing a property they will look at the prisoner's MO (Modus Operandi, their manner of working) to see what other burglaries on their books could be linked to that prisoner. They then visit the happy bunny in prison to see if he is prepared to do a deal on owning up to these crimes. The deal is very simple. If the prisoner owns up to the unsolved burglaries that the police believe he has committed, they will try to ensure that the sentence he receives is concurrent (no real extra time would be served, as all the sentences for the crimes would run concurrently). If, however, he refuses to cooperate with the police, it is likely that he will be charged for the other crimes once sufficient evidence has been gathered. This is normally after he has been sentenced for the crime he was originally caught for with a strong chance that he will end up serving another sentence consecutively (on top of the sentence he is already serving for the original crime).

More than once I have had a prisoner proclaim that he has been 'set up' by the police for crimes that he did not commit and I have no doubt that, in the eagerness to produce results on the 'clear ups', the police are under tremendous pressure to simply get the job done. The majority of police that I have come across, however, work very hard to ensure that they have got the right person for the burglaries, although it was very odd once listening to two prisoners who had inadvertently owned up to each other's crimes and who still had the front to whinge about it.

We sometimes got requests from solicitors and barristers for a television and video to be provided for a legal visit so that they could view video evidence. On one occasion, a team of lawyers who were visiting a 'bacon' had requested a TV and video. As I was patrolling the corridor to ensure that none of the prisoners had decided to kill their legal representatives, I noticed that the legal team in with the 'bacon' were watching a video film of two little girls being sexually abused by the accused. I immediately switched off the power from outside so that it stopped the viewing of this evidence and was met with a torrid of complaints by a complete arse of a lawyer who could see no problem with viewing this evidence, even though other prisoners and visitors could clearly see what was on the screen from the room opposite. They eventually agreed to have a screen put up against the window so that no one could see the film.

This particular 'bacon' was residing on one of the normal houseblocks as he had refused to accept the protection rule which would have enabled him to be housed with the rest of the 'bacons'. He had told the other prisoners on his wing that he was in for fraud charges. However, unlucky for him, the prisoner who was in the legal visits room opposite to his had witnessed the disgusting video and promptly informed the wing that he was a 'bacon'. The next day, the prisoner was nearly kicked to death on the exercise yard. He survived his injuries but received just two years for sexually abusing his own granddaughters.

There is an area within the Visits Hall that has rooms provided for what are known as closed visits. These are very much like what you see on all the good American films about prisons; a tough Perspex screen divides them so that the prisoner and visitor are unable to touch or pass anything to each other. They have to communicate through an inbuilt intercom. Each room has a CCTV camera and they are monitored, although this still does not stop some of them from re-enacting the scene from *Midnight Express*, where a British guy serving a sentence in a Turkish prison gets his girlfriend to expose herself on a visit so that he can masturbate. There is nothing more embarrassing than having to tell a prisoner to stop wanking in the closed visits room.

This particular wanker was placed on report and brought in front of the governor the next day on a charge of 'Failing to comply with a direct order' – that is, to stop wanking immediately. He denied the charge so the tape evidence of the incident had to be played (much to the amusement of the segregation senior officer who was a gimpy pervert himself). The governor asked the prisoner to explain why he pleaded not guilty when the video clearly showed what he was doing and that I had entered the room and given him an order to stop. His defence was that had had reached the point of no return and that nature had taken over his senses and his actions and that he was therefore unable to comply with the order. In my opinion, it was a pretty canny defence and I would have found him not guilty as charged for his sheer audacity; however, the governor was not amused and gave him two weeks loss of canteen.

There have been many embarrassing moments in the Visits Hall but perhaps none more so than a particular visit for one of our hardened bank robbers who had a reputation amongst the prisoners for being a really tough bastard. Although he was never too much trouble for staff, we would not have relished having to pile in and restrain him if he ever decided to kick off.

Whenever he had a visit, it was always from his mother, a really nice lady who was always polite to staff. We had never once seen him have a visit from a wife or a girlfriend but, on this particular day, we noticed that some female called Sharon was visiting him. As soon as we let Sharon into the hall I had to look twice as, before me, stood a very tall 6' 6" very slim person with long blonde hair, immaculately dressed in a mini skirt and a pink blouse. What particularly caught my eye, however, was that she had the biggest feet I had ever seen on a woman and an Adams apple that could have knocked you flying. I was not the only one who had noticed this. The rest of the Visits Hall, which was nearly full at the time and extremely noisy, suddenly fell silent. The very tall blonde walked straight over to our hard bastard criminal and embraced and kissed him passionately, before sitting down where the two of them held hands and gazed into each other's eyes. Suddenly, the shouts started to ring out from around the hall of "Show us your cock!" and "It's a bloke in a dress!" or "You'd make a fortune in here, mate, come on, show us your cock!" The hard bastard prisoner simply stood up and surveyed the hall, as if to try and catch who was shouting the insults. The hall fell silent, so he sat back down and continued his visit with the person who was clearly his partner. He obviously did not care what the rest of the prison thought or said and, because of his reputation, he knew that no-one would have the guts to say anything directly to his face.

We have had many principal officers in the visits group but I remember one who had come from Wandsworth and who had a bit of a Cliff Richard look about him. Once, when he called a meeting with us all to discuss problems with the visits and to talk about how we could improve them, we decided to try and keep the meeting going with a Cliff Richard theme to it. So, for our amusement and entertainment, we set ourselves the challenge of trying to mention as many Cliff Richard songs as possible. So, on the day in question, the conversation went as follows:

PO: "Right now, I need to understand what the main issues and problems are with the visits as we need to try to improve the capacity of the amount of visits we do each day."

1st Officer: "Well, sir, it's like this. We have some very disruptive visitors and none more so than prisoner Smith's wife, she's a bit of a 'Devil Woman'."

2nd Officer: "Sir, it's even worse when she has 'The Young Ones' with her."

3rd Officer: "It's always worse at this time of the year, sir, it being near Christmas and all that 'Mistletoe & Wine' as she's clearly had too much wine at times."

PO: "Has anyone tried having a word with prisoner Smith about his wife?"

1st Officer: "Sir, I have, but he tells me that it's because she's a 'Gypsy Woman' and has had the 'Best of Me' and 'She's So Beautiful' and headstrong. He said that he has tried to tell her to keep the noise down, however he said 'We Don't Talk Anymore'."

PO: "Well, we cannot allow one visitor to clog up the system and disrupt the visits. If 'Next Time' she continues to act in this way we will look at banning her or placing her on closed visits as this may be our 'Only Way Out'. It is my 'Millennium Prayer' that we 'Constantly' improve the visits and have the best visit system 'In the Country' and I want this achieved by 'Summer Holiday'. Now, stop fucking about with trying to include Cliff Richard songs in this discussion, and get the job done."

With that we declared the PO the winner and he gained a lot of respect from us, because he clearly had a great sense of humour.

The Visits Hall can also be a very sad place, however, as most of the visitors have never been involved in perpetrating any crime and are normal everyday people. The only difference is that their loved ones have been stupid enough to risk committing some crime or other and, having been caught, ended up incarcerated in one of Her Majesty's residences for the duration of their sentence.

Chapter Ten

Fraggle Rock

"You are now cleaners of Her Majesty's Prison Healthcare. This is a very privileged job and I expect you to perform your duties well as you never know when Her Majesty may wish to check on how clean you keep her establishments. I therefore want it shining like the Queen's crown jewels."

Fraggle Rock is an endearing term used within the prison service for the wing where prisoners with mental health issues are kept. However, the use of wings specifically for people with mental health problems was stopped and they were then kept in the prison healthcare centre, where they affectionately became known as Fraggle Rocks.

For those of you who are either two young, or too old, or had far better things to do with your lives, there used to be a children's television series called Fraggle Rock which ran from 1983 to 1987. Wikipedia describes Fraggles as tiny humanoid creatures, about 22 inches tall, that come in a wide variety of colours and have tails that bear a tuft of fur on the end. Fraggles live a very carefree life, spending most of their time playing, exploring, and generally enjoying themselves.

Other than the description of the tail and their height, this is very close to the description of the prisoners that were held within the healthcare unit of the prison.

The healthcare unit was set out on two levels. The lower level had a 22-bed unit made up of 12-purpose built cells that were about three times the size of a normal single cell with doors twice as wide, so that patients could be easily placed within the cells and nursing staff could work within them as and when they needed to. There was an 8-bedded ward and two special cells, one that had all its walls, floor and ceiling padded with a non-destructible soft material and the other which was similar to the strip cells of the segregation unit. There were two interview rooms for the doctors, an office, communal recreation room and disabled showers and baths, as well as a kitchen and storerooms.

The upper level had offices, a pharmacy, four surgery type rooms, a dentist, X-ray room, opticians and an outpatients department.

I was aware that a new scheme had started up to encourage prison officers to work alongside the nurses in the healthcare and train as healthcare officers so that they could have a dual role of prison/healthcare officer. I decided to apply for this role as it would be a great challenge, not to mention that I was fast running out of places to work in the prison because no one else wanted me.

The idea of prison officers working within healthcare alongside nurses was not a new concept, but simply someone deciding to re-invent the wheel yet again since an earlier decision to remove the nursing prison officer grade had not worked. Coupled with this, a policy decision to phase out discipline staff from the healthcare was also not working as these units were becoming 'no go' areas and many nurses who were recruited to work in the prison simply resigned as it was too dangerous for them to work there.

There are different types of prisoners who tend to become residents of the healthcare unit. You obviously can have the run-of-the-mill type prisoner who is not well and needs to be kept an eye on within the healthcare unit. These type, however, are actually very rare as 90 per cent of prisoners would not want to spend any time at all in Fraggle Rock. Then there are those who wish to use the healthcare as a hiding place. These are usually prisoners who would normally be held on the vulnerable prisoners' wing but have managed to upset someone on this wing and do not want to spend their time in isolation in the segregation unit, which is the normal option to keep them from being harmed by the person they have upset. So, they choose a different option which is to harm themselves in order to get placed within the healthcare unit. There are also prisoners who are nearing the end of their days and are in the healthcare before being relocated into an outside hospital to die. Other prisoners are in healthcare because they had been discharged from hospital with either a mobility problem or a treatment programme that requires regular observation. Then there are the mentally ill.

Most prison hospitals have a percentage of mentally ill people as up to three-quarters of prisoners admitted to prison healthcare units have mental health problems. One problem in treating these prisoners is that the Mental Health Act does not cover prisons, so inmates cannot be forced to undergo treatment. It is becoming increasingly hard to find suitable places for these prisoners who require treatment in a more appropriate environment and inmates can be waiting for as long as eleven months to be transferred to hospitals for specialist care.

Defendants who are suspected of being mentally ill are often remanded in custody for psychiatric reports. Facilities within our prisons to deal with people who have mental health problems are very limited and conditions are poor. Not only do they have to cope with the shock of entering prison, they also face the stress of not knowing what will happen to them. Many are experiencing prison for the first time and know little about the system.

This appalling misplacement of people with mental health problems only increases their suffering and drives some of them to self-harm and sometimes, tragically, to take their own lives.

The average cost of a prison place is £38,753 per year, which is not far short of the cost for a bed in a therapeutic psychiatric hospital. So how can it be possible that in 2007 we have closed most of the large therapeutic psychiatric hospitals and instead are putting mentally ill patients into our prisons rather than supporting them in the community which was always the intention with the closure of the old style large psychiatric hospitals? (That's enough of me on a soapbox for now.)

Most of my colleagues thought that I was mad to want to work in Fraggle Rock until I explained to them that I would be working within a small unit with a number of nurses to look after. They then began to see the rationale for my decision.

The real reason that I had decided to apply for the healthcare, however, was because I knew that this would be a very challenging and rewarding place to work where I would have the chance of learning new skills, which I may be able to put to good use if I were ever to leave the prison service. Also, they did have some very pretty nurses working there.

Three of us applied to work in the healthcare and they required four, but we still had to go through an interview and give a presentation as to why we believed that we should be chosen to work within the healthcare unit. Our interviews were conducted by the acting head of healthcare who was a principal officer and the senior nurse in charge of the healthcare, both of whom I had taught interview and presentation skills to two weeks prior to this interview.

I was offered the job but was disappointed to find that we would be used as discipline officers until the prison service agreed the type of training we would be receiving, as healthcare within the prison would need to achieve the same standards as the National Health Service. This was at the time that responsibility for prison healthcare was being taken away from the prison service and transferring to the NHS through local primary care trusts who would be responsible for ensuring that all prisoners had access to the same NHS service as you or I.

If a prisoner required healthcare services, they simply made an application to their spur officer during applications, which were carried out each day. Alternatively, they could approach the nurse that attended their houseblock with the daily drug run, the nurse would make a note and place them onto the list, depending on which healthcare professional they needed to see.

Prisoners could choose to see a nurse, doctor, dentist, physiotherapist or optician and were usually guaranteed to see whoever they wished within 24 hours of their request. The healthcare at Highdown Prison met most of the prisoners needs as there was always a nurse on duty, day and night, and we were even able to call a doctor out during the night (although he may not be very sober or indeed particularly happy to be dragged out to a prison in the middle of the night).

There was a well man clinic and even some alternative medical treatments such as acupuncture. If the prisoner was suffering from any ailment that required more than a paracetamol, then they would be dispatched to an outside hospital.

I was concerned that, if we were to meet the standards set by our National Health Service, we would end up with concerted indiscipline from the prisoners, as this would mean prisoners having to wait up to a week to get an appointment to see their doctor and be left waiting on the phone for hours until the receptionist decides to pick it up as the ring tone was interrupting her chit chat with her friends. They would then be charged £6 or so for their prescription. An infinitely inferior service to what they were already receiving in prison!

So, after my hopes of learning new skills, I was simply to work within the healthcare unit and provide security for the nurses. The other two officers, Tracy and Steve, were equally pissed off that we would have to wait for the prison service to make its mind up before we could be trained as healthcare officers (or, in prison jargon, Scab Lifters).

The healthcare unit was always very full and one of my targets was to clear out any malingerers who were trying to make the healthcare their home. There are many reasons why prisoners do this. The obvious one is because they feel very vulnerable and want to cling onto the nurses who have much more time for them than an overworked prison officer. They also prefer the environment and the relaxed regime within the healthcare unit as, instead of being locked up for up to 23 hours a day, they get the chance to be out of their cells and watching television in the day room. The day room is like any other institutional dayroom with comfy chairs, a television and a hot water urn. There are games, puzzles and an odd collection of books. I say 'odd' because they were either Janet and John type children's books or very gruesome murder books. Some particularly nasty bastard had removed the last few pages from all the gruesome murder books to provide a rather cruel and wholly unexpected ending. However, knowing most of the clientele in the healthcare, they would rather eat the books than actually read them.

Another reason was that they could ensure that they received their medication on time which also gave them an opportunity to whinge that they needed even more or barter with others to create some weird and wonderful cocktail that would give them an ever bigger and better high.

It always amazed me how much the druggy goppers knew about medication. They would ask the nurses for their medication with an informative flair that most pharmacist would be proud of. "Guv," (even the nurses would be called guv) "my panic attacks have started again, could I have 40mg of benzodiazepine? Also, my head is banging, so I need 500mg of DF118 and my Tom Thumb (Bum) is really hurting because I had to pay back in kind what I owed to Erica, the wing poof. Could I have 200mg of diazepam, and a packet of condoms?" (Yes, they used to be able to get these in prison, too.) "Oh! And do you have the ribbed strawberry flavoured ones and some E45 cream for the old Tom Thumb?"

Of course, most nurses were very used to the many excuses that a prisoner would give to obtain extra medication and would simply palm them off with two paracetamol, which they would still try to sell. Although they could sometimes get a result, which was a referral to see one of the few doctors who visited our prisons. We could never get enough doctors who were stupid enough to want to work in a prison taking care of Her Majesty's guests. But the trick was that, when a prisoner managed to get an appointment with one of them, they would bend their ear with such a story of woe and horror, that the doctor would gladly prescribe anything to get rid of them.

There were three kinds of genuinely frightened and vulnerable prisoners: the celebrity criminals like FF 8282

Archer, or the convicted liar, known as Jeffrey Archer (who was held in Belmarsh prison), Ronnie Knight and Ronnie Biggs; the very mad and the very bad, Hannibal Lecter types; and the bacons (sex offenders) who have committed such a ghastly crime that they do not want to reside with the other bacons, because even the normal run-of-the-mill sex offender is so appalled by the crime they have committed that they are likely to harm the even bigger bacon. I guess that makes them gammons! These types are usually held within the healthcare on a suicide watch.

One of these 'things' was Roy Whiting who had murdered little seven-year-old Sarah Payne. When the news broke in early August 2000 that the police had found who they believed to be the killer of Sarah Payne and he was coming to Highdown, I was on duty in the healthcare unit. I remember the healthcare governor telling us to prepare to accept him as a patient and that he would be on a 2052SH, which is suicide watch, the number of the prison form given to the book in which we write observations about prisoners who we suspect may try to harm themselves. Although he was only being sent to Highdown on a charge of dangerous driving, the police were convinced that he was the one and they needed more time to gather enough evidence to secure a conviction.

When he arrived he was brought straight to the healthcare unit and interviewed by one of our full time nurses called Sue. I remember her coming out of that interview, visibly shaken by the experience, but too professional by half to reveal to me what had been said. The interview had, in principle, been a medical interview bound by clinician-patient confidentiality rules and, of course, Whiting had been very well aware of this when choosing to divulge certain information to Sue during the course of that interview.

As I located him back to his cell, he had such a smirk on his face that I made him sit on his bed, told him to keep his hands by his side and made it clear to him that failure to comply with this order would be seen as an attempted assault on me. Faced with such a personal threat to my safety, I would, of course, be compelled to send him into a world of pain that would not leave any mark on him but, having attacked me, he would then spend the next few nights in the segregation unit.

I then made it very clear that he should not even think about 'bragging' to any of the prisoners about what he had done or try to frighten any of our nursing staff in any way. I informed him that we were all fully aware of why he was with us and that I saw it as my duty to ensure that he would be attending court to face up to the crimes he had committed. A good friend of mine, who was a healthcare nurse, was with me and Whiting was glaring at him the entire time. As far as I was concerned, you could see the evil in this thing's eyes and the desire to kick seven bells of shit out of him was great – but not as great as the risk it would have of him gaining even an ounce of sympathy in court by turning up clearly having been on the wrong end of a beating.

On 27 September 2000, Whiting admitted taking the car and driving dangerously. He was sentenced to 22 months' imprisonment. This then gave detectives the opportunity and time they needed to carry out forensic tests on his Fiat Ducato van and, on 6 February 2001, following the police enquiry, Roy Whiting was formally charged with the murder of Sarah Payne. He was then remanded in custody for this charge and the trial started on 14 November 2001 at Lewes Crown Court.

Our staff then had to escort this thing to court each day. He would always smirk at the escort staff to wind them up as he was clearly trying to get a reaction that may have prejudiced his case in some way. However, everyone knew what his game was and behaved impeccably throughout, even though they had to sit next to this thing in court and only just a few feet away from Sarah's parents.

As a prisoner he was always very demanding and, when he was being processed through the reception area, all you would hear from him was, "I want this," or "I want that." Finally, on 12 December 2001, he was dispatched to court for the last day and for sentencing to be passed. I had the great pleasure of leaning into his ear and whispering, "You know what you need, you gopper? You need to get a life – and that's exactly what we're all hoping you'll get from the judge."

Roy Whiting was convicted of the abduction and murder of Sarah Payne and sentenced to life imprisonment. The trial judge, Mr Justice Curtis, said that it was a rare case in which a life sentence should mean life. This was only the 24th time in British legal history that such a recommendation had been made. Whiting was duly sentenced and the trial judge recommended that he should never be released.

In some respects, the real horror of the case is that this thing had abducted and sexually assaulted an eight-year-old girl on 4 March. He was arrested a few weeks later after a man, who knew Whiting, had come forward after hearing that the abductor's car had been a red Ford Sierra. Three months later he admitted to the charges of abduction and indecent assault and was sentenced to four years in prison. The maximum sentence could have been life for such a crime, but the sentence was reduced because he had admitted to the crime. A psychiatrist who assessed Whiting after his conviction said that he was likely to re-offend once he was released.

Working in the healthcare was not all doom and gloom, however, and there were times when we did have some light relief. We had one prisoner who was in for arson and who was as mad as a box of frogs. I was given the task of trying to call some of the secure mental hospitals to see if they had a bed for him as, although he was a convicted prisoner, he was clearly in need of treatment. The task I was given proved to be impossible because, as soon as I gave the hospital details of who the prisoner was, they would very quickly interrupt me to say that they were full before promptly hanging up. I later found out that this was because the acts of arson were always committed against the hospitals he was staying in and he was very well-known on the secure mental hospital circuit.

He was a bit of a sad figure though, I have to say, and would very rarely venture out of his cell to socialise with other prisoners except to ask them for cigarettes. He was a constant chain smoker, which would result in him using all his week's supply of tobacco in two days and then spending the other five days asking everyone he met for a cigarette. If they turned him down he then would call them a 'cunt', which was fine as most of the other prisoners were used to him and just ignored him. However, it did not go down quite as well with one of the nuns who visited the healthcare from time to time or, indeed, the new governor, although, I have to say, I was rather inclined to agree with the prisoner about the new governor.

Another strange thing that this prisoner would do was to talk to a pot plant that we had outside. He would spend at least 20 minutes talking to the plant every day, asking if it was alright and advising it to cheer up because he believed that the plant was sad. One day, I managed to hide a speaker amongst the plant's leaves and connected it to an intercom so that, when he started speaking to the plant, he was so happy that it was able to reply back to him. I know that you're probably thinking that this was no way to treat someone who has a mental illness but, ask any mental health nurse, and you will get similar stories of horseplay from them, I'm sure. What is real ill treatment of people with mental health problems is locking them up in prisons without proper treatment for their condition and in an environment more likely to exacerbate their problems than to in any way alleviate them.

There was a time when this prisoner found himself in trouble when he was caught stealing cigarettes from one of the Yardie wheelchair gangs. This was a group of three Jamaican lads who had all, at separate times, been shot by rival gangs in Jamaica and were rendered wheelchair bound for the rest of their days. Now, life in Jamaica was hard, but as a disabled Yardie, it was even harder, so to help pay the bills, they had volunteered to bring drugs to England, hidden within their wheelchairs. We were so full in the healthcare unit that I had asked the gang to inform their top Yardie to stop the wheelchair ploy because our customs boys had well and truly sussed that one out and we were rapidly running out of space for the wheelchairs in the prison.

The mobile Yardie who had caught the prisoner helping himself to his cigarettes went ballistic and, in good Yardie tradition, produced a weapon, a broom. I arrived in the nick of time to stop our mad chain-smoking prisoner from becoming an attachment to the broom and put myself between him and the domestic appliance-wielding Yardie. I asked him, "Do you intend to hit someone with that broom or were you just about to start sweeping the floor?" To which he replied, "Just sweepin', boss, just sweepin'."

The Yardie gang was a real drain on our resources because the last place they needed to be was the healthcare but, because it was impossible to fit their wheelchairs through the standard cell door on the wings, there was literally no other place to hold them but in the healthcare unit as the cell doors were much wider. They were always rude and sexually abusive towards the female nursing staff and would bully other prisoners, so we constantly had to keep them in check which used up far more of our time than dealing with three regular prisoners. I thought I had heard all they could throw at us until I heard one of them tell a probation officer, collating pre-sentence reports, to "go suck your momma's pussy, you blood clot". The probation officer said he had heard it all before and just ignores it but I did not ignore it and decided to place the prisoner on report under Prison Rule 51, paragraph 19/YOI Rule 55, paragraph 21, for being disrespectful to any officer, or any person (other than a prisoner) who is at the prison for the purpose of working there, or any person visiting a prison.

Everyone said that I was wasting my time as the penalty that could be imposed, seven days cellular confinement for a repeated offence could not be carried out and he would simply be allowed to remain in the healthcare unit to continue to abuse its staff. Not to be deterred, I set about arranging how this could be done in order to teach them a lesson. I contacted the segregation unit, told them of my objective and asked if they could help me by agreeing to help lift the prisoner in and out of the cell as necessary. Normally prison officers would not volunteer to lift a prisoner unless they were applying some form of control and restraint, but as I got on well with them and most were good mates of mine, they were more than pleased to help.

The day of the adjudication arrived and the prisoner was wheeled before the governor in a temporary adjudication room, which had been set up within the healthcare. The governor conducting the adjudication was the healthcare governor: a well respected and well thought of man with many years experience in the service. He also knew that I had made sure that any award of cellular confinement could be carried out. By now, the prisoner had got wind that something was wrong and tried to show remorse for being so abusive. This was not accepted, however, because there had been fifteen previous cases, and he received a sentence of seven days cellular confinement, with a loss of all privileges, which meant that he would spend seven days in a small segregation cell and would not be allowed to have any of his possessions with him: no radio, no television, no books (other than a Bible), no canteen, just his meals and his own thoughts to make him reflect on what he had done. As soon as the sentence was dished out, he was duly wheeled to the segregation unit where his specially prepared cell was awaiting him. As I lifted him into the cell to start his punishment, he started crying and saying how sorry he was. That's when, for the first time, a prisoner got to me. But, he needed to learn that you cannot go through life being so abusive and disrespectful to people and we needed to show the rest of the gang an example.

It worked. Seven days later our wheelchair Tourette's sufferer arrived back to the healthcare in triumph and, although the gang continued to be very vocal and demanding, they were always far more respectful to the staff. The point had been made.

Like the segregation unit, we had to choose our orderlies very carefully as we needed to trust that the prisoners working in the healthcare would not attack any of the so-called vulnerable prisoners within our care, or bully any of our healthcare clients for their medication. We needed to be confident that they would simply get on and do a good day's work.

One of these workers was a South American drug smuggler called Rodrigo, who had many skills, one of which was dancing, as he used to be a lap top dancer in a gay club. He was a great worker, keeping the place spotless and always willing to help in communicating with Spanish speaking prisoners. One particular day, I mentioned to him that I always enjoyed dancing but could never master the tango. He promptly offered to teach me the tango, so there we were on the ward in front of my colleagues in the healthcare being taught the tango by a gay lap top dancer, when, of course, in walked the new governor in charge of the prison. To say that he was not impressed is an understatement. I thought he was judging me harshly, I have to say. After all, it was only my first lesson.

We have had some very strange creatures visit us in the healthcare, but none stranger than one prisoner who had transferred to us from Feltham prison. Feltham is a Young Offenders Institute and when the baby criminals become 21, they are sent to the big boys' prisons. This particular come-of-age criminal had hidden three D1 batteries and a three-foot length of wire flex up his bum.

Now, I am not sure if he had forgotten to attach them to something or if he had simply read the instructions incorrectly, but he had to be admitted to the healthcare until they could be safely removed. He also had another strange hiding place. Apparently, he had self-harmed several times in the past and had slashed himself across his belly to such an extent that, on more than one occasion, he had managed to put his intestines on show. As he kept repeating this form of self-harm, the scar plus the rolls of fat had produced a kind of pouch that was hidden by the rolls of fat on his lower belly, which enabled him to hide razor blades, phone cards and such like, that he had stolen from other prisoners. If he was about to be searched by staff, he would manage to open up the scar enough so that it would bleed, which would result in the officers calling on the assistance of a nurse. In the meantime, he'd use the opportunity to hide the items elsewhere but I never liked to imagine exactly where with this particular inmate.

The healthcare had two specially adapted cells where the cell door could be locked back so that it remained open and a locked gate was used to contain the prisoner and prevent others from attacking them. These cells would be used for prisoners who were on what is known as 'constant watch'. For some strange reason, they used to use nurses for this process, who were usually bank nurses as we could not afford to use our own team of nurses as they were already understaffed. I could never understand why it was necessary to pay in excess of £20 per hour to have a trained nurse sitting outside a locked cell watching a prisoner in case he attempted to commit suicide.

Nurses are very rarely trained in first aid and bank nurses were not trained to recognise the different methods of attempted suicides within a prison as there are many different ways. But, here's the best bit, nor did they have keys because they were not regular staff and did not have an essential key talk by our security department. So what possible use could they have been, other than being a pair of eyes that could raise the alarm in the event of the prisoner managing to, for example, regurgitate a boot lace, carefully tie it round his neck, attach the other end to the bed, then slowly turn himself around and around until the tourniquet around his neck begins to choke him. This was just one of the many ingenious methods prisoners have come up with. When this was pointed out to the governors, a decision was made to allow officer support grades to carry out constant watches. This was just as stupid; however, because although these guys were a very valuable assistance to the work we did, they were not trained and certainly could not lay a hand on a prisoner so, instead of simply placing a prison officer on the constant watch, they continue to use nurses.

When I was working nights, I was asked to report to the healthcare along with the principal officer in charge of the prison at night (known as the night orderly officer), as the officer and nurse based in the healthcare had seen something odd about a prisoner and wanted our advice. When we got to the healthcare, we looked through the inspection flap on the door of the cell and could see that the prisoner was lying in his bed. He appeared to be asleep, so I asked what was wrong with that and my colleague said that the prisoner's face was very shiny and looked wet. We tried calling the prisoner to wake him but got no response so the night orderly officer decided to open the cell door. But as we approached the bed, calling the prisoner to try and wake him up, it dawned on us what the problem was. He had tied a clear plastic bag over his head and had suffocated himself. The plastic bag had formed into all the contours of his face and this is what gave the appearance of him having a wet, shiny face.

When the doctor arrived he informed us that the prisoner had clearly been dead for some time as the body was very cold and stiff due to rigor mortis. As the temperature was mild in the cell, rigor mortis would usually only have set in about 3-4 hours after clinical death. The prisoner had been in the healthcare due to a minor ailment and not given any sign of depression or any other indication that he would commit suicide.

Two nights after this sad incident a colleague and I were checking the double gates on the walkways when I received a call on my radio from the night orderly officer to report to the healthcare unit to help deal with a difficult prisoner. When we arrived, we found the orderly officer at the cell door of a very noisy prisoner who was hell bent on making sure that no other prisoner could sleep because he had run out of cigarettes and was demanding that we should give him a cigarette or he would continue to make a noise until he got one.

Suddenly the night orderly officer opened the cell door and went to grab the prisoner. We took this as our cue to assist him in restraining the prisoner using correct Control and Restraint methods, which we did with great speed and professionalism. We relocated the prisoner in a strip cell at the end of the healthcare, where he would be less likely to disturb the other prisoners.

Normally, if we have to restrain a prisoner in sight of other prisoners, we receive a lot of abuse. On this occasion, however, we were cheered by the rest of the healthcare who were also making interesting suggestions as to how we could improve our Control and Restraint methods, such as: "Kick his fucking head in, Guv!"

We located the prisoner into the strip cell using the standard method of C&R; laying the prisoner flat on the floor, the officer restraining the head of the prisoner (which was me) would place the prisoner's legs into a figure of four positions, so that he would be unable to kick any one. His hands were placed high above his back and held in place by me, who was now leaning on his legs. The other officers then left the cell and, when they were all out, they informed me that it was clear for me to leave, which I did by quickly releasing the prisoner, who was still lying face down on the floor, while I backed out of the cell, still facing the prisoner, guided by my colleagues, until I was clear of the door. The door was then shut and locked.

I checked to make sure that the prisoner was getting up off the floor and he was just sitting on the floor shaking his head and looking very bemused and sorry for himself. The orderly officer asked if we were all okay and then enquired, "Why the fuck did you wrap him up?" (that is, use correct Control and Restraint method.) We were puzzled and replied, "Well, you grabbed him first so we just moved into assist you." "You stupid fuckers," he replied, "I'd only grabbed him to stop him from falling over because he'd lost his crutches."

The prisoner had a ligament injury to his ankle because he had been kicking the crap out of his wife. When he was arrested by the woman police officer, he was abusive and had shown very little respect for anyone female he came across, including the magistrate who remanded him in custody. When he arrived in our reception area, he was greeted by the reception senior officer who was also female and, true to form, promptly referred to her as a "fucking slag". The female officer in the healthcare had had enough abuse and threats and was concerned that he was banging his cell door and keeping all the other prisoners awake, so she called the night orderly officer and that's when we came in.

The prisoner was released from prison the following day because his wife dropped all charges. He never visited us again and I'd like to think that he had seen the error of his ways but somehow I doubt it.

There are times when I have had to draw on my skills as a hostage negotiator to get the job done. On one particular occasion, we had a prisoner who had been sectioned under the Mental Health Act and who was going to be transferred to a secure hospital for treatment. On the day that the prisoner was going to move, the officers who were to escort him to the hospital came down to the healthcare unit where our happy bunny was and simply went straight to the cell, without consulting the nursing staff, to give the prisoner a clean set of prison clothes ready for the escort, as the prisoner was only wearing a dressing gown. As soon as they gave the clothes to the prisoner, he went absolutely berserk, screaming all kinds of abuse, launching himself at the wall trying to smash up the cell.

The escort staff very quickly shut the cell door and came running to our office to deny any responsibility for the prisoner's outrage. I must admit I did not have a clue as to why this prisoner was so upset. Eventually, the principal officer in charge of the reception area came over to try to calm the prisoner down but he only lasted about ten seconds before the prisoner spat in his face and tried to eat him. We managed to rescue the PO because we were running short of them but, by this time, I had managed to pick up on some of the issues that seemed to be upsetting him; his love of Manchester United Football Club and his hatred for anything that was not in the club's red colours. The tracksuit that was thrown into the prisoner was blue and the prisoner believed that he would be playing for Manchester United and was just awaiting a call to join the team.

However, as the prisoner was trying to explain this amongst the 101 swear words, it was not altogether immediately clear. When I finally managed to pick up on what was upsetting him so much, I suggested to the PO who was still trying to wipe the spit from his face, that I might be able to calm him down, get him to put some clothes on and get him on the minibus that would be taking him to the happy farm.

The PO agreed that I should give it a try on the basis that he was certainly not prepared to be spat upon again. So, I simply got a red tracksuit from our clothing store, asked the staff to unlock the cell door of our mad friend and started shouting even more loudly than him at imaginary orderlies, demanding to know who had given this pile of shit to this player, proclaiming them not to be our team colours. I then threw the blue tracksuit out of the cell, ordering it to be burned, and presented the prisoner with the red tracksuit, telling him to hurry up as I had arranged for the team minibus to pick him up to take him to the match as we needed him to play for the team. The prisoner's eyes lit up and he complied with my instructions. I then led the way out of the healthcare, through the reception area, and straight onto the minibus whilst encouraging the prisoner to chant for his team and wave at the paparazzi (prison officers) who would be lining the route. They managed to get him to the hospital and the officers successfully transferred him into their care and, as far as I know, he sadly never did get that chance to play for his team.

After about eight months of working in the healthcare, I started to feel 'fraggled out' myself. By this time, the prison service had finally made a decision to train discipline officers as healthcare officers and allow them to receive formal nurse training. After my eight month stint, I knew that I could not give my full commitment to this profession and made the decision to return back to houseblock 3 as a discipline officer.

'Madness takes its toll. Please have exact change.'

Chapter Eleven

First Night

When I arrived back at houseblock 3, I found that there had been a few changes since I had last been there. By now, all cells had a power socket whereas before they simply had a fluorescent light, which most prisoners hot wired into to power their radios. This practice was a chargeable offence and caused a lot of adjudication work. It was also very dangerous as quite a few prisoners had given themselves a nasty electric shock and managed to blow all the cell lights on the landing, which made them very popular with their fellow prisoners. We objected to the installation of these sockets, as we believed that they could be used to harm staff if, for example, the prisoner were to wire up the door handles so as to electrocute the officer as they grabbed the metal cell door handle. We were assured, however, that the trip fuse would be so low as to prevent anyone coming to any harm if the prisoner tampered with the socket. The worse that would happen would be for the fuse to simply blow.

We were also told that the introduction of the sockets was to stop prisoners from wiring up to their lights and reduce the need for them to have heavy batteries in their cells which have been used as weapons. Prisoners would place them in a sock to form a nasty cosh. What our managers failed to tell us, however, was that they also intended to remove all the hot water boilers located on each spur to provide hot water for the prisoners to make tea. Instead, prisoners were all to be given kettles so that they could brew their own tea in the comfort of their own cell. The next stage of this radical transformation of the prisoner's living accommodation was to provide in-cell television, for which the prisoners would pay 50 pence per week rental.

So now we had accommodation for about 700 prisoners, all with en suites, colour television and tea-making facilities. The Holiday Inn up the road complained that we were proving to be unfair competition. I started to question why the prison service seemed to be making every effort they could to make prison a very soft option. They had certainly made sure that prison would no longer serve as a deterrent for the would-be criminal. I believe that the powers to be knew exactly what they were doing, because they could see that the prison population was increasing at an alarming rate and the cost of prison places was very expensive due to the manpower needed to run them. By making the cells into nice, little, self-contained bijou apartments with all mod cons, they could save on recruiting more staff by keeping the prisoners banged up longer and being brainwashed by watching Richard and Judy on daytime television.

The extra bang up seemed to piss the cons off, although I blame the daytime television programmes myself. No sooner had the nice facilities been installed, prisoners on houseblock 4 decided to have a sit down protest in the yard due to the amount of bang up they were getting. Their complaint was that they wanted to be out of their cells associating with their fellow prisoners every evening. However, we did not have enough staff and the Home Office was not exactly going out of its way to recruit more staff, so we had no choice other than to bang them up.

My view is straightforward. If they had not had such an easy regime in the first place, allowing association amongst prisoners every night of the week, we would not have been facing this problem. As far as I am concerned, there is an important lesson to be learned here for prisoners. Again, it is quite straightforward thinking. If you do not like being in prison, then do not commit crimes that will get you put into prison. Having prisoners out of their cells so that they can follow useful rehabilitation programmes is one thing we should be doing, however having them out of their cells so that they can play with their mates, make phone calls, pass drugs to each other, settle old scores in the washrooms and generally bother us with stupid questions is certainly not, in my mind, conducive to returning them back to the community, rehabilitated and ready to make a useful contribution to society. And, in any case, staffing these evening associations costs lots of money.

A sit down protest is exactly what it says on the can. The prisoners are allowed out for their one-hour per day walk around the exercise yard. On this particular occasion, the officers supervising the exercise on the yard had noticed that the behaviour of the prisoners was not normal because, when prisoners go on the yard, they will always walk around in a clockwise direction. Only rarely would you see the odd prisoner walking the other way around and this was usually because they were indeed odd. On this occasion, however, several prisoners were shooting about in all directions and appeared to be rallying support for something. An officer radioed in to ask the senior officer of the houseblock to attend the yard so that they could speak to him.

When the senior officer met the officers on the yard he agreed that it looked like the prisoners were up to something as they were now starting to gather at the opposite end of the yard. The senior officer went back in and informed the duty governor and the orderly officer that it looked as though trouble may be brewing on the yard of houseblock 4. The officers had read the situation correctly; something was indeed brewing and when it came to the time that the prisoners should have returned to their houseblock, they simply sat down on the yard and started to shout abuse at the officers.

All the officers withdrew from the yard and contingency plans were started to deal with a sit down protest. CCTV cameras were trained onto the yard and we were able to identify the main organisers of the protest. Several futile attempts were made by the principal officer of the houseblock to warn the prisoners that they were in breach of prison rules (like they did not realise this already – duh!) and, at the risk of stating the blindingly obvious, went on to inform them that, if the protest continued, they would end up finding themselves in a lot of trouble. Perhaps unsurprisingly, his request was met with even more abuse. However, by now, some prisoners were starting to give in and return to the houseblock of their own accord and it was very clear that the organisers were getting very upset with them. They started to redirect their abuse and threats away from the prison officers towards their fellow prisoners who were, by now, returning to the houseblock in droves.

It was a very hot day with the sun beating down on them and we noticed that prisoners in the cells that backed onto the yard were passing water out to the remaining protestors. Clearing the prisoners from these cells rapidly put a stop to this way of aiding and abetting the protest.

Contingency plans for this type of protest were put into action and a call went out for assistance from neighbouring prisons for Control and Restraint teams. After about three hours, the Control and Restraint teams had arrived and were in place ready to clear the yard and one final warning was given to the 50 or so prisoners that remained. Encouraged by their ringleader, however, they simply shouted further abuse at the PO who had made the request. The word was given for the C&R teams to move in and they entered the yard in such extremely good formation that even a giddy guardsman would have been impressed with, coming to a halt about 20 feet away from the prisoners who now seemed to be showing the first signs of alarm and concern. And concerned they should have been because the next thing to happen was for the prison attack dogs to be brought onto the yard. Their handlers led them to the front of the extended line of the C&R teams and they were certainly the biggest, snarling, most vicious looking dogs I had ever seen. At this point, the prisoners had started to climb over each other to get to the back of this, by now, quaking, nervous bunch of prospective dog food.

Although the prisoners did not realise this, the dogs were only on the yard to prevent an escape. They would not have been used directly to break up this protest as they would not have been able to distinguish between a member of staff or a prisoner. Plus, it's not allowed, as some tree-hugging politician would complain. It did not take much longer for the prisoners to comply with orders and surrender to the teams. The ringleaders were summarily dispatched to the segregation unit and most were subsequently shipped out to other prisons. They had been on the yard for about five hours and most of them had severe sunburn from being exposed to the sun for such a long time. What surprised me more than anything is that not one of them sued the prison service for failing to provide sun protection cream.

Houseblock 3 had become the induction houseblock and it was being proposed that a detox unit also be set up here. As I had just left the healthcare, the managers on houseblock 3 and the PO in charge of the new detox management programme known as CARAT (Counselling, Advice, Referral, Assessment and Throughcare), thought that I would be an ideal person to work on this unit. And there I was thinking that carrots are a simple root vegetable, used to good comedy effect by Bugs Bunny!

By 2001, the number of prisoners with a drug or alcohol problem was on the increase and it was estimated that 80 per cent of all remand or convicted criminals that entered a prison had a drug or alcohol problem. So, to tackle this increase, the prison service introduced the Counselling, Advice, Referral, Assessment and Throughcare programme, with a multi-disciplinary team of health service professionals, drug workers and prison officers. It was suggested that Highdown should have a spur on a houseblock dedicated to ensuring that prisoners with a drug problem were able to go through a careful detoxification programme and be monitored and helped to become clear of drugs and alcohol. It was hoped that the Throughcare part of the CARAT would ensure that, when the prisoner was released, they could continue their treatment for their drug or alcohol problem back in the community.

The greatest challenge that any detox programme has is to combat the supply of drugs within the prison. I have already explained how easy it is for drugs to enter the prison and sometimes you do not even need a drug dog to sniff out the drugs as even a prison officer with a full blown cold and stuffed up nose could smell the drugs either being used or being prepared. The CCTV cameras would pick up hundreds of 'lines' hanging out of the cell windows. A line is the method that is used to pass a small item from one cell to another. Prisoners construct lines from torn bedding and they are long enough to reach the next cell either below or to the side of them. They rarely pass items above them as, to get the momentum needed to swing the line to the cell above, could result in the loss of the item altogether so, if you were in the cell above, you would make your own line and lower it down to collect the package.

Whenever we conducted a cell search, we were guaranteed to find torn bedding made into a 6-metre line. When I first started as a prison officer, I would place every prisoner on report for damaging prison property and the prisoners would end up being fined about £5, which was in excess of the cost of the item. I was told by a more experienced officer that I would get fed up with wasting my time over the paperwork and save the 'nicking of the goppers' for when we needed to as they had got tired of telling the governor that he needs to fit wire mesh grills. The governor apparently believed that this would be inhuman. My prisoner officer colleague was right, though. You are so busy and the pressure is on you to ensure that you perform all your duties and get the roll in on time that you end up by simply removing the line and giving the prisoner a quick bollocking.

However, we were under pressure to prevent the destruction of the bedding as the prison would be running out of sheets and blankets and, as they would be nearing the end of their financial year, the management would insist that we crack down on the prisoners.

We would, of course, carry out the orders given to us and the governor would then find that he had a 200 per cent increase in adjudications. This would not look good on the statistics, so he would then tell us to use a system called IEP, Incentives and Earned Privileges. This is a system whereby a prisoner may gain or lose certain privileges within the prison so prisoners have the opportunity of gaining extra privileges through good behaviour, but losing those privileges if they misbehave.

The regime is based on a system which places a prisoner on one of three levels: basic, standard or enhanced. Most prisons operate a similar system, which starts prisoners on either the basic or standard level. The privileges that can be earned affect a prisoner's daily life and include: the number of hours allowed out of their cell; the number of visits allowed above the minimum requirement; access to more of their own money to spend in the prison shop or on phone calls (on top of their prison wages); and the chance to have a television in their cell. So we would place all the prisoners who did not heed our warnings on the basic IEP regime, which increased the amount of prisoners on the basic regime by about 200 per cent and which, again, looked bad for the statistics. So we told the governor to fix wire meshes to the windows, which he still did not do.

Before I re-joined the houseblock 3 team, I had the chance to look around other prisons to see how they operate their detox units and was impressed to see that they have sealed separate units and all prisoners are searched going to and from these units. There are mesh grills on all the windows and the detox prisoners are kept separate from the rest of the prisoners. They have their own visiting times and these visits are conducted under a closed visit scheme. If they wish to attend a church service, they are kept separate at the back of the church. The general idea is to try to prevent any contact that will allow drugs to enter the detox unit. These prisoners are in prison because they have committed crimes to feed their addiction and have, therefore, already demonstrated that they are prepared to go to any lengths to feed their habit. It is, therefore, important that we help them by ensuring that they have no means of obtaining drugs whilst they are on the detox programme. Detoxification from opiates normally takes in the region of 10 to 15 days. This in itself does not strengthen their resolve to stay off the drugs and they therefore need Throughcare programmes to educate them and help them build defences to reject and stay off drugs.

Highdown had decided that it did not want to go to any added expense so the managers were tasked with operating the detox unit as a normal spur and they would be allowed to mix with the other prisoner. We found that most of the prison's drug barons were all trying to re-locate to houseblock 3 as they knew we would be doing nothing more than herding together a ready source of willing customers, who would pay anything for a fix. The management were a bit pissed off that I would not work on this unit and I watched good officers get very despondent, very fast, once they started working there.

In 1996 prisoners had a new challenge to their drug taking habits when Mandatory Drug Testing (MDT) of prisoners was introduced, although those who where receiving medication and help on the detox programme had to agree to be tested at least once per week to qualify them to remain on the detox programme. Prisoners have always been adaptable and immensely resourceful when it comes to avoiding being caught which brings with it the possibility of added days to their custodial sentence.

One such ingenious method was to get a fellow prisoner, who had not used drugs, to supply a sample of their urine in a small bottle, which they attached to their penis with a thin thread so that it hung down behind their penis to prevent it from being viewed when they are strip-searched. After they are searched, the prisoner is given a sample tub into which they have to provide a sample of their urine which, of course, they are allowed to do in private. The prisoner simply empties the sample from the drug free prisoner into the tub from the bottle attached to their penis and hands the bottle to the officers conducting the MDT. However, I have known this to back fire as to get a sample of drug free piss in prisons can prove to be a challenge and, at times, a prisoner may pay anything up to four cigarettes for a good sample. More than once, the so-called good sample, which is always verified at an outside laboratory, has come back positive and the prisoner who conned the cigarettes in the first place is hopefully long gone by then to another prison otherwise he is very likely to soon be suffering from 'tuna on the brain' syndrome.

In the eyes of the management at Highdown, I was beginning to become something of a loose cannon as I had the irritating combination of experience and an opinion. This seemed to worry the inexperienced pretenders amongst their ranks, who were growing in number.

Soon after the setting up of the detox unit, a new PO was appointed to houseblock 3. I knew him as he had worked at Highdown before as a PEI but I was surprised to hear that, when he was promoted and worked at Brixton Prison, he managed to upset most of the staff there and had even received threats from them. I was surprised because, when he worked at Highdown, he always seemed to have a good sense of humour and seemed to have plenty of bottle for the job. When he arrived back at Highdown, he was tasked by one of the governors to set up a new concept in prison called the First Night in Prison (FNIP). He was also short of a senior officer and asked if I would be prepared to act up as a senior officer on houseblock 3 and take forward setting up of the First Night in Prison programme.

I had always moaned about the poor quality of managers and decided to be the change I wanted to see and accepted the offer.

If I was to set up this First Night in Prison programme, the first thing I needed to find out was why the prison service had decided to put effort into this piece of work. The answer was because the years 2000–01 had seen a spate of self-inflicted deaths of prisoners in England and Wales. It would seem that increasing numbers of acutely distressed and vulnerable individuals were overwhelming the system.

Suicide in prison is a very sad reality of prison life and the prison service is constantly trying to improve how they prevent them. At the time that I worked as a prison officer, we had a system that was known as 2052SH. The 2052SH was the name of the form used to record events and observations made by prison staff about a prisoner who is suspected of being at risk from suicide. A 2052SH could be opened by anyone and healthcare staff and prison officers would interview the prisoner and an assessment would be made about how vulnerable the prisoner is to self-harm. Depending on their assessed level of vulnerability, they would usually be located in a shared cell as the policy was not to allow anyone who has a 2052SH form to reside on their own. Also, everywhere that the prisoner goes, the form must follow and comments must be updated in the book in relation to any change of location and observation about the prisoner.

Men in prison are five times more likely to commit suicide than those in the general population. Mental illness and overcrowding are possible explanations. One in five men in prison, and nearly 40 per cent of women, have attempted suicide at some time – rates that are much higher than in the general public. And, at some stage in their sentence, most prisoners will experience personal distress, mental health problems, drug dependency, or a lack of family support – all factors which increase the risk of suicide. Prison staff are under enormous pressure to predict who is at risk of suicide. On top of all this, overcrowding makes it extremely difficult for staff to prevent someone intent on taking their own life. From 1995–2004 there were 12 suicides in Highdown and I would guess that there were probably at least a further one hundred serious attempts. The statistics showed that the most vulnerable were those on remand and the new arrivals to prison.

Suicide in prison key points:

- Two people per week take their own lives in our prisons; this has almost doubled since the early 1990s. This is despite the prison service having invested far more time and resources in suicide prevention work during the same period.

- Over half of those who take their own lives are on remand.

- Overcrowded local jails like Highdown suffer from the greatest number of suicides.

- Over half of all suicides since 1 January 2004 took place in a quarter of all jails.

- In addition to the 95 people who committed suicide in 2004, a further 228 required resuscitation following a recognised suicide attempt.

- There were 17,678 recorded incidents of self-harm in prisons in 2004 (some of these will have been from serial self-harmers).

- Over half of all prisons are overcrowded and, in September 2005, the overall prison estate was overcrowded to 111 per cent of its capacity; 14 prisons (11 of which operated as local prisons) were overcrowded to over 150 per cent of capacity, with a further 21 prisons overcrowded to between 125–149 per cent of capacity.

- Seventeen thousand two hundred prisons were doubled-up in cells meant for one in August 2005.

At the prison service college, we were taught how to recognise the signs of potential self-harmers and what to do about it, as well as first aid training to deal with a range of different suicide attempts. I could never imagine how much I would use these skills and I am very proud that my direct intervention has saved the lives of other human beings (now, now Kelly, you're getting soft).

There are many 'stranger than fiction' stories that have circulated the prison service. One of these concerning suicides was when a prison officer found a prisoner hanging in a cell. The officer immediately hit the alarm bell and went into the cell to try to save the prisoner. He grabbed the prisoner around the top of his legs and lifted him up to take the weight off the ligature in an attempt to save the prisoner's life. However, the prisoner weighed about 18 stone and the prison officer was only about 12 stone (when wet), therefore when the ligature came loose from its fixing on the ceiling, the full weight of the prisoner came crashing down on the officer. Meanwhile, the seventh cavalry arrived (officers responding to the alarm bell) and saw that one of their officers was lying on the floor with a big hefty prisoner on top of him. Assuming that their officer comrade was being attacked by the prisoner, they quickly restrained the prisoner using correct C&R methods and proceeded to march the prisoner off to the Seg, not appreciating that this particular prisoner was not cooperating in the usual way as they dragged him towards the segregation. The officer who had attempted to save the prisoner eventually managed to get to his feet and informed his colleagues that they should be taking the prisoner to a morgue and not the Seg, as he was dead.

When designing the first night in prison programme, I first had to think about how distressing the effects would be if I had been banged up. I looked at our reception procedures and the process that every prisoner goes through before they are located onto a houseblock.

Prison receptions are very busy places when they are receiving prisoners and the officers are under enormous pressure to process the prisoners in and out of the reception area as quickly as possible. It is therefore not difficult to lose focus on individual needs such that a prisoner coming into prison for the first time, who is probably very nervous and scared but trying to put on a brave face to ward off others, can easily be overlooked and treated like all the other very noisy demanding prisoners.

There was one officer who had decided that he would use the following talk for prisoners who have never been in prison before:

Reception Officer: "Is this your first time in prison?"

Prisoner: "Yes sir."

Reception Officer: "Well, let me tell you about some of the delightful things in store for you! Do you like football?"

Prisoner: "Yes sir."

Reception Officer: "That's good. You'll like Mondays, because you will be out to play football on our state of the art astro-turf football field. Do you like board games?"

Prisoner: "Yes sir."

Reception Officer: "Then you will love Tuesdays as that's when you will be allowed out of your cell to play any number of wonderful board games we have here with the other prisoners. Do you like films?"

Prisoner: "Yes sir."

Reception Officer: "Then you will love Wednesdays too as it's the director's chair night and we show the latest releases to be seen and welcome you comments on them. Are you gay?"

Prisoner: "No sir."

Reception Officer: "Then you will fucking hate Thursdays!"

Other than with the reception programme, I never did get the chance to work in the reception area unless I was re-deployed there due to the shortage of staff. Because there is a need to have experienced officers working in this area, reception can attract some officers who think they know it all and, as the work involves no personnel officer work or prolonged prisoner/staff contact, they tend to treat the prisoners with an air of indifference. Some reception officers can also view the houseblock officers as a hindrance to their structure and procedures, which I must admit we often were. However, they were not the only ones who would be busy trying to get everything done. It is also worth keeping in mind that reception staff are more likely to be attacked than any other officer in the prison.

This is because the newly delivered, straight off the street and never been in prison before, 21-year-old prisoner, has very little respect for anyone, let alone someone in uniform. They have probably decided to get drunk at a club in Croydon, have re-arranged the facial appearance of some other reveller with the use of a glass or knife, verbally abused the police, who would have called him mate, and treated the private court staff with contempt. Then, when asked to take their hands out of his pockets, not to lean on the desk and answer the question concerning his incarceration, next of kin and so on, they throw a tantrum as if they are in a Tesco aisle and their mum won't let them have a sweetie. They usually throw their arms about everywhere and, as I have had to put in more than one statement: 'The prisoner came at me with flailing arms and I feared for my safety and that of those around me, I therefore used correct Home Office approved Control and Restraint techniques to prevent him from harming himself or others.'

I observed how one reception officer met and greeted the new prisoners and he simply said, "Right, stand still and smile at the camera. Now get behind the curtain and show us your cock." At this point, the prisoner will be kitted out in the very best 'no dad tracksuit' and deprived of any belongings that he is not allowed to bring into the prison, which will be nearly everything.

They are then placed in a holding, caged cell, along with all sorts of other prisoners, some of whom are new, others who are returning from court and some who are transferring in from another prison. They would be given a meal if it was around tea time and then transferred to the houseblocks as soon as the reception staff had a chance to breathe and empty the cage as it would be getting impossible to squeeze any more in.

New prisoners are delivered to the houseblocks by reception staff who simply drop them off and get back to reception as soon as possible so that they can get on with the mammoth task of trying to process all the prisoners before the evening role needs to be submitted so that everyone can go home. This would normally happen around 8.00pm, just after bang up for the evening when everyone was doing their best to locate all the returns that we would have from reception. New prisoners would then be allocated any empty cell that could be found for them by the office officer. Spur staff would then be told that they have a new prisoner for their spur complete with their bed kit: two woven woollen blankets and two sheets, a pillow case and a towel (that's if they have not been reduced in size by the previous owner to make a line), a breakfast pack consisting of a small packet of cheap breakfast cereal, long life milk, two teabags and four sachets of sugar. They will also be given toothpaste, a toothbrush, a razor, soap, and a toilet roll, a plastic plate, a bowl and a mug. The new arrival would have to pick up all these items and follow the officer to their new humble abode.

More often than not they would be placed into a shared cell where the other two occupants (originally these were all two man cells, now they were three man cells) had taken the pillow from the third bed and made sure that the worst mattress was the only one left for the new prisoner to sleep on. There was many a time that I would be found making sure that the prisoner had a pillow and a decent mattress, although the pressure that was placed on us to ensure that we got the evening role in on time, and staff were not kept back late, often prevented us from being able to achieve this. These new prisoners would then be at the mercy of whomever we had just banged them up with. More often than not, the other inmates were just normal run-of-the-mill prisoners who would fill the minds of the new intake full of crap about what prison life is about.

Sometimes these new intakes would be placed on their own in a single cell and, thankfully very rarely, they would self-harm. In my time as a prison officer, I have opened up three cells the next morning to find that these new prisoners, spending their first night in prison, had committed suicide, not to mention the number of countless serious attempts that I encountered. As far as I was concerned, that was three too many.

The odd thing about the 2052SH book and monitoring system is that, in my experience, most prisoners who actually committed suicide had not even been placed on the 2052SH register in the first place and staff were totally unaware of any problem.

So I felt I had a good understanding of the problem and decided to draw up a simple to use system that would combat some of the glaring failings in our treatment of new prisoners. I knew that my biggest problem would be the reception team and their senior officers who were under constant pressure to get prisoners through the reception area as quickly as possible.

I set about ensuring that there would be a dedicated team of officers on houseblock 3, tasked specifically with the First Night in Prison programme. Ideally, these officers would also be the induction officers who would run the induction programme.

Although the prison was only ten years old, most of the cells were in various degrees of decline and were in need of a *Changing Rooms* makeover. There was not one cell that was completely fitted out as it should be: all had their small store cupboards broken into one way or another; some had no table in the cell; others had a very wobbly table with table legs that were loose and ready to use as a weapon; others had chairs, although this depended on how many prisoners were expected to be crammed into the cell; and most of the mattresses were worn so thin they would not even be classed as a duvet.

So I selected six multiple occupancy cells on 'A' spur houseblock 3 to become the First Night in Prison cells. They were called multiple occupancy because they were designed to hold only two prisoners but, as the overcrowding started in the early nineties, management decided to call them multiple occupancy cells so they could squeeze even more prisoners in.

I managed to get some paint, new beds, new mattresses and pillows and some new bedding that had not been reduced in size to make a line, a television that worked and had an aerial and kettles that had not been shit in. I also managed to get hold of some cell furniture that had not been transformed into the latest design of prison weaponry. I then made sure that the prisoners, who were to be employed to clean these cells ready for the next intake, would not allow the cells to be robbed by all the other prisoners on the spur.

I then looked at designing an interview room on houseblock 3 for the FNIP prisoners because we would need to interview them to ensure we had all the relevant information we needed, as well as being able to provide them with as much information we could as to what would be happening over the next few days. I also wanted to make sure that we gave them a brief overview of the prison (remembering, of course, to make sure that no one told them about Thursdays!) and its regime, and to have a chance to find out from them if they had any questions and let them phone someone to arrange a visit, so that items could be brought in for them.

Prison rules were always changing to ensure that they were only ever ten years behind the times and a recent change had forbidden any cigarettes or tobacco to be brought into the prison. Before this change, newly remanded prisoners could bring in cigarettes or tobacco provided that the packet was still sealed. The message did, however, eventually dawn on our security departments that someone could arrange to have packets of tobacco or cigarettes resealed once the tobacco had been enhanced with a special Jamaican woodbine brand. So, all their cigarettes and tobacco were taken off them at a time when they probably needed a smoke more than ever to help calm them down. Their money was also taken off them and given to the cashiers who would open up a prison bank account for them so they could spend money at the prison canteen and replenish their cigarettes and supplement their wonderful prison diet with sweeties or biscuits to dip in their tea. The only problem with this was that most of our new prisoners did not arrive until a Thursday or Friday and the cashier would not get around to creating their account until the following Monday or Tuesday.

So I set about making arrangements so that we could provide the new FNIP prisoners with a FNIP 'goody bag'. The contents of this bag would depend on whether they were a smoker or non-smoker and would be made up to the value of £5, enough to see them through until their weekly canteen allowance when they could spend their own money. The cost of these packs would be re-paid back from the prisoner's account.

Once they had been interviewed, made their phone call, picked up their goody bag, breakfast pack and bedding, they were shown to their new home, tucked in and read a bedtime story about what happens in prison on a Thursday night (I never did find out what the reception officer thought might happen on Thursdays, however I do believe my talk was far more informative for them!).

When the scheme started there were the usual stumbling blocks. After the first day of the newly refurbished cells being made ready for use with all their new bedding and furniture, an officer had left all the doors open and it took the rest of 'A' spur just three seconds to strip the cells bare of everything they wanted.

The reception staff believed that they always knew best and had no concept of helping a fellow officer make a good plan work. Our new prisoners were always the last ones to be processed, which slowed the whole procedure that we had to go through with them, which meant that the FNIP officers were always the last ones to leave the prison because they were still trying to locate the FNIP prisoners into their cells. So I tried reasoning with the reception officers but they always seemed to have a great excuse as to why they could not prioritise the new prisoners and get them through to us. It did not help that they were also at the mercy of the newly privatised escort staff who would drop Highdown prisoners off last as the other prisons where they were dropping off would simply lock them out if they were not there on time. Our governors were very reluctant to lock the prisoners out as they knew that the area manager would simply order them to let them in. However, by the time they did this, precious time would have been wasted and the prison role would be even later. The role should have been in by 9pm every evening but, due to these delays, the role could sometimes be as late as midnight and the management would still expect the staff to be back on duty in the reception at 6.30am.

The reason why the privatised escort vans were late is because these companies were operating for profit and, to maximise their profits, they cut back on the amount of escort vans they had and, instead, performed multi-drops at different prisons. In the past, when we were in charge of our own escorts, we would simply deal with our own prison and it would be as rare as rocking horse shit to get a late role in.

Eventually the reception staff decided to muscle in and assist the FNIP officers. They felt they had used it to make their point about the late roles and they could see the benefits the FNIP scheme would have on reducing the amount of suicides within prison.

The FNIP scheme ran well after these small glitches and locally we were confident that we were reducing the number of suicide attempts amongst prisoners. On one occasion, we had a visit from Phil Wheatley, the then deputy director general of the prison service and I had the pleasure of showing him around. We were also visited by a contingent of Russian prison officers who were over here to see how our prisons work. They commented that their army barracks were more brutal than our prisons and, when we asked about the risk of suicides in their prisons, they laughed and said that there was not enough room in their cells to wipe their arses, let alone kill themselves.

The scheme that I designed was used by other prisons and the governor who instructed my PO to get the scheme set up received an award. This was very nice for him. As for the other officers and I, both within the reception area and houseblock 3 who had worked hard to make the scheme work, we received bugger all except for several hours of accumulated Time Off In Lieu for the many late roles. I was demoted back to an officer because I had served my purpose and I was too 'gobby' and not a 'yes man' for the governor's tick box schemes.

Sadly, the FNIP scheme fell apart after a year as the overcrowding situation within our prisons became critical and it was near impossible to try and keep the FNIP cells vacant for the purpose of FNIP prisoners. There was also a new form introduced because of the murder of an Asian prisoner, Zahid Mubarek, by a racist cellmate. The form asked questions about whether you were a racist or homophobic or known to commit very violent acts. If the prisoners said they were, they would be placed in a single cell. It took the criminal grapevine just two weeks to get this message through the system so we were faced with quite a few prisoners who would claim that they were homophobic so that they could gain a single cell.

There are prisons where the FNIP scheme is working very well and these have dedicated units designed, and sometimes built especially, to provide a more effective first night in prison programme along with good effective detox units. Admittedly, money was found within the budgets for these prisons to ensure that they were built. I had a budget from my award-winning governor of £500 to spend on setting up the First Night in Prison programme. Interestingly enough, they found enough money in their budget to have their car park painted with specially marked car parking places where governors could park close to the prison gate so that they would not have too far to walk. Now that's what I call getting your priorities right.

Chapter Twelve

"Trouble at t' Mill"

Before I joined the prison service I had always been involved with the trade union movement and decided that, although I would join the Prison Officers' Association (POA) when I started work for the prison service, I had no intention of becoming actively involved. I had always managed to get myself far too involved with unions because I could never tolerate the injustices that were sometimes meted out to workers by piss poor managers. I would end up becoming a shop steward or union branch official, with my neck on the chopping block, because no one likes a gobby trade unionist.

The Prison Officers' Association is able to trace back its roots to the First World War, although it was not until 1939 that the government formally recognised the POA. In 1994 the Courts decided that, under Section 8 of the Prisons Act 1952, prison officers had the powers, authority, protection and privileges of a constable. Essentially, this meant that it was illegal to induce prison officers to take industrial action and break their contract of employment. Because prison officers were in the 'Prison Service' as described in Section 280 of the Trade Union and Labour Relations (Consolidation) Act 1992, the POA could not be a Trade Union. Consequently, the

Certification Officer advised the POA of his intention to remove its Certificate of Qualification.

In 1994, however, the government passed the Criminal Justice and Public Order Act. And Section 126 of the Act gave the POA the status and immunities of an Independent Trade Union. Section 127, however, made it unlawful for prison officers to take industrial action, which removed any chance of the POA being an effective bargaining force on behalf of its members.

The Labour party, in opposition at the time, promised to return our full trade union rights but, once elected, they took a bloody long time to get around to making the necessary changes to a law that was unfair and out of place in any democratic society. In 2004 the Joint Industrial Relations Procedural Agreement was agreed and the government announced the withdrawal of section 127 of the Criminal Justice Act 1994, which effectively made it illegal for prison officers to take industrial action. They had also set up the Independent Prison Service Pay Review Body (PSPRB). There was little evidence that this review panel was independent, however, until they recommended a 2.5 per cent increase, which was then carved up and had its value reduced by paying the award in two stages. This caused such disquiet and anger amongst prison officers that they were forced to show their disgust at the blatant disregard for their fair pay claim and the recommendations of the independent pay review panel by staging a one day strike on 29 August 2007.

It was interesting to note that the Labour government soon introduced new legislation to prevent prison officers from ever taking this action again under the Criminal Justice and Immigration Act 2008. Prison officers have no desire to ever want to take industrial action and simply want to be treated with respect and the dignity they deserve. Perhaps not surprisingly, they also expect the prison service to honour their agreements and to set up another agreement that will bring back the trust of prison officers.

HMP Highdown had a very active branch and meetings were well attended. There was always some kind of local dispute going on with our governors because they would always be trying to reduce staff and make conditions for us unsafe. When I arrived at Highdown, branch officials were very experienced prison officers and trade unionists and the governor of the prison was a very decent and intelligent man who cared about his staff although he did have a habit of constantly stopping officers who were not wearing their name badge.

Officers, in the main, were very reluctant to wear a name badge for a number of reasons; my objection was that I did not want to wear anything that could be used as a weapon against me and, given that the badges had a 2cm long safety pin to attach them to your uniform, that constituted a potential weapon to be used against me, in my opinion. The majority of prison officers feared that, if they were forced to wear name badges, this would allow criminals to track them down, identify where they live and launch revenge attacks, especially if they had an unusual surname. But, our governor had a bee in his bonnet about them and was very keen that they should be worn. On one occasion, he stopped me to ask who I was and made a great show of looking for my name badge. I told him my name and he asked how long I had been in the prison. I came smartly to attention, saluted him and replied, "All fucking day, sir!" made an about turn and marched off in the opposite direction. He never did ask me my name again.

Eventually the branch committee changed and the officials we had either retired or moved to another prison. We ended up with some officers who believed that, by becoming a branch official, you could further your career prospects, as a spate of branch officials had been given temporary promoted positions. They spent most of their time at odds with the rest of the branch as they were known to be in the management's pocket.

We had one deputy governor at Highdown who was ruthless and ensured that he had most of the branch officials on temporary promotions and with a string of promises to keep them under his control. The branch officials who had sold themselves in this way were eventually voted out of position but not before they had destroyed the reputation of the POA at Highdown and stitched up several of the membership.

But, like a complete sucker, I could not resist getting back on the union soapbox and placing my neck on the block. Not content with some lesser role within the branch structure, I became chairman of the POA at Highdown. I have always hated piss poor managers and, it has to be said that, some of the management team were so bad they would have trouble running a bath, let alone a prison. Most had been promoted to the level of, and indeed beyond, their incompetence.

It constantly amazed me that most of the management team at Highdown were under the illusion that, because they had positional power, their orders had to be obeyed. But, of course, what they did not grasp was that, once they had reached the point of having to order their teams, they had lost the ability to lead: an ability they had never possessed in the first place.

When I became branch chairman, I made a promise not to accept any temporary promotion but, just as soon as I was elected, the governor offered me a temporary promotion. I declined the offer, of course, so he promoted another member of the branch committee. All we could do was hope that she would not end up doing the governor's bidding for him as she was a pretty strong willed character.

The committee comprised a branch secretary, a branch chairman and five committee members. Even with seven of us, we had our work cut out because officers were constantly under investigation for one alleged offence or another. The prison service's code of discipline means that, if a prisoner accuses an officer of anything whatsoever, the governors and line managers are duty bound to carry out a simple investigation to ascertain if the prisoner is simply lying and causing trouble which is not uncommon.

Most investigations into officers could have been dealt with locally by their line manager but, because we had such a high proportion of very inexperienced managers who found themselves out of depth in a car park puddle, simple investigations were pushed up the ladder further. They then tended to become full blown investigations into what should have been no more than straightforward performance management issues to be dealt with under the line manager's sphere of responsibility.

A fine example of this is when a prisoner on houseblock 1 had decided to commit suicide and managed to get a job where he could gain access to a store cupboard at the rear of the food serving area. The prisoner simply waited until the coast was clear, went into the store area and hung himself.

The officers who found him summoned help and desperately tried to save his life but to no avail. They were very upset and two of them were sent home in distress. The prisoner was well liked by the officers and had never given staff any reason for concern, so his suicide came as a complete shock to everyone involved.

When these sorts of incidents happen, they have an effect on everyone who works in the prison but none more so than with the officers who have been in contact with the prisoner on a day-to-day basis. Like hospitals and other similar institutions, officers develop a shield of black humour, which is no more than a defence mechanism to help them deal with what is a very distressing situation. A healthy person needs a variety of coping mechanisms at his or her disposal, as there is no single coping mechanism that will be right for every situation. Humour is recognised as a healthy response to dealing with stress and should be one of the many tools one carries in one's repertoire.

One of the officers who had worked with the prisoner came on to his shift in the afternoon of the incident and heard the news about the prisoner from the gate staff. He was visibly very upset by the news but, by the time he arrived on the houseblock, he was making quips about "one off the role" and asking "is this the swinger's houseblock?" One of his friends and colleagues made a complaint and reported him to the principal officer in charge of houseblock 1, who sought guidance as to what he should do from the deputy governor. The deputy governor demanded that the officer be brought to his office; so he was marched down to see the new deputy governor who was a nasty, vicious man with an appalling track record of bullying staff. He suspended him from duty pending an investigation and snarled at him that he would ensure that the officer would never work in his prison again.

This was a clear breach of their own guidelines on performance management and, although the comments that the officer had made had upset some staff, there was very little thought as to the feelings of the officer himself. No consideration was given to the possibility that this behaviour was his way of dealing with the news and that it was an instinctive defence mechanism to deal with something that he was clearly distressed about.

I was asked by the officer to represent him as he was being charged under the disciplinary code of practice and made sure that I had regular contact with him and that our committee gave him as much moral support as we could. We knew that management would not bother with him and, in fact, they had made very little contact with him whilst he was on suspension. The first time he saw someone from the prison, other than the branch committee, was when he was told to attend an investigation interview being conducted by staff from the area office – some three whole weeks after he had been suspended.

During the investigation interview, the officer broke down several times and the interview had to be stopped until he had recovered. It was very clear to the interviewing staff that the officer had been badly affected by the whole sorry saga and the actions of the prison service had simply added to the stress of all concerned. I explained to the interviewing staff the advice that has been given by prominent psychologists concerning the use of coping mechanisms but they went off and compiled the usual non-committal type of investigation report, which included the recommendation that a disciplinary hearing should now be held. These hearings are conducted by the governor in charge of the prison.

The governor of the prison at that time was a 'time-served' governor who had come up through the ranks and had many years experience in the prison service. I hoped to present, not a defence of the offence with which the officer was being charged, but more of an explanation of mitigation as to why he had used black humour as a coping mechanism to deal with his distress. I also explained why I believed that the whole incident had been mismanaged and how I felt that this officer was just as much a victim of the incident as the rest of the staff on houseblock 1. The governor simply could not give a shit and decided to back up his deputy governor by finding the officer guilty as charged of serious unprofessional conduct and the governor had the officer forcefully transferred to another prison.

The compulsory transfer of the officer to another prison was not strictly a punishment award but, under our conditions of employment, we are a mobile grade, which means that we can be ordered to work at any prison the service wishes to send us. However, by transferring the officer, the governor was making sure that he would not be able to appeal against the move so the officer found himself in a classic 'Catch 22' situation.

The governor started to try and lecture us about morals until I cut him short by telling him how appalled I was by how this officer had just been treated by him and his henchmen. I told him not to lecture me about morals when he clearly had none himself. I think it was at this point, almost precisely, that I placed my neck firmly on the proverbial chopping block. My problem is that I just cannot keep my mouth shut and when I see such injustice being meted out to my colleagues, I just have to let rip. This number one governor had a very privileged position and was being paid a very good wage, courtesy of the taxpayer. The care and welfare of all his officers were part of his duties and, as far as I was concerned, he had failed spectacularly and quite despicably in this particular responsibility.

The officer who was accused of upsetting his colleagues had never denied that he had made an inappropriate comment and was extremely remorseful for the hurt that these comments had caused his colleagues. The officer who had made the complaint simply wanted his line manager to deal with the issue and never imagined for one moment that it would be escalated to such a level and was horrified to find that the governor had shafted a friend and colleague. The acting principal officer who had simply asked for advice from the deputy governor was embarrassed by the whole incident and wished that he had simply used his own judgement and dealt with the incident himself.

If the governor and deputy governor did this to set an example, then they had well and truly succeeded, because they gave us a perfect example of how bloody unfair they can be.

A good friend of mine secured the role of the training principal officer and one of his first tasks was find two volunteers to help out on what is known as course role play. The education course was about investigations and was designed to teach new governors how to conduct an investigation. These courses were being run at the Prison Service College at Newbold Revel. So my PO friend suggested that he could think of no better candidate than the branch chairman and his good self. Not only would we be able to learn about how the other half try to investigate their staff, but we could also have a very good time sampling the cultural delights of Newbold and sharing our wealth of knowledge and expertise with the new recruits up there (getting pissed in the bar and talking bullshit to any stupid sprog that would listen).

I was very impressed with the course; we were asked to play out different types of scenarios to put the new governors through their paces. The tutor was called Mick and he was a typical, very large, hairy-arsed screw, who knew his job extremely well. He had spent many years in the service and we had a great time swapping typical anecdotal stories. What's more, he had a good sense of humour, and set us some entertaining challenges to really test out the new governor grades.

I played two characters in two separate scenarios; the first of these was an officer who was very new in the job and, during a prisoner escort to a local hospital with a prison officer of 20 years' service, the prisoner escapes whilst I had been left alone with him. I had been left on my own because the other officer wanted to make a few phone calls and have a cigarette or two outside. The other officer was blaming me and I was behaving like a complete Wally, apologising for letting the prisoner escape. My first task was to see if I could get the female governor to be taken in by my pathetic excuses. I knew that I had achieved this when I managed to get through a whole load of rubbish about all my problems with my wife, my kids, my mortgage, my in-laws and so on. No-one stopped me so I went on to tell her about how much everyone picked on me in the prison and that the only friends I had were the prisoners themselves. I then decided to go in for the kill and spun her a story about how sick my dog had been and that it had been put down that very morning. I took a calculated pause, kept my head down and gave a little sniff as if I were trying to hold back tears and regain some composure. With that, I heard her start to sniff back tears, too, and when I looked up she had tears rolling down her face. Who says you can't make role play seem real?

The other test I had was to see if these governors could control the interview, ensuring that they have the interviewee next to the microphone. Mick had taught them how to ensure that, when they bring the interviewee into the room, he does not sit in the wrong chair. The tip he gave them was that, as they get up to answer the door, they should place their notes and papers on their own chair so that the interviewee would make for the chair with no papers on it. The challenge that Mick had given me was to get to the interviewer's chair. So, I knocked on the door, shook the interviewer's hand and held onto it, still shaking it vigorously as I sat down on top of his paperwork on his chair. This so flustered the interviewer that he spent the next five minutes trying to negotiate his papers back from me.

It was such a useful opportunity to get a chance to see how governors are taught to investigate staff and it certainly assisted us in the amount of local investigations that were held at Highdown.

The role of a POA branch chairman can be very demanding and I welcomed any distraction that allowed me back onto the houseblocks to work as a prison officer rather than a trade unionist. There was one occasion when I had spent most of the day negotiating with management over a proposal to reduce the number of prison officers and the evening back on the houseblock to supervise the serving of the evening meal.

As the officer in charge supervising the serving of the meal, my duty was to take the prisoner hotplate workers down to the kitchens to collect the meals. I needed to ensure that there were sufficient meals to serve the prisoners on the houseblock and then return to the houseblock and simply let the hotplate workers lay out the array of culinary delights ready for the serving of these meals. We had also been issued with white coats to wear whilst we were carrying out these duties. I have to say that I was a bit pissed off to have to wear it, particularly as I would not be handling any food.

I could hear that the prisoners had already been opened up, ready to receive their evening meal, and I could also hear officers sending some of the prisoners back for not being dressed correctly.

"Right, first six, away you go. And where do you think you are going, looking like Elvis Presley? Do your shirt up!"

"Next six, hold it right there. You are not going to the hot plate with flippy floppies on, go and put some proper shoes on."

"Oh, come on, guv, I've got to wear these as I've got a medical condition," pleads the prisoner.

"You will have a medical condition if you don't get some proper footwear on, it's called hunger."

So there I was, standing by the hot plate, clip board and pen at hand, ready to tick off the confirmation sheet that records which type of meal the prisoner had requested. I must have looked like I had the right hump, when a long-serving prisoner I knew from when I first joined the job, came straight up to me and asked, "Two choc ices, please."

This had me roaring with laughter. Both the prisoner and I knew that this was straight from a *Porridge* sketch where Fletcher walks up to Officer Barrowclough and asks for 'Two choc ices, please' which gets Barrowclough dribbling on about the importance of hygiene to explain the white coat. I then spent most of the evening talking to this prisoner about the television series and it was interesting to hear him saying how much prison had changed, even going so far as to admit that there was far too little respect and far too many drugs.

We were constantly finding ourselves at odds with our management because they could never see the benefit of working with the trade union. Most of the lower management were very inexperienced; they rarely managed staff in a positive manner and were always using threats of discipline against the officers.

I was always there to defend the staff whenever they needed me and faced all kinds of challenges and obstructions from the managers. Somehow I knew that choosing to be a trade union rep was a very limiting career choice because I was bound to piss off people with my ability to not sit on a fence.

I found myself getting too passionately involved with my union work and my wife had noticed a change in my health. I no longer came home and recited stories about what had happened that day at work. I began to hate going into work because we were so undervalued, so very short of staff with even more pressure being placed on us to accept more and more reductions in staffing levels so that we could compete against the private prison sector in a system called market testing.

People who knew me before I became a prison officer had also said that I had changed and I suppose I must have done. When I became a prison officer I would use the uniform as if I was putting on a stage costume and stepping onto a stage to perform the role of prison officer. At first this was probably done to shield my nerves and allow me to carry out my duties. Eventually, however, the actions and habits of survival within the prison environment were becoming ingrained within me, to the extent that when someone was talking to me outside the prison, I would be observing everyone else around me. Some people thought that I was not paying attention to what they were saying but I was simply reacting to the prison regime. I had got used to talking to prisoners or staff while always ensuring not to be so distracted by the conversation that I would miss any possible danger or incident that needed my attention.

I realised that I would always be very wary of strangers and on my guard when I was walking about in crowds. I also noticed that I had become a nightmare for any salesman. They did not stand a hope in hell of getting me to buy from them if I did not want the item, as I had spent most of my career saying 'no' to some of the best conmen you could ever get in prison.

I decided to resign from the service on 5 August 2005, as I wanted to try to ensure that I would not become one of the 'average prison officers' who drop down dead just 18 months after they retire. It was a hard decision to make because I had, for the vast majority of my career, thoroughly enjoyed my time as a prison officer of Her Majesty's prison service. I am proud to have worked with some of the finest colleagues I have ever worked with, and equally proud that I was able to help save the lives of many prisoners and prevent harm coming to others. I did, however, stay up all night on 4 February 2007 to make sure that I beat the18 months.

Two months later, however, I was rushed into hospital with chest pains and was diagnosed with a heart condition that I know was caused by having such a stressful career. The stress was very rarely from prisoners; it was the constant back-biting, cut backs and poor management practices that caused me the most stress of all. "Governor, the staff are revolting," one prisoner once told me. "I know," I replied, "and the prisoners are not nice either!"

Chapter Thirteen

"How to run a prison service" – According to Chairman Jeff!

At present, each prison place is costing you, the taxpayer, an estimated £40,000 per year and the population now stands at around 80,000 prisoners. This means that it is costing around £32 million per year to house our current prison population, give or take a pound or two.

So, now we know how much it costs us, are we getting value for money? Let's begin by looking at the statement of purpose of Her Majesty's Prison Service:

'Her Majesty's Prison Service serves the public by keeping in custody those committed by the courts. Our duty is to look after them with humanity and help them lead law-abiding and useful lives in custody and after release.'

'Her Majesty's Prison Service?' A proportion of the prison service is private and run to make a profit, so I would hardly refer to them as 'Her Majesty's Prison Service', unless Her Majesty now employs mercenaries.

With the increasing number of escapes from court escort custody, all from private firms who now service the escorting to and from courts, they are hardly complying with the 'keep in custody' bit, either. The prisons themselves, however, do have a very good record of keeping prisoners in custody, unless they were to start lowering the category of many of their prisoners so they could be placed in open condition prisons, therefore making more room in our overcrowded state prisons. Funnily enough, this is exactly what they did at the end of 2006 and suddenly found that they had a 200 per cent abscond rate. Most of the prisoners who have absconded from prison should never have been categorised as being able to serve time at an open prison. Whoever made the decision to re-categorise category 'C' prisoners to category 'D', allowing them to be housed in open prison conditions, had clearly not read my description of a category 'C' prisoner: prisoners who can't be trusted in open conditions but who are unlikely to try to escape. When a prisoner 'has it on his toes' from a Cat D prison, he has not actually escaped but has simply absconded from an establishment with open conditions, rather than having effected a proper escape from an actual prison with walls and razor wires, in the true meaning of the word 'escape'. So, again, the 'keep in custody' bit of the prison remit is certainly not a roaring success here, either.

Because our prisons are so full, our offending behaviour programmes are ineffective because we simply do not have the capacity to place prisoners on these courses. My experience, however, has been that these programmes have very little effect on the prisoners. Latest figures from 2003 show that 61 per cent of adult offenders were reconvicted within two years of their release with a staggering 73 per cent of young offenders, aged 18–21, being reconvicted in the same period. And when you look at the reoffending rate for male adolescents (aged 15–18, it shoots up to 82 per cent. Most of the reoffending programmes simply do not provide the practical skills that prisoners need to enable them 'to lead law-abiding and useful lives in custody and after release'.

So, as the prison service is not meeting its statement of purpose, it is clear that it is 'not fit for purpose'.

I could spend pages dribbling on about statistics and putting forward arguments for and against prison, but I doubt that anyone would want to read it. There have already been far too many studies compiled by many different pressure groups of one persuasion or another. The prison service itself has a large workforce of staff whose sole duty is to compile shed loads of manufactured figures to show how well they are doing. We have an increase in crime; despite any clever excuses about crime reporting techniques, there is no doubt that crime has increased. The prison population in England and Wales has soared in recent years – up 85 per cent since 1993. In January 1993 – when the prison population began rising – there were 41,561 prisoners in jail in England and Wales. The current population is over 80,000 and climbing. Britain has the unenviable record of locking up more people than any other European Community country.

Prison is not working.

So, what actually is a prison? According to *Chambers 21st Century Dictionary*, a prison is defined as: 'Prison, noun. **1** a building for the confinement of convicted criminals and certain accused persons awaiting trial. **2** any place of confinement or situation of intolerable restriction. **3** custody; imprisonment.'

The general public would like to see most of our prisoners locked up and the key thrown away. The reality, however, is that we have always had crime and the perpetrators of crime must be dealt with in a way that achieves two results: punishment and rehabilitation.

Psychologists have it right when they proclaim that, in order to reduce crime, we must rehabilitate. On the one hand, however, trying to operate a 'one size fits all' cognitive programme for prisoners who could not give a shit is not only futile, but it is also a sheer waste of time and money. We first need to look at the causes of crime and one of the major influences on the massive increase in crime has been, without a shadow of a doubt, drugs.

Society in Britain witnessed a major change in the attitude to drugs by our teenagers during the late eighties and little effort was put in to prevent the growth in drug taking. The whole pop culture and modern day icons seemed to make drug-taking a fashion, much like the heady days of the late '60s, except this time the message given out was not 'love and peace' but 'live for now and fuck everyone else' with a large dose of the me, me, me attitude. It did not take long for the pop culture to feed on this frenzy by promoting some very sinister genre like gangsta rap. Gangsta rappers often try to defend themselves by claiming that they are describing the reality of inner-city life, and that they are only adopting a character, like an actor playing a role, which behaves in ways that they may not necessarily endorse. That's utter bollocks! They have quite deliberately brought over a culture that they developed somewhere either in New York or Kingston Town and have sold it to youngsters in Europe. We now see many of our teenagers trying to mimic these negative icons. We did not have such high levels of gun crime, gang on gang violence or violent robberies until this crap Afro-American rubbish hit our shores and turned our 'E' dropping druggy teenagers into menacing gangsta fans with even more attitude and very little respect, even for themselves.

So, if we are going to make prison work, we have first got to decide what we want from our investment of good taxpayers' money. Do we simply want to lock them up and keep them away from society until their release date, achieving no real deterrent and ending up with them going straight back to their miserable, thieving, robbing, and drug taking ways? In other words, basically continue to do what we are doing now. Or do we want to give them a real chance to change their lives and rejoin the rest of an ordered, decent, society?

The prison system that we have now is simply divided into categories of security risk, with only a few prisons having specialist rehabilitation programmes which, unfortunately, are just not effective enough to curtail the reoffending rates.

We need to radically look at how we deal with this ever-growing criminal population. Most prisoners have no skills or abilities that are of any use to society and which would encourage them to lead law-abiding lives. The majority are so fucked up on drugs that they have no, or very little, chance of ever coming off them before they kill them. We have a very liberal attitude to offenders and, at times, it seems as though we spend most of our time and money trying to protect their human rights and paying them compensation for refusing to give them detox medication to reduce the effects of being without their source of drugs, until they can get some in on their next visit.

To deal with prisoners who are hooked on drugs and committing crime to feed their habit, we need to make sure that we first detox them and then ensure that they do not have any chance of getting any kind of drugs whilst in prison. This will only happen if we have specially designed detox units in prisons that allow no physical contact with any likely source of drug trafficking. Once they are clear of drugs, they need to be educated about how they can prevent themselves from being tempted to go back to drugs. We would then need to give them skills and opportunities so that they can rejoin society and have a real purpose to their lives and a chance to fit in and contribute.

We should look at improving our state funded drug rehabilitation centres as, given the chance, these centres can do far more effective rehabilitation work with drug users than a prison because they can work with the drug user in their own environment.

Our prisons should be divided into three main categories. The first of these should be a remand and assessment prison, where prisoners can be held on remand waiting for their day in court and then, if sentenced, assessed as to what their educational or training needs are to prepare them to function legally in society. The prisoner would need to sign up and agree to this reoffending programme. The assessment would look at how best to maximise the prisoner's chances of earning a decent living and, if need be, the medical rehabilitation programme that would be best suited to them if they are addicted to drugs or alcohol. Once processed and free from drugs, they would then progress to the next prison.

This second prison should be designed as a training prison. I am not, however, talking about the many prisons that are already scattered about the prison estate claiming to be training prisons. These prisons are poorly equipped and even those that do have modern facilities and equipment have very few spaces available to cope with the amount of prisoners within the system. The training prisons I am talking about should be able to teach real skills that can be used by the prisoner. I was amazed that one of the courses being run at Highdown, for example, was bookkeeping and payroll. Now, let's get real. How many prospective employers would employ an ex-con in their payroll department?

These training prisons should have the facilities and the staff to take prisoners out as working parties to work on and repair the infrastructure of our country and, at the same time, to learn valuable building skills. In my view, any state funded building should be built using prison labour force. Although, admittedly, the labour force should only be made up of those prisoners that do not pose a danger or threat to society. The sentence that they have been given should reflect the period of time in which they will perform this work. At present, under the Criminal Justice Act, prisoners who have been sentenced to less than four years are only expected to serve half of this sentence in prison and the other half in the community. We should, therefore, ensure that the second half of this sentence is designed so that the prisoner is working for the community.

The third type of prison would simply be a prison that holds prisoners safely, keeping them banged up. These are the prisoners that the public will never want to release back into society, or have failed or refused the option of a training prison. These prisons should be secure units, designed to hold all types of prisoners who clearly do not wish to conform or participate in society. Despite what the prison psychologists would have us believe, there are is a large section of the prison population who are quite literally beyond help and who will never change. The best that we can do is 'bang 'em up' and keep the public safe. But, if we are going to simply 'bang 'em up' we do need to ensure that it is done safely and provide sufficient numbers of officers to perform the task and minimise the risk of harm to both staff and other prisoners.

As for prisoners who have mental health problems, they should be held in the correct secure hospitals. Prison is absolutely no place for people who are mentally ill.

We need also to look at our judicial system and review why we send people to prison in the first place. We need to consider whether it is not possible – and indeed preferable – to sentence more offenders to community work and rehabilitation orders. Under the current sentencing regime, prisons try to be all things but consistently fail to deliver results.

We should also be tough on crime and stop the rot in our society; if neighbourhoods stood firmly together they would beat crime in their areas. We do not need pretend police officers (community support officers), we need proper police officers. And we do not want the ones who are afraid to get stuck in and call criminals 'mate'. Whenever did it happen – and how was it allowed to happen – that officers of the law started to refer to potential criminals as their 'mates'? If criminals are indeed their 'mates', then we are in deeper shit than I first imagined.

We should have zero tolerance to all crime and come down very hard on anyone who promotes anti-social behaviour or other similarly negative, destructive and violent attitudes, especially those who use the entertainment industry to do so.

Prison officers are always being hounded by the press and are usually wrongly addressed by the press as prison guards or warders. They are prison officers, not guards or warders, members of Her Majesty's Prison Service and very proud of what they do. Prisons are not nice places and they hold not nice people. I can assure you that prison officers are trustworthy, honest, hardworking servants of the crown. Yes, there have been a few who have let down the good name of prison officers. Like any profession, you will get people who are not always professional. Being a prison officer is a very tough job and is regarded as one of the most stressful occupations with the average life expectancy of a prison officer of just 18 months after they have retired. The government tried to help us out by increasing the retirement age of prison officers, until someone pointed out that having an ageing 65-year-old prison officer rolling around on the floor trying to restrain a very violent, 22-year-old fit, young prisoner, was maybe not such a good idea after all.

There were times during the year that fights in prison, where I either had to stop a prisoner from hitting someone else or prevent them from attacking me, averaged out at about two per week. Now, unless you're a professional boxer, this is a very unusual level of violence for any one person to face week in and week out whilst going about their work. I admit that not all prison officers face this level of violence on such a sustained basis as it depends on where you are working in the prison and how much direct contact you have with prisoners on a daily basis.

Officers are verbally abused and face all kinds of levels of danger; they witness some really harrowing events during their careers and now the prison officer training programme actively encourages officers to grass on their colleagues for any form of slight lapse in professionalism. They have managers who actively encourage a fear culture amongst staff and constantly use threats of dismissal to get everyone to conform to whatever hare-brained, stupid idea is passed down from some tosser at head office who is clueless when it comes to dealing with prisoners.

A prison officer should be able to rely on the rest of the service to back him or her up. Every time a prison officer has to unlock and open a cell door he has no idea what is going to face him: it could be anything from a cheerful, "Good morning, guv," to a disdainful, "Fuck off! You screw bastard." On the other hand, it could be an attempted suicide, which would need all your wits and clear, calm thinking if you were going to stand any chance of saving the life of another human being. At other times, it could be just another frightened prisoner who has spent their very first night in prison and has a barrage of questions to ask but the officer will have very little time to stop and deal with them as they have a whole landing to unlock. Or this could be the cell door of a very violent prisoner who simply wants to hurt a screw; he will not be bothered which screw it is, as we are all the same to him.

These officers should be able to count on every single person employed in the prison service, from their line manager all the way back to the director general of the prison service, being there to back them up. Sadly, though, it has been my experience that they are not.

The prison service spends more on prisoner clothing than it does on the uniforms that they expect the officers to wear. Officers are no longer issued with the smart full number one dress uniform, as they are now seen to be a waste of money. At some establishments, they have even issued cheap tracksuit bottoms and polo shirts, replaced the traditional prison service cap with a baseball cap as it was too intimidating and provided a cheap looking fleece, which is better suited to serving burgers than ensuring that prisoners serve time.

Our chiefs in the prison service seem to have forgotten what their duties are as employers as well as the real purpose of prisons. As employers and managers, they have a very privileged and important position to manage staff and to ensure that they can perform their duties in a safe manner. The prison service is a public service, which should be providing a service to the public by keeping in custody those committed by the courts. The service has a duty to look after them with humanity and help them lead law-abiding and useful lives in custody and after release; not employ shit loads of civil servants to push paper around that has less than dodgy statistics telling themselves and their political masters about how well they are doing, whilst prisons are bursting at the seams and prison staff being placed under increasing and intolerable pressure.

For normal law-abiding people, prisons are not nice places to be; they are a totally alien environment, full of unknown threats, noise, smells and a complete lack of control over your environment and your dignity. The formidable walls shield a world that the public know very little of, or indeed care very much about. The slamming shut of the cell door is claustrophobic and drives home the sense of helplessness and vulnerability. They are not nice places.

However, to a habitual, drug-taking felon who would not think twice about kicking the shit out of an old aged pensioner, or sticking a knife several times into your body because you were preventing them from robbing you, because he needs the money for drugs, these cells feel very like the 'hovels' they have come from. Their lives are spent going from a high to such an extreme low that forces them to get money by any method to buy more drugs. They will live in complete squalor, sometimes amongst their own shit and filth because cleaning it up interferes with their cycle of drugs and crime. They are so far gone that they hardly notice the filth as they live in fear of the lows, the rival gangs, the pusher they owe money to, or the fellow druggies who will slit their throats, given half a chance. The lack of respect and isolation from the rest of the world leads them to mix only with their own kind. Then there is the risk of disease and hunger as it is more important for them to buy drugs than food and they often lack clean clothes and bedding, because they have probably soiled the ones they had. For them prison is a safe, clean environment.

Compared to life on the outside, prison is an easy option for them. To their fellow prisoners, they can pretend that they are a hard-nosed criminal who takes no shit from screws, they will tell any prison staff about their flash, make-believe car and the decent bird they have on the out. They will be fed three very decent meals per day, have clean bedding each week or more if they need it. They will be housed in a cell with a colour television and en suite facilities, get a chance to associate with their peers and pretend and brag about the good times they only wish they had. They will be protected by the prison officers when they end up in the shit because they have been caught stealing off their fellow prisoners even though they publicly scorn prison officers by referring to them as 'screws', and would not think twice about assaulting them or accusing them of all kinds of mistreatment. Some of them may even pay attention to the detox programme and stay away from drugs for a while and embark on a keep fit programme and develop a measure of respect, clean living and a sense of security. Until they get out, that is. For them prison is great, although you would never hear them admit it for fear of losing too much face.

If we are going to combat the ever-growing crime wave and the swelling prison populations, we must build bigger and better prisons, detox and educate the prisoners, provide them with real, achievable and sustainable options for a lifestyle change and monitor and support their release back into society.

Home detention curfews are a joke because the sentence they were given was a custodial one to protect the public, otherwise the judge could have given the criminal a telling off and sent them off with the fashionable Home Detention Curfew (HDC) tag fixed to their leg. My understanding of crime and punishment is that, if someone commits a crime, they are given a punishment by the judge. It is our duty to carry out the punishment and, in the case of a prison sentence, the punishment is to be kept away from the society they have violated for a period of time set by the judge.

I also believe that our duty should be to attempt to rehabilitate the criminal in an effort to instigate a change in their lifestyle that would make them worthy of being back in public. So how does a HDC tag fit in with that? It doesn't. It is simply another hare-brained idea to try to reduce prison numbers. It is just the same as the last great idea from the head office twits who came up with the Criminal Justice Act, which simply halved custodial sentences for those serving less than four years. These are both daft ideas because the prisoners we have the most chance of changing are those that have a sentence long enough for us to work with them, using whatever offending behaviour programme and skills training that will give them the option of a lifestyle change.

All we are doing by bringing them into the prison system for a few months and then throwing them back out again is costing the taxpayer shit loads of money. For the average robbery, for example, it will cost about £30,000 to secure a conviction and, along with the rising cost of prison places, times the average length of sentence (which is around 42 months), this equates to a total bill for the taxpayer of around £100,000. The prisoner will serve about ten months on remand and will only serve around eleven months actually in prison, which will not give the prison staff enough time to achieve any chance of rehabilitating the prisoner. It is never very long before they are reconvicted and brought back to prison, only to go through the expensive cycle yet again with absolutely nothing to show for the massive financial investment by the taxpayer.

There is always plenty of debate as to why crime is on the increase and I can only hope that they find a solution to these increases someday soon. Until then, however, we have an increasing prison population with stark evidence that the prison system does not work. We need to restructure the prison regime, sentence prisoners for a length of time that allows for them to be properly rehabilitated, build bigger prisons that are not for profit and look after and support the very brave prison officers who work hard in them day after day, facing challenges that most people would never dream of having to face in their daily working lives.

"Now, listen up you goppers. I'm harsh but fair. I want you to know I treat you all with equal contempt."